ENOUGH

AS SHE IS

Also by Rachel Simmons

The Curse of the Good Girl

Odd Girl Out

*Odd Girl Speaks Out: Girls Write About Bullies, Cliques,
Popularity, and Jealousy*

ENOUGH
AS SHE IS

How to Help Girls Move Beyond
Impossible Standards of Success to Live
Healthy, Happy, and Fulfilling Lives

RACHEL
SIMMONS

HARPER

An Imprint of HarperCollins*Publishers*

HarperCollins books may be purchased for educational, business, or sales promotional use. For information, please email the Special Markets Department at SPsales@harpercollins.com.

FIRST EDITION

Designed by William Ruoto

Library of Congress Cataloging-in-Publication Data has been applied for.

ISBN 978-0-06-243839-3

18 19 20 21 22   LSC   10 9 8 7 6 5 4 3 2 1

For Estee

CONTENTS

INTRODUCTION
NOT ENOUGH AS SHE IS

To be a girl today is to enjoy historic promise. Our daughters come of age in a world unbound by the limits their mothers faced and unrecognizable to their grandmothers. Girls are glass ceiling–busting, selfie-taking world changers. For the last twenty years, my job has been to teach, study, live with, and listen to them.

But there is something troubling stewing beneath the surface of all this success. There are the girls so riven by anxiety about school that they can't sleep at night—like the high school junior who obsessively refreshes her school's online grading system, first after school, then after sports practice, then after dinner, before bed, and then again when she wakes up, to calculate her GPA down to the minute.

There are the girls who cluster after finishing an exam, each competing to tell the other how badly they just failed, because it makes them feel better to anticipate failure—and who collapse, inconsolable, when they score less than an A-. There is the girl who posts a selfie, then refreshes her screen repeatedly, only to delete her post for fear it hasn't gotten enough attention. There is the girl who can't hear a class lecture over the voice in her head wondering if she ate too much at lunch, and if her thighs look too fat against her chair.

For too many girls today, the drive to achieve is fueled by brutal self-criticism and anxiety that they will fail. We are raising a generation of girls who may look exceptional on paper but are often anxious and overwhelmed in life—who feel that no matter how hard they try, they will never be smart enough, successful enough, pretty enough, thin enough, well liked enough, witty enough online, or sexy enough. No matter how many achievements they accrue, they feel that they are not enough as they are. This book is about how to help your daughter redefine success and pursue it on healthy terms, without sacrificing her self-worth, and to be well and whole in a world that often isn't.

Our culture is pummeling girls with toxic messages about success, and we are bearing witness to an epidemic of stress that is consuming young women from the inside. It has quietly become a mental health crisis for them, their schools, and their families, one that will only worsen if we don't sound the alarm.

The data is shocking. According to the Monitoring the Future survey cited by Jean Twenge in her book *iGen*, girls' depressive symptoms increased by 50 percent from 2012 to 2015, more than twice as much as boys. In 2015, UCLA's annual Cooperative Institutional Research Program (CIRP) Freshman Survey, which includes responses from 150,000 full-time students at more than two hundred colleges and universities, logged the highest levels of unhappiness ever recorded in female first-year college students. The survey reported that twice as many females as males said they felt depressed frequently or occasionally; twice as many girls also said they were "overwhelmed by all I have to do." The number of girls in these categories had shot up 25 percent over just fifteen years. At the same time, the number of girls who ranked themselves as most competitive among their peers rose by nearly 15 percent, while men's numbers remained nearly stagnant. Last year, the Girls' Index, a national survey of twelve thousand fifth- through twelfth-grade girls, found that the number of girls who describe themselves as "confident" declines more than 25 percent throughout middle school. Confidence bottoms out in ninth grade, where it remains stagnant for the rest of high school. Success for these girls isn't a lifeline; those with a GPA higher than 4.0 were the least likely to say what they thought or disagree with others, because they wanted to be liked. Led by Dr. Lisa Hinkelman of the nonprofit Ruling Our Experiences, the survey displayed a nosedive in girls' confidence alongside a simultaneous spike in a desire to change their appearance.

It's true that girls have never been more successful, but they have also never struggled more. Girl competence does not equal girl confidence. Nor does it equal happiness, resilience, or self-worth.

Each year, I teach thousands of young women around the United States. My college orientation programs help new students transition to college life and recover from their high school hangover. As a leadership development specialist at Smith College, I develop workshops for undergraduate women that cultivate resilience, self-compassion, and confidence. I spend most weeks during the academic year traveling to high schools and universities all over the country, where I work with students, parents, and teachers. And I serve as a scholar in residence at the Hewitt School in New York, where my job is to integrate research on girls into curriculum development, student workshops, and parent education.

I am tired of the headlines that trumpet the success of girls, as if good grades and college enrollment were the markers of a life well lived. It's time to dispense with the myth of the so-called amazing girl. We have allowed superficial criteria to influence our judgment of how girls are doing. When I listen to girls talk about how and why they achieve, and at what cost to their bodies, hearts, and minds, *success* is not the first word that comes to mind. We have long understood that low-income girls face multiple risks to their health, but new research finds that affluent adolescent girls are shockingly vulnerable. High school girls in affluent suburbs report using cigarettes and marijuana at nearly twice the normative rate. From depression and anxiety to body shame, they exhibit more adjustment problems, across more domains, than any other group of American youth—yet continue to push themselves to achieve.

Why are girls struggling? Psychologists call it "role overload"—too many roles for a single individual to play—and "role conflict"—when the obligations of the roles you play are at odds with one another. Both conditions are known to induce high levels of stress. In the so-called age of Girl Power, we have failed to cut loose our most retrograde standards of female success and replace them with something more progressive. Instead, we've shoveled more and more expectation onto the already robust pile of qualities we expect girls to possess.

"Women today have to succeed by traditionally male standards of education and career, but they also have to succeed by the traditionally female standards of beauty (not to mention motherhood)," Duke University's Susan Roth has written. Girls have to be superhuman: ambitious, smart and driven, physically fit, pretty and sexy, socially active, athletic, and kind and liked by everyone. As Courtney Martin put it in *Perfect Girls, Starving Daughters*, "Girls grew up hearing they could be anything, but heard they had to be everything."

An "anything is possible" mentality among American girls has thus wound up as a mental health crisis. A single-minded focus on giving girls access to every opportunity seems to have put into motion just the opposite: a double-digit gender gap in depression, anxiety, and confidence. In 2016, for the first time ever, a majority of students entering college described their mental health as "below average." The number of teens who agree with the statement "I can't do anything right" has skyrocketed since 2011. Our 24-7 success-seeking culture has pushed girls to pursue achievement at the expense of all else, including the vital relationships that nourish them with self-esteem and resilience.

The embrace of achievement over attachment is threatening not just girls' wellness but, ironically, also their ability to succeed. Relentless success-seeking keeps girls from taking healthy risks and becoming creative, original learners. It costs girls their courage, curbing their ability to figure out who they are and what really matters to them, exactly at the moment when this developmental task must be undertaken.

There is also the matter of gender differences, many of which intensify in adolescence. UCLA's Linda Sax defines gender differences as the different "values, confidences, aspirations and patterns of behavior" that distinguish the lives of girls and boys. These differences aren't hardwired. They are mostly the product of socialization: the informal, out-of-class schooling girls get every day from peers, media, and family. These norms carefully instruct a girl in how she should act, look, and talk.

A large body of research tells us that differences in how girls and boys are raised lead girls to behave, feel, and even think differently than boys, and in ways that can make adolescence uniquely challenging for them.

By age six, anxiety will be twice as prevalent among girls as boys. As a girl enters adolescence, she will be twice as likely as her brother to suffer from depression. She will perceive stress more often than her male peers. She will get less sleep. Her self-esteem will drop across a range of domains: in sports, appearance, and self-satisfaction, to name a few.

Some of her depression will be caused by overthinking her every move (*Should I have said that in class? Is she mad at me?*), which will shunt her motivation and limit her problem-solving skills. Some will be caused by the self-criticism that girls are more likely to visit on themselves. And some will be caused by shame, the unshakable feeling that she is an unworthy person, an emotion that emerges in adolescence and follows her into adulthood. By late adolescence, her self-compassion will decline to its lowest level of any group of youth.

During this period her body will change in ways that may make her uncomfortable and self-critical. In contrast to a boy, whose puberty confers the high-muscle-mass, lower-body-fat ideal the culture asks of him, a girl will gain an average of forty pounds of body fat. She will be pulled inexorably away from the thin ideal nearly everyone around her demands that she fulfill. She will engage in self-objectification, or excessive body monitoring (*Do I look okay? Look at my stomach roll*), which is linked to eating disorders, depression, body shame, academic trouble, impaired personal relationships, and even diminished political action on college campuses.

If she is affluent, her body dissatisfaction will exceed her peers by a measure of three standard deviations, an extraordinary margin. She will be more likely to struggle with depression, anxiety, aggression, and delinquency. She will also express the most envy of any group of youth, which researchers speculate is caused by "the frustration of always falling short of perfection." The researchers who study these girls call their findings "especially troubling."

When she taps on her phone, she will be more likely to visit a visual platform like Instagram or Snapchat, where she will feel pressure to construct a physically flawless, hypersocial digital life through a carefully curated stream of videos and pictures.

If she is considered a high achiever, she will be more vulnerable to interpreting even minor failures as a sign she's not smart. This mindset will encourage her to avoid healthy risks, catastrophize setbacks, and even cheat. As her GPA rises and she builds out her résumé, she may be prone to imposter syndrome, the belief that she's a fraud just waiting to be found out.

As she enters college, she will be more likely to rank herself lower than men on nearly every measure of intellectual ability (despite no measurable differences in actual ability). Throughout college, she will get less exercise but seek counseling more often than her male peers. In college, one in four of her female peers will be sexually assaulted.

And as she walks across the commencement stage to get her diploma, she may not only be less confident than the men lined up behind her, but she may also be less confident than when she started college. In 2012, Boston College released data showing its female students graduated less confident than when they began, while male students became more confident. Focus groups told administrators appearance pressure, hookup culture, and the housing lottery (prone to "mean girl"–style expulsions of women from suites) were to blame. Not surprisingly, administrators expressed shock at the findings. "It did not fit" with their experience of the confident-seeming women in the classroom and around campus.

We have long known that as girls approach adolescence, their self-esteem declines. Psychologists call it a global "loss of voice," a grim milestone usually reached just before puberty. As little girls they might be feisty and spirited, forceful and stubborn, but as the unwritten rules of young womanhood sink in, these once fierce voices become muted or even silent. They learn what it means to be a "good girl": pleasing others, being "nice," and playing by the rules. In classrooms, *this is what I think* is replaced by a halting *I'm not sure if this is right*. An *oh yeah!* is traded for a tepid *I guess*, an *I want that* for an *I don't know*. Bodies that once leaped and straddled fold inward.

In order to be well liked by others, they learn to lock up strong, authentic feelings like anger or disappointment. Be nice, smile a lot, and keep your friends; trade your voice for your connections. The result, as books like *Reviving Ophelia* and *Meeting at the Crossroads* showed us in the 1990s, is a loss of confidence and increased striving for perfection.

For most of my career, I was certain this was what held girls back from achieving their potential. If girls could break the shackles of their inner Good Girl—if they could speak up, self-promote, and take their seat at the table—all would be well. "It's not enough to open the doors for girls," I wrote in *The Curse of the Good Girl* in 2009. "We have to give them the confidence to walk through them."

But I've had a change of heart. Telling girls they need to develop more confidence is code for just another thing *they* have to fix, work on, and be better at. Likewise, to say girls are suffering because they're "too perfectionistic"—a judgment I heard constantly in researching this book, not just from adults but also from girls themselves—is a simplistic excuse that lets everyone off the hook but the girls themselves. Both are ways girls can feel that something is wrong with *them*, when in fact I have come to see that something is deeply wrong with our culture. Over the last decade, the rise of social media, arrival of college admissions mania, and ever more ruthless pressure to be thin have tightened the rules of success for girls in punishing ways. As an educator and researcher, I've watched each of these cultural forces pulse a set of toxic messages to girls that clash with the most vulnerable parts of their unique psychology and undermine the development of a confident, authentic self.

Today, a new, equally toxic trade is being offered to girls, especially the ones who have access to the schooling, parenting, and other resources needed to strive for admission to a four-year college. If they once traded their real thoughts and feelings for relationships, they now trade close connections with peers for the pleasure of outperforming them. They give up their curiosity and authentic interests in exchange for narrowly drawn, external markers of success. They learn their achievements must seem effortless and self-generated, that needing help signifies incompetence, that peers are their competitors, and that success means stardom in every domain and at the highest level. If girls once approached adolescence and heard *This is what it means to be a "Good Girl,"* they are also now told, *This is how you become a Supergirl.* Supergirl is the new baseline: to be any less is to be nothing at all.

In 2014, the Making Caring Common project at Harvard asked ten thousand American middle school and high school students to rank the values most important to them. Over 80 percent picked high achievement or personal happiness. Just 20 percent picked caring for others. The students ranked self-interest above fairness. The study shined a light on the growing influence of an ethic of individualism in American families, one that prioritizes upward mobility, independence, and external markers of success, and which associates material wealth with happiness.

Relationships are not dispensable to healthy development; they are fundamental to it. Close, authentic relationships with peers and adults give girls the courage to try new things, express themselves, and face down failure. For fifty years, we've known that girls' identity development happens in close concert with their relationships; they will develop their values, purpose, and self-worth through connection to others. This has mostly to do with how girls are socialized: from almost the moment they are born, they learn to take care of others and rely heavily on feedback.

But the new rules of success are driving girls to disconnect from their most nourishing relationships in order to pursue an elusive ideal of achievement. One girl refuses to tell a close friend which schools she is applying to for fear of competition; one consistently misses meals to study longer at the library. Another travels thousands of miles away from her parents to please them by attending a "brand name" college. Each values ambition over connection, and each surrenders a vital channel to her wellness.

At two all-girls high schools in 2016, where students were overwhelmed by stress and tense peer relationships, researchers traced girls' lack of well-being to a "pervasive belief" that professional status and financial gain would lead to happiness. Girls were hearing these messages from parents and from the media. It was the "intense pressures to perform," the psychologists wrote, that threatened girls' ability to develop relationships that offered meaningful social support.

Traditional psychology tells us the goal of adolescence is to separate from our parents and prove we can stand on our own. But my work and that of others has challenged this assumption. Adolescents, especially girls, are most resilient when they are connected to others. Girls themselves agree: a wide-ranging review of studies in 2012 found that "the need to maintain relationships with peers is of greater importance [to girls] than success through winning."

The idea that adolescents just want to be left alone by adults is simply inaccurate. In a 2014 study I helped design for the nonprofit

Girls Leadership, 77 percent of high school girls said they turned to their mothers first for advice to achieve their goals; 86 percent said parents, more than friends, helped them be braver. Other studies have found that even as college students want more autonomy, they also continue to seek the approval and validation of the adults who are most important to them.

These ideas are at the heart of Relational-Cultural Theory. First defined by psychologists Jean Baker Miller and Irene Stiver, RCT argues that all people grow through their most important relationships, not by separating from them. Growth-fostering relationships allow us to be authentic with our thoughts and feelings in ways that make us feel empowered to deal with conflict or manage change. They also inspire an increased sense of self-worth. All of this moves us toward maturity and adulthood. RCT argues that separation from others is not progressive and that isolation is a primary cause of human suffering.

Yet over the last decade, media coverage of girls has told us just the opposite: the savviest young women avoid committed relationships so they can pursue success. A woman at the University of Pennsylvania told the *New York Times* that marrying young was "either proof of a lack of ambition or a tragic mistake that would stunt her career." In her book *The End of Men*, Hanna Rosin argued that the transactional sex of college hookup culture was a girl's shrewd response to an overscheduled life, one that conferred job mobility without forcing her to commit to any one person. Relationships, in these tellings, are a distraction from a girl's goals.

In fact it's the other way around. It is the pressure to pursue their ambitions that is sundering girls from the relationships they need in order to thrive. In a 2014 national study where, for the first time on record, teens reported higher levels of stress than adults, the American Psychological Association found 17 percent had canceled social plans because of stress. Between 2000 and 2015, the number of teens who got together with their friends nearly every day plummeted by over 40 percent, and girls' social self-confidence declined at double the rate of boys'. UCLA's 2015 Freshman Survey found that over the last ten years, the proportion of first-year college students who said they spent sixteen or more hours a week socializing with friends dropped by nearly half over ten years, to just 18 percent. It is women who were more likely to say they were spending less time with their friends.

Social media is a culprit here. Psychologist Jean Twenge, who studies generational trends, has found that teens who visit social networking sites every day, but see their friends in person less frequently, are most likely to agree with the statements, "A lot of times I feel lonely," "I often feel left out of things," and "I often wish I had more good friends." She reports that teens' feelings of loneliness have risen steadily since 2013 and are now at an all-time high.

Learning to be a girl is a process that unfolds over many years. "If you ask a room full of first-grade girls 'Who's the best runner in this class?' every single hand will go up," an elementary school principal once told me. "'*I'm the best runner*,' they'll say," she went on. "But if you ask that same question of a group of fifth-grade girls, they point to the best runner."

Ask a group of ninth-grade girls that same question, and there might be silence. Or if they point to the best runner, she might smile weakly, deny it, look down, or say, "Nah, I'm not that good."

To be an adolescent girl, writes Claire Messud in her novel *The Woman Upstairs*, is to "never let on that you are proud, or that you know you're better at history, or biology, or French. . . . You put yourself down whenever you can so that people won't feel threatened by you, so they'll like you. . . . You learn a whole other polite way of speaking to the people who musn't see you clearly." The changes that wash over girl children slowly are as subtle as they are profound.

"It doesn't even occur to you," Messud writes, "as you fashion your mask so carefully, that it will grow onto your skin and graft itself, come to seem irremovable."

Many of us get uncomfortable talking about the things that make girls and boys different—and not for nothing. For thousands of years, the belief that women and girls were different justified their degradation and inequality. Partly for this reason, more recent legal efforts to achieve gender equality have argued that women should be treated the same as men because they *are* the same as men.

Calling attention to gender differences can also make them seem bigger than they really are. Women and men on balance are more alike than different. Emphasizing difference can reinforce the destructive stereotypes that hold women back and distort public opinion about female potential.

But if you're parenting or teaching an adolescent girl, you know that she can be different from her brother. This book argues that to ignore that difference is to miss the unique ways our girls struggle during this stormy period of development and neglect the most effective strategies to support them.

I reject the idea that difference makes girls less capable. But I argue they and their parents need special knowledge, support, and awareness to usher them through the challenges of twenty-first-century adolescence and into adulthood. To raise and teach a girl well during this period, we need a different kind of report card to evaluate her health and potential.

There are two things this book will give you. First, a language. So much of what girls face is unspoken but deeply felt. Without words for what they are going through, they think they are alone; worse, they think it is their fault. But when you know what something is and what it means, it changes you. Take overthinking. When I tell girls what it is, why it happens, and what to do about it, they are palpably relieved. These obsessive thoughts, they realize, don't mean they're crazy; there is a name for it, things you can do to manage it. Change is suddenly possible.

Second, this book will give you strategies you can try right away. I am an educator above all. My passion is converting research into skill-building curriculum, so people can change the way they think and act. I want you to imagine each chapter as a workshop you're taking with me. This book contains nearly a decade of my research and teaching on the subject of girls and confidence. It is also the first I have written since becoming a parent to a girl myself.

Parenthood is an exercise in what journalist Jennifer Senior called "all joy and no fun": meaningful moments dwarfed by an endless, daily grind. It is one that disproportionately burdens mothers. Out of any stage of parenting, from infancy to adulthood, it is during middle school and the teen years that mothers bottom out on measures of well-being and satisfaction, a 2016 study by Suniya Luthar and Lucia Ciciolla found.

Girls aren't the only ones battling blows to their self-worth. Despite all the hours we sink into parenting—time that has increased exponentially for both mothers and fathers in the last two decades—our confidence as parents has bottomed out. I blame three pernicious cultural messages that make us question our own instincts:

1. *You have complete control over your child's development. If you don't, you must be doing something wrong.* Forget genetics. All you have to do is read the right books, attend some lectures, and peruse the parenting blogs. If you're smart and committed enough, you should be able to program your child into a miniature superhuman. A cottage industry of parenting experts (yes, guilty as charged) now implies they have answers parents don't, and it has gutted parents of their innate confidence and authority along the way. As Jessica Lahey writes in *The Gift of Failure,*

parenting has been transformed from an instinct every human has to "a skill to be studied and learned."

2. *You can never do or be enough as a parent.* Despite being told we're all-powerful, or perhaps because of it, we're constantly besieged by the fear that we're not good enough parents. The insecurity forces us to compete with others and see our peers' shortcomings as quiet signs of our superiority, and vice versa. It also, Lahey writes, pushes us to be "ever-present, ever-helpful, ever-reminding, ever-rescuing."

3. *Your child's success or failure defines you.* It's impossible not to identify with your child's ups and downs, and anyone who tells you not to probably isn't a parent. Most of us have poured the lion's share of our focus, resources, and heart into our kids for as long as they've been alive. But there's a point where this crosses over into something much more destructive to the parent soul: a worldview that says, *as my child goes, so goes my worth as a parent and person.* This myth firmly entrenches our egos in our kids' everyday lives. It also, says Lahey, drives us to interpret the moments our children are safe, successful, or happy as "tangible evidence of our parenting success."

To become a better parent, you must take as a given that there are always factors beyond your control. Despite what you may fear in your worst moments, you are not exclusively to blame for your daughter's struggle. That's why the first part of this book is devoted to ways the culture has changed and exacerbated challenges for girls.

I approached this project by posing two questions: What chips away at a girl's sense of self? What bolsters her in the face of challenge? I began imagining this work as a recipe I was building (coinciding with a newfound love of cooking). I wanted to cull the "ingredients" of confidence. This book is that recipe, and each chapter is an ingredient. To "cook a girl" successfully, I've found, you need to be clear on the forces that act against her as much as what she needs to be strong. Each chapter begins with a list of challenges your daughter might be facing in a particular domain, followed by step-by-step directions to teach you how to guide her through it.

For this book I interviewed ninety-six girls, almost all between the ages of fifteen and twenty-four, the age when adolescence concludes; for this reason I refer to them as girls throughout. The majority of girls were middle-class and from high-achieving schools. One of my interviewees was assigned female at birth and identified as nonbinary. Most of these conversations occurred one-on-one. Most were students at three universities in the Northeast: one elite, residential, and small; another a largely commuter college; and one a large state university. Two of the schools were all-women colleges. Through colleagues and my travels, I met high school students who were mostly from the Northeast and attending coed public and private schools. Postgraduate interviews came to me similarly. I also interviewed over forty adults: parents, researchers, college and high school administrators, and school counselors. One-third of the girls I interviewed identified as people of color. For ease of reading, girls are identified by their race only when they have mentioned it in an interview as directly relevant to their story. An appendix contains more information about each girl mentioned in the book; their names were changed to protect their privacy.

As always in my books, it is the girls' voices that guide me (and, again for ease of reading, I trimmed the word *like* from some of their statements when the word was used liberally in a sentence). For the two years I spent writing this book, they spoke to me on Snapchat and Instagram, in my office, in their dorm rooms and food courts, by e-mail and video chat and text. They told me when I was wrong and when I was in their heads. What these voices helped me understand is that teaching girls the skills to speak up and take charge is only part of how we'll help them thrive. A life well lived isn't just about doing and accomplishing more, nor is it about depending only on yourself. We need to make the same kind of investment in teaching girls the skills for self-compassion and mindfulness, so they can tame the tendency to ruminate and catastrophize, and have a healthy mindset to cope with failure. We need to help them talk back to a toxic culture and claim success as more than the sum of college résumés and filtered Instagram feeds. We need to help girls not just lean in, but lean inside.

Despite what girls may be hearing from parents and learning in school, income and academic achievement will not determine their happiness or life satisfaction. Neither will materialism. An exclusive focus on these are linked to lower levels of life satisfaction, no matter what your income group. Emotional health is what matters most. I want girls to prioritize self-care, nourish their most important relationships, and seek support as much as they strive to succeed.

Success itself is not the problem for girls. It's how they are expected to pursue it: the rules they believe they must follow, their beliefs about themselves as they achieve and fail, and the habits and values they develop as a result. These habits, of mind and behavior, are being learned as girls enter young adulthood, taking their first jobs and leadership positions, doing the work of figuring out who and what they want to be, and learning the mechanics of how to be a grown-up. What they learn in these formative years may stay with them throughout their lives, making late adolescence precisely the moment when we can help them develop healthier habits to last a lifetime.

Girls should be able to succeed without sacrificing themselves. We owe them the tools to develop a strong sense of self so they can say, with conviction, "I am enough just as I am." Their lives will be changed for the better if we succeed.

ENOUGH

AS SHE IS

1

The College Application Industrial Complex

You have to be better than everyone else—even yourself.

—ALLISON, SEVENTEEN

From the moment they are old enough to understand what college is, middle-class kids enter a toxic system I call the College Application Industrial Complex—a swirling mix of anxious parents, obsessively checked online grading systems, college counseling, and my-life-is-over-if-I-blow-my-SATs terror. The Complex demands that students excel at absolutely everything, so they can craft themselves into the perfect specimens worthy of college admission.

It is an exhausting competition with a single goal: acceptance, preferably early decision, by a top university or college. In this system, being anything less than amazing can feel catastrophic. A *Hunger Games* mentality emerges in the most ambitious communities, where students (and their parents) interpret a peer's success as a threat to their own. The stakes feel impossibly high; they suggest that if you don't identify a new planet or cure a disease by the time you turn seventeen, you're not only not extraordinary, you're mediocre. Even middle school students have begun to feel like their lives are building toward a single day when they will hear "yes" or "no" from the college of their choice.

From the outside looking in, girls appear to be champions in this arena. But in my work with girls, parents, and teachers over the last decade, I've seen something very different. Applying to college exacerbates vulnerabilities girls already bring to the table: fear of failure, low confidence, and the desire to please. Anxiety about college acceptance preys on girls where they are psychologically weakest, eroding the assets they need to thrive in adolescence and beyond. This chapter is about the ways college admissions mania uniquely harms girls, and how you can buffer your daughter against its most toxic elements.

"If life were one long grade school," Stanford professor Carol Dweck has said, "girls would rule the world." She means that school offers the kind of orderly, rule-based environment where girls tend to thrive: classrooms where you wait to speak, are praised when you have the right answer, keep a neat notebook, and hand in assignments on time. This is likely the reason girls outnumber boys in college, and why their grades are better, too. The problem is that these behaviors often backfire for girls. Needing to get everything just right can lead to crippling perfectionism, fear of failure, and a lack of resilience in the face of challenge.

College admissions mania arrives to exploit these traits in girls. What they learn as they apply leaves a lasting imprint on their motivation, sense of purpose, and self-worth. Girls arrive in my office on campus with a high school hangover that plagues them well into college, and beyond.

I have spent nearly a decade teaching young women to resist the Complex's most destructive messages, and I share them with you here. Be warned: many girls bring a healthy dose of cynicism (*this is the game, I have to play it*) and snark (*oh, so you don't want me to get into a good college?*) to the conversation. I don't blame them. It's a form of self-defense.

But keep talking. Even if she isn't agreeing, she is still listening. When I talk with parents around the country about how to support their daughters in the Complex, the first and last thing I say is this: you are the strongest buffer between your daughter and the messages she is receiving. Her school won't stand up to them. Her peers won't stand up to them. Yours may be the only voice of reason she hears. Suniya Luthar has urged parents to protect their children from the Complex, just as inner-city parents work to shield their children from gang violence.

It won't be enough to tell her that she'll get into a good college no matter what, and that she'll be happy wherever she goes (though both these things are likely true). Girls want to know you get the root causes of their stress, and that you are willing to engage with them on these issues.

THE MESSAGE: Be amazing at everything you do

THE RESULT: Diminished self-worth and relentless stress

Constant pressure to be extraordinary will inevitably make your daughter feel like she is falling short. She will never know the sense of satisfaction that comes with crossing a finish line because there is always another race to run. Nor can she stop to take a breath and enjoy the scenery. The messages she hears, shared as both consolation and warning, are that everyone else is doing more; that college admissions are arbitrary, confusing, and heartbreaking, even when a résumé is virtually perfect; and that the competition has never been fiercer or more threatening.

A high school senior put it to me chillingly: "You have to be better than everyone else—even yourself." In no time at all, the sense that *I don't* do *enough* quickly becomes a deep-seated belief that *I* am *not enough.* "I always judge myself," sixteen-year-old Rebecca told me. "I have this little voice in my head being like, you could be better at this, you could be better at that. It takes a toll on me."

When your baseline is a sense of deficit, you can't be grateful for what you have. Lily, sixteen, told me, "I'm not appreciating what I have in the moment because I'm always striving for something else. If I'm always so hard on myself, always pushing myself for the better thing, then how can I be happy with the accomplishments in that moment?"

Although it may seem obvious to you, your daughter needs to hear you say that no one can sanely excel at everything they do, nor should they want to. Will a life in which she does everything perfectly be a happy and healthy life for her? Focus on what is sacrificed on the altar of perfection-seeking: Self-worth. Curiosity and exploration. Hobbies. Sleep. Challenge the standards being imposed on her. Let her know you reject them.

Reflect together on your family's values. This is a time to talk about the big-picture questions your family has tried to answer in the way that it lives: What matters more, getting ahead or finding meaning in your work? How does your family define "success"? What does it mean to have a good life? Is it time spent together at home? Faith? Service? Lifelong learning? Travel adventures? Cultural events? Cultivating relationships? A spotless GPA and schedule that is built around studying may get her into the college of her choice, but at what cost? Narrate what you stand for as a family in contrast to what she is hearing outside of it.

Every morning at breakfast, or whenever you have consistent time together, cultivate a family practice of gratitude. It can be simple: "Today, I'm grateful the sun is out." "I'm grateful that I'm healthy." "I'm grateful that I get to see my best friend tonight." If you're not together, text with her about it, or do it on the phone.

A reminder of what she has can help mitigate the longing for what she doesn't.

THE MESSAGE: Avoid new ventures, especially where you might fail

THE RESULT: Diminished curiosity, exploration, and healthy risk taking

The girls I met told me high school was a time to get smarter about what you already knew. It was not when you asked new questions. New ventures could make you look like an amateur to an admissions committee. "By ninth grade, your experimental time in life is over," Emily, sixteen, told me, without a shred of irony. "You have to know what you want to do because as soon as you start high school, you're too old to start anything."

Instead, as they undertook a new activity, the only question many students found themselves asking was, "Will this look good on my college application?" Questions such as "Do I really want to study this?" and "Does this interest me?" became irrelevant. This at the very moment when a girl should explore, listen to her evolving interests, and take risks to figure out who she is. But in the Complex, she hears the opposite: Play it safe. Specialize. Trade what you love to do for what looks good and feels safe.

The cost is a steep decline in healthy risk taking. The ability to take a risk—to try something where she might fail and face down an unpredictable outcome to prove to herself she is stronger and braver than she thought—is a core ingredient of confidence. It is also a muscle. When she stops taking risks, that muscle atrophies, and so does her confidence.

Girls don't need any more help avoiding healthy risks. Gender differences in this domain are prominent. A meta-analysis of 150 studies by James Byrnes and colleagues found that men were more comfortable taking risks in almost every category. The widest gender gap, notably, was in intellectual risk taking.

Hannah was a passionate activist in high school. She loved her creative writing work and a local internship. "But I constantly felt the need to not screw up, to achieve the most I could, to be perfect at the things I loved," she told me. "It took away from my focus on exploring and enjoying."

The Complex can indeed turn school into a clinical means to an end. Allison, a seventeen-year-old senior at a public school in New York, was waiting on an early decision from an Ivy League school. She had excelled in her classes but felt little investment in her education beyond where she would go to college. She was unable to take classes she wanted, like wood shop and poetry. Her sacrifices made her bitter. "If I don't get into a top-tier school, it's like, 'What was all this for?'" she told me angrily. "If it wasn't to get into a good college, then it's all for nothing." The whole process felt "sad and pathetic."

When I asked her if college could be a refuge where she pursued what she really cared about, she laughed drily. "I want to learn what I really want," she told me, "but in reality it's like, go to elementary school so you can do well in middle school, so you can do well in high school, so you can go to a good college, so you can do well in a good college, so you can get a good job, so you can make a lot of money, so you can raise kids to make them do well in elementary school. And then when I'm retired that's when I'll have fun."

This isn't an easy conversation to have. After all, it's more than fair for a girl to worry about how her college application will look. But the so-called shoulds and have-tos of her life must live in balance with pursuits that she genuinely cares about. Obsession with appearance cannot dominate her life, or it will gut her of joy—in learning and in life.

Ask your daughter if she feels pressure to choose success over challenge. If she has the guts to say yes, give her your sympathy. She's likely only doing what she thinks is required to succeed in the Complex. Keep asking questions: Is she taking that class because she genuinely likes it, or because she thinks she should? What are the things in her life that she values more than getting into the right college, or getting good grades?

Deans of admissions are increasingly turned off by applications that smack of dilettantism. "No child should have a six-page résumé. That to us isn't impressive," Debra Shaver of Smith College told me. A flashy summer experience rarely inspires her or her team. "We talk about a deep engagement in something. I love the kid who's the chair of the dance cleanup committee for three years," she said. "I love the kid who has the part-time job."

In 2016, Harvard's Making Caring Common project launched a two-year initiative to reshape the college admissions process. "Turning the Tide" has enlisted over one hundred deans from around the country (including Yale, MIT, and Kenyon) to expand admissions criteria to prioritize ethical engagement and diminish the power of external achievements.

If there were no pressure to get into college, what would she be doing with her time? The measure of success in conversations like these isn't a U-turn in her behavior or course of study. It's taking the time for her to reflect on what she genuinely cares about, and affirm what you stand for as a family.

What if she calls you a hypocrite? How can *you* possibly tell her to take chances when you've ridden her so hard about getting into college? The answer is that both can be true: you can want her to succeed by society's standards, *and* talk about the places your values reject them. This isn't an either/or choice: you're not either a slave to the Complex or a radical outlier. She can be nimble: how and when she gives in or pushes back is up to her. Your job will be to guide the conversation, and occasionally bite your tongue when you disagree with where she lands. You will easily support some choices and struggle to find a way to respect others. You are also entitled to change course as a parent. Perhaps you realize you've been pushing too hard, even letting the Complex speak through you. It's okay to say so to your daughter; she will respect and trust you more if you do. You can look at resisting the Complex as a journey you take together, knowing that the values you define for yourselves will help both of you be healthier and more whole.

Reward her for taking risks. If she's willing to try a tough class because she's interested, go with it. When my students face a challenge and worry about not excelling, I ask them: What is the *minimum* benefit you could gain from this situation? Sure, I know they want an A on the test or whatever the ultimate success looks like. But what is the least they might gain from this experience? Is it learning something new? Toughening their test-taking muscle? Try this with your daughter. If she can find some value beyond the outcome she is aiming for, she is likely to be tougher in the face of not getting it.

Above all, play the long game. It's easy to have tunnel vision about college acceptance and put that goal at the center of all her plans. Resist the temptation. Short-term choices have long-term consequences. To size up every decision through the lens of high performance is to set her up for a narrowly defined life that may bear painful repercussions later on.

Casey, nineteen, played three varsity sports and participated in student senate, student council, and the civil rights team at her rural Maine school. After her parents got divorced, her mother moved to a nearby town. "Do you want to come over for dinner?" she would ask her daughter. Casey would decline because of work.

Today, Casey told me, "I feel guilty because I won't consistently be home ever again. I wish I could get that time back." Should her mother have been tougher? Casey may not have listened, but the message would have registered. When you take a strong position, it may be years before they can appreciate it. Think back to a time when your own parents made you do something you hated at the time but thank them for now. Hold on to that as you face her resistance.

THE MESSAGE: What you accomplish matters more than what you learn

THE RESULT: Loss of intrinsic motivation

Girls who make choices based more on appearance than on genuine desire give up a vital learning asset: their autonomy. Autonomy is a core ingredient of intrinsic motivation, the drive to learn simply because you enjoy it. Researchers suspect this may be a learner's most precious resource. Intrinsically motivated people are more resilient in the face of challenges. They are less anxious and depressed, and have lower levels of burnout. They have better relationships, get better grades, and have higher levels of psychological well-being, to name just a few benefits.

We most want to learn when we can do it freely and without oversight. When we suspect someone is trying to control our performance through extrinsic motivators—say, by offering rewards, threatening punishment, or tendering certain kinds of praise—our intrinsic drive declines.

In his book *Drive*, Daniel Pink shares one of the most famous studies to prove this point. Researchers split preschool children up into three groups: The first was an "expected award" group, where the children were told they'd get a blue ribbon certificate if they drew with markers and paper. The second group was the "unexpected award" group: the kids were asked to draw, and when the session ended, researchers could give them blue ribbons if they felt like it. The third group was the "no award" group: these kids were asked if they wanted to draw, but a reward was neither promised nor handed out at the end.

Two weeks later, the teachers put out paper and markers during free play. The children in the "unexpected award" and "no award" groups drew just as much, and as enthusiastically, as they had before. The kids who were promised the blue ribbon showed less interest and spent less time drawing. These were the children whose autonomies had been undermined. Their freedom to choose whether or not they wanted to draw had been undercut by the control of an offered reward.

Professors Edward L. Deci and Richard M. Ryan, pioneers in the study of motivation, say girls are more vulnerable to having their intrinsic motivation threatened by the offer of a reward or punishment. Because girls are socialized by adults to please others, they tend to care more about feedback from teachers and parents—and so are more sensitive to feeling controlled.

Females, Deci and Ryan have found, "pay particular attention to evidence of having pleased the evaluator when praised." Multiple studies find that girls show more negative outcomes when they are praised in ways that encourage them to keep performing at a high level. In one study, praising elementary school students for fixed traits and abilities, like being "smart" or "nice," undermined intrinsic motivation for girls, but not boys. Other studies have found that emphasizing "extrinsic values" like good grades, college acceptance, and financial success is particularly damaging for girls' wellness, and that girls are more vulnerable when a parent's emphasis on achievement is delivered with high doses of criticism.

None of this means girls will work less hard or less well. But it does suggest that any school initiative emphasizing extrinsic rewards, such as online grade books, may burden girls especially. A popular trend in education, online grade books allow students, and usually their parents, to view an updated grade point average at any moment in a semester. Constant access lets families know where their children stand; it also encourages obsessive checking, not unlike the ways girls look at their phones to count the likes they've racked up for a post.

Educators at Harpeth Hall, an all-girls school in Nashville, issued a white paper in 2016 questioning the use of the technology, writing that "the joy of learning diminishes as [students] focus narrowly on the numbers and improving the numbers." Constant parental monitoring, they wrote, lessens "the space girls have in their lives for risk taking" and independent struggle. The system may burden high achievers with perfectionist tendencies, who "are more likely to equate their self-worth with their grades." In a survey, students at the school said their confidence was most inhibited by the tendency to compare themselves to others; online grading could exacerbate this, the educators said. At least six girls' schools have taken a stand against online grading. Paul Burke, the head of Nightingale-Bamford in New York City, has said online grade books "rob students of the chance to be what they call the 'authors of their own education.'"

A girl who is low in intrinsic drive is more likely to adopt what Dweck calls "performance goals," where she is driven more by the wish to be judged competent by others, and avoid criticism or failure. Getting an A on a French test is an example of a performance goal. Mastering the past tense, on the other hand, is a learning goal. Jennie, a twenty-year-old tennis prodigy, had relied on performance goals her entire athletic career. "All I could hear [in my training] was 'best tennis player in the world.' I never thought about, this is how you hit a forehand. This is how you hit a backhand." For students with performance goals, writes Dweck, "the entire task choice and pursuit process is built around children's concerns about their ability level."

By contrast, a girl will pursue a learning goal because she wants to master a challenge or increase her competence. In one study, Dweck taught a group of middle school students a set of scientific principles. She gave half of them a performance goal, and the other half a learning goal. Students with the learning goal scored higher on challenges, worked longer on their tasks, and tried more solutions before giving up.

Performance goals aren't necessarily bad. The desire to compete and outdo someone else can be excellent motivation. But when this is what most drives you, the outcomes aren't positive: research cited by Judith Harackiewicz finds higher levels of depression and anxiety, along with more challenge avoidance and helplessness. Attaining these goals is linked to increases in unhappiness instead of well-being, and even fiercer attempts to be perceived as perfect.

Performance goals dominate the college application process, where it's not uncommon for girls to display a disconnect between where-I-want-to-go and what-I-want-to-do. "They have been working so hard, but they don't know what they've been working for," a college counselor at an all-girls school told me. "They're beating themselves up, they're not sleeping, they're eating poorly, they're making themselves wrecks, and they haven't taken the time to figure out what their interests are and what they want." In 2015, the largest annual survey of American college freshmen found that over 72 percent of women said the most important factor in their college search is a school's "good academic reputation," compared to 66 percent of men. In 2009, more women than men said they chose their college because it was where "my parents wanted me to go."

Students like Jennie, who are largely driven by performance

goals, are less likely to achieve mastery in their learning. "I didn't necessarily love tennis," she told me, "but I loved the idea of being the best tennis player in the world. Because of that I could never become the best tennis player in the world."

Encourage your daughter to choose at least one pursuit per semester that is more a "want-to" than a "have-to." Call attention to what she genuinely loves to do: perhaps it's mentoring a younger child, coding, studying fashion, or playing music in a band. Yes, she may tell you that a certain class will "ruin" her GPA, or that she has "less than no time" for her hobby. Try not to give in. Teenagers are many things, but they are largely not forward thinking. At certain times, they will need you to intervene.

THE MESSAGE: Having lots of choices = control over your life

THE RESULT: False sense of control; taking setbacks personally

For high-achieving girls, life is a series of go-heres and get-theres: from school to activity to social event to internship. Implied here is that it's not only the substance of your life that matters, but also its structure. It's not just, *if you get this grade, you'll succeed.* It's, *if you do this activity, take this class, or play this sport, you'll succeed.*

All this sends a destructive message to girls: the schedule of your life is just as important as your performance within it. That if you work hard and make all the "right" choices—sleep this many hours, take this class, lead this club, do this service project, make this review sheet—you should be able to get what you want. This reasoning creates a girl who harbors a satisfying but ultimately false sense of control over her life.

Sociologist Barry Schwartz has shown that people who have lots of choices—say, about where to go to college, which activities to pursue, or what to major in—can be lulled into an illusion of control. They believe that if they can make *any* choice, then they should be capable of making the *best* choice.

The problem with this logic is that if a girl gets to steer her own ship, she's also to blame if it springs a leak. If things don't work out for her, it must be because of something *she* failed to do. Depression and shame typically follow. Schwartz called this self-destructive reasoning the "paradox of choice."

Remind your daughter that having a full schedule—and, in the most extreme version, having your life mapped out—won't necessarily make her happier, smarter, or more successful. Let her know that she should not mistake having a plan for having a purpose. In his studies of young adults, Stanford professor William Damon found that "it is the people who seem to be most on track who express the most severe misgivings."

Challenge the assumption that having a full schedule gives her control over how life turns out. Have there been times when she thought she was in control of something but actually wasn't? When she worked hard and did her best, expected to excel, then fell short? What did she learn from that experience? Most of us gain humility and perspective. Through this conversation, help her respect that there are forces larger than herself at play. Besides this, there are other times when she'll just plain make the wrong choice. Talk about a time that happened, too, and what she learned. Mistakes are sometimes the only way we get to figure out what we genuinely want out of life.

When our children are young, we are told to offer them choices as a way to give them a sense of control without turning them into despots. Do you want pasta or pizza? Do you want to go to the playground or to Grandma's house? This is a practice worth returning to. If she has too many choices, and you worry she feels overly responsible for her own destiny, narrow the scope of her choices to only a few. Do you want to play a sport or be the president of student council? Do you want to run the student newspaper or start a nonprofit? You pick, but pick only one.

This kind of restriction may only be feasible in high school. But your job, as the parent of an adolescent, is not to be the hero—at least not right now. And if she's really angry, let her blame you. When a teen is faced with a choice she doesn't want to make (but may on some level accept as necessary), blaming Mom or Dad works well. "My dad [or mom] is making me" come home early, take off that shirt, you name it. Throwing your parents under the bus is a terrific strategy.

THE MESSAGE: You must find your life's passion by high school

THE RESULT: Forced passions lead to big, costly decisions

In the last decade, it's become fashionable to suggest that having passion is a golden ticket for students at every level, whether you're applying to college or for a first job. It has become a proxy for "having your whole life figured out." This is college admissions mania at its most absurd and unfair.

To figure out what you truly love, you need at least two resources: time to explore what you care about and the freedom to screw up doing it. This is precisely what the Complex yanks away as your daughter enters high school. It's an outrageous paradox: we give students the narrowest of paths to follow to admissions success, squashing their ability to pursue the full range of what they truly love, while pressuring them more than ever to do just that.

Ideally you pursue a passion because you love to do it, and not necessarily because you excel at it. True passion is powered by curiosity, a thirst to answer a burning question: How fast can I run? When does a chorus start to sound good singing together? How do you get people to pay attention to global warming? The question is what fuels you. This kind of passion requires being comfortable with not knowing the answer. I don't know if I'm fast. I don't know how many hours of practice it takes. I don't know if a bake sale will work.

In the Complex, it's never okay not to have the answers. Curiosity can't breathe in this atmosphere because passion comes with rules: First, you have to find your passion early. It's all but implied that if you haven't found your passion by puberty, you're screwed. Then, what you "love" must not only look good on a college application, but you better be exceptional at it, too.

Not surprisingly, many girls feel like failures at finding their passions. "I don't even know what I want for dinner tonight," Jessica, sixteen, told me, much less what was her passion. "Because I spend most of my time working, I don't have time to explore myself and get familiar with what I love or what I'm good at," she said.

Jessica knew what she *did* love didn't fit the bill. "I love tennis," she said, "but I'm not about to become Serena Williams, and can't study tennis in school." Watching her peers enter every robotics competition within a two-hundred-mile radius, then take "three thousand four hundred twenty-three math classes," Jessica forced herself to throw out random ideas—business, tech—that would be marketable to a college. "I often feel like I must figure out what I love, so I can do it in high school, study it in college, and then get a job so I don't fail." One high school girl participated in a nationally regarded coding program for girls, took AP computer science, marketed herself as a coder to colleges—but told her friends she hated computer science. "I'm just going to use it so I can get in," she said.

But passion can't be forced on a person, nor can it be rushed. Forcing it may not just divert her from discovering what she might actually love to do; it can also lead to her pouring some of the best years of her life into something she's not sure she cares that much about in the first place. It can influence other choices she makes, like where to study, live, and work—only to wake up years later and realize the passion was forced and not real. "Fake passions," wrote author and Grown and Flown blogger Lisa Heffernan, "crowd out real ones."

Instead of inspiring girls to discover what they love, passion pressure becomes yet another box to check, and another expectation to fulfill—and so ends up making girls feel like they've fallen short yet again. Passion has been distorted into a tool used primarily for self-focused, external achievement, the opposite of what a passion should be. Nor does it help that, as girls are now expected to succeed across a wide range of areas, specializing in just one has become harder and harder—which only makes them feel worse. Debra Shaver, dean of admission at Smith College, thinks passion pressure is ridiculous. "Passion is something you discover in college or beyond. I'm constantly surprised and annoyed by admission deans who declare that they're looking for 'students with passion.' I think it creates unnecessary anxiety in students. Finding your passion is a journey of self-discovery. It takes time."

Passion arrives on its own schedule. It cannot be planned for. To rush a child to develop one is akin to asking her to walk before she is ready: she will try and she will fail, and you both will feel frustrated and dejected. It will become yet another way she worries that she's falling short.

Be clear that you don't expect her to force a feeling she doesn't have, or to fudge one on an application. Question the absurdity of being expected to know what you love by the ripe age of seventeen. I found tennis at thirty, cooking at forty. When did your passions arrive? Let her know. Normalize the reality that passion finds us at different moments in life.

Instead, focus on cultivating purpose in your daughter. Purpose, writes Damon, is the "intention to accomplish something that is at once meaningful to the self and of consequence to the world beyond the self." Purpose is likely what passion used to be, before the Complex distorted it. Purpose isn't a synonym for public service or altruism. Engaging with a goal that is "bigger than yourself" might mean creating a new app or starting a business. The point is to expand beyond more self-oriented goals like "getting good grades" or "getting into the right school."

When you have a sense of purpose, you know why whatever you are doing matters to you personally, and why it matters to the world. Purpose is the deeper reason we pursue our everyday goals. Yet only about 20 percent of adolescents have a sense of purpose, Damon has found, and its value has seen a steady decline. In 1967, fully 86 percent of first-year college students endorsed a meaningful philosophy of life as an essential life goal; only 42 percent did so in 2004. But purpose may be making a comeback, and educators are increasingly turning to the trait as an antidote to Complex insanity. Research has shown that adults with purpose are more confident and comfortable with themselves, and have higher self-esteem. The findings are similar for young people.

The Echoing Green Foundation's Work on Purpose curriculum helps young adults clarify their purpose, identify their competencies, and find meaningful jobs. One of their many useful activities asks participants to reflect on questions such as these:

+ What issues or ideas make your heart beat faster, whether because you are so deeply compelled by them, because you are angered by them, or because you are overjoyed by them?

- What is the primary topic of the articles you always read, and the movies, books, and TV shows that most attract you?

- Who are "your people"?

- When you imagine the world you want to live in, what three words come to mind?

- Have you ever stood up for anyone? Who? Why? Who would you stand for, and why?

- What social or environmental problem do you ache to see solved?

In a formal program, these questions are usually answered in writing, but they can also work well in conversation with an active listener such as yourself.

Damon encourages adults to act as matchmakers to help connect a child's beliefs to a particular need or opportunity. This is an ongoing process and rarely occurs in a single aha moment. Instead, Damon likens the process to grass seeds spread in a yard: "only some will sprout, and we have no idea which ones." When you talk with your daughter about her day, listen for signs of her enthusiasm. You may hear her light up about work for an organization, a lecture she attended, or something she read. Ask her why she liked it, and why it matters to her. Ask her why it matters to the world. What would she like to do about it next? Then, offer to help her deepen her interest (but not in ways that, straight off the bat, will "look good" to a college). Perhaps you can get her a book by the person who gave the lecture, or brainstorm ways to expand her volunteer work.

Girls from low-income backgrounds, many of whom attend

college to better their family's circumstances, often possess a driving sense of purpose. Isabel, who came to college in New England from Cuba, was roiled by the comments her friends made about finding their passion early on. She ultimately chose to disregard them. I asked her where she found this calm. In part, she practiced asking herself what genuinely mattered to her. Most of all, she said with great clarity, "supporting my family is the priority over other things."

THE MESSAGE: Everyone is doing, being, and succeeding more than you are

THE RESULT: Pervasive insecurity; tense, competitive relationships

Your daughter feels quite certain that everyone is doing and being more than she is. Her peers are spending more time working, getting better grades, scoring higher on tests, applying to better schools, having more fun, and looking more beautiful. Try to suggest otherwise and you'll be told: You. Just. Don't. Get it.

It's not true, of course. But the delusion makes perfect, if not troubling, sense: if you are beset by your own perceived shortcomings, you'll miss signs of others struggling. Or, maybe you know your peers are suffering, but you discount it because they have been able to achieve despite it. If you think nothing you do is enough, it's easy to imagine your peers are leaving you in the dust. Thoughts like these force girls to compete with and compare themselves to friends. And they threaten the fabric of some of girls' closest relationships.

"Your closest friends can become your strongest competition," Maya, eighteen, wrote to me. "You start to evaluate them like an admissions counselor and personal trainer. Their grades, their body, their clothes—you are in competition with them rather than offering unconditional support. There can still be a strong, loving relationship, but the element of competition is always there." Girls begin to see one another not for who they are, but through the lens of the culture's unforgiving demands.

"Everyone around me is checking the boxes," Kayla, nineteen, told me. The floor in her dorm, where everyone was an honors business student, was tense. "Even though you might like the person you're living next door to," she said, "you want to beat them out. You want to be better than them at the end of the day." When competition begins to eat away at connection, resentment and even paranoia can follow. College women talk about the challenge of having friends with the same major. "It's hard to be happy for each other sometimes," one junior told me. Better, her classmate said, to find friends studying something totally different. "They literally have no idea what your successes even mean!" Her friends laughed knowingly.

"When I'm not completely secure or comfortable with one part of my life, a way for me to feel better about it is to almost put people down and just brighten my spirits," Lily, sixteen, explained. "I selfishly think or strive to be better than them in whatever way I can be. It can lead to me being mean to someone, I guess."

The loving friendships Rebecca had built with peers in high school began to fray as her peers sank deeper into the Complex. She began hiding the fears about her own inadequacy that she most needed to confide. Now she saw signs of her inferiority in the triumphs of her friends. Megan, one of her closest friends, "gets everything," she told me, "like every award. It makes me look so worthless. Why am I not getting those awards? It makes me feel like I'm going to be a failure because she's so successful."

While there is nothing wrong with going head-to-head academically with a capable opponent, the problem is when it becomes personal and destroys relationships. This happens more often than it should. In the 2017 Girls' Index, 41 percent of girls in grades five through twelve said they did not trust other girls; 76 percent said most girls were in competition with one another. Socialized to be nice at all costs, girls struggle to be fully honest as a rule, especially when it comes to disclosing non-good-girl feelings like competition and jealousy. Many hide these feelings to survive, so their feelings go underground. Girls stew, grow resentful, and become lonely. Add to this a culture of scarcity and insecurity around success, and relationships are endangered.

There are two things you can do here. First, make clear that the most noble competition separates performance from relationship. In other words, how well a friend does in school or life should have nothing to do with how much you trust or like her. This will not only spare your daughter's friendships, but it's also the right way to approach competition as a rule. Girls who are encouraged by their parents to personalize their conflicts become women who do the same in the workplace, where the behavior can backfire in dangerous ways.

Second, remind your daughter relationships matter. If your family believes in the value of women supporting women, this is the moment when you say so. This is when you name the toxic lesson she has been taught about seeing other girls as threats, and remind her of all the women in your lives who have helped you socially, professionally, financially, and spiritually. If your daughter loves one of your close friends, sit down together and talk about a time when you overcame a challenge to your friendship. Applying to college will arguably be the most competitive moment of her life, but the lessons about principled competition that she will learn here from you will serve her for much longer.

If a friend's success makes your daughter feel insecure, work compassionately with your daughter on owning that. Validate her insecurity and make sure she understands it's a by-product of the Complex, not necessarily a personal shortcoming. But if she wants to save those relationships—and she should, unless there is more to the story—encourage her to face her vulnerability and share it with the friend. Share a time with your daughter when you confided a fear to a friend, and it paid off. If your daughter remains silent and never speaks to the friend, the secrecy and resentment will eat away at the friendship from the inside until very little remains.

RESISTING THE COMPLEX

"I've always been the good girl," Natalia told me. "I did my homework, got good grades, did some sports, and paid attention to what my parents told me." She was eighteen and repeating her junior year at a boarding school abroad. Not long ago, she told me, "I felt like I had lost my motivation. I felt like I would lose my personality in the long run if I didn't change."

Natalia's parents had been pressuring her to become a lawyer or a doctor with a secure salary, but she'd always loved fashion journalism. Her resistance to her parents filled her with guilt. "I have everything," she told me. "I have a nice family, we have nice financial circumstances, I'm doing great at school, so I shouldn't complain at all. I didn't want to look like I wasn't appreciating what I had. But this was really killing me."

She tried so hard to contain her feelings, and felt so afraid of them spilling out, that she began to dissociate. She tried to stop feeling. "I became neutral about everything," she told me. "My mother kept asking me, 'Can you even smile?'"

As it dawned on Natalia that she was losing herself, she began to see how she had traded her own desires for her parents'. She didn't love piano. Her mother did. She didn't want to enter creative writing competitions. Her dad did.

Natalia had always carried around the secret, agonizing feeling that she was not particularly good at anything. Suddenly she wondered if her mediocrity came from lack of inspiration rather than her actual potential. "I wasn't motivated because I wasn't interested," she told me. "What I was good at is learning and doing what other people tell me to do."

She came to Courage Boot Camp, a four-week program I designed to help girls identify and take healthy risks. "I wanted to be able to fight for myself," she told me. Natalia was determined to confront her parents and tell them the truth. Each week, she named and took a small risk toward her goal. Her peers in the Boot Camp freely shared whether they had succeeded or even tried to take risks, and that delighted Natalia. It was the first time she was given permission not to excel, and it freed her.

When she decided she was ready, Natalia called her parents and told them she wouldn't be pursuing medicine or law. They were angry, as expected. Her father warned her that success in creative fields was rare. Out of anger, her mother took a potshot: Natalia wasn't special enough for that kind of pursuit. Natalia cried but held out. Afterward, she told me, "I felt like I was brave. I made a mature decision to talk about this. I became a better person because I wasn't hiding anymore. I wanted to find my own way, even if that was scary for them."

Several more painful conversations followed, but Natalia has never been happier. "I'm much more relaxed and joyful," she told me. "I think I make more jokes. I feel like I want to have more fun." She was on her way to finding herself.

When we worked together, she developed a practice of asking herself questions like, "Are the things that I am doing meaningful to me? Are they pleasurable? Is my mind telling me that I should be doing different things with my time? Is my heart telling me that I must change my life?"

One of Natalia's favorite activities was the "I Love" exercise, which I learned from Buddhist psychologist Tara Brach. Using a timer, and for one minute straight, I had Natalia sit opposite a partner and say everything she loved that came into her mind. For example, "I love dogs, I love running, I love cheese." Her partner listened, then they switched. The activity reminded Natalia of what she most valued, anchoring her to herself at just the moment when she worried she was drifting away. Try this exercise with your daughter. Discuss what surprised you and what you found interesting. Was it hard to think of the things you love? How often do you do them? How can you incorporate doing more things you love into your life?

I conclude all my orientation programs with a graduation ceremony. I stream "Pomp and Circumstance" through the speakers. The girls know they are getting a certificate for participating. They just don't know what it says.

Before I call the first name, I read the Gothic lettering on the piece of paper made to look like a diploma. It is a Certificate of Failure, authorizing each girl to start the next chapter of her life by letting go of the need to be amazing at everything she does. "Having honorably fulfilled all the requirements imposed by the overlords of high school," it says, you are

> hereby certified to screw up, bomb, or otherwise fail at one or more relationships, hookups, friendships, emails or texts, classes, extracurricular activities, or any other choices or decisions associated with college herein and forevermore . . . and still be a totally worthy, utterly excellent human.

The girls laugh. Then they take them back to their new dorm rooms and put them up on the wall. One even put hers in a broken frame, to double down on the point. Every girl needs a Certificate of Failure. Don't forget to give your daughter one, too.

2

Girls and Social Media: The Virtual Second Shift

Social media is a way to show everyone what kind of person you are and what kind of girl you are. It creates a me I am in front of other people.

—MAYA, EIGHTEEN

Maya's phone was the first thing she peered at through half-open eyes after silencing the alarm. She looked at it on the bus to school, then between and during classes, toggling among six different accounts. At night, she often sat naked and shivering on her toilet, shower running, trying to thumb one last message before pulling back the curtain and stepping in.

Adolescent girls dominate social media's visual platforms: places where girls post pictures and videos of themselves, their friends, what they eat, where they go, and what they do. In 2016, 58 percent of Instagram's 400 million unique visitors were female; teen girl usage dwarfs boys' usage there and on Snapchat by double-digit margins. Girls get and send more texts, post more pictures, and have more followers and friends online than boys. They own the social Internet.

One of my passions is to keep pace with what girls are doing on social media, translate it to parents and teachers, and write curricula to help girls and parents navigate the challenges of life online. I spend hours hopscotching between Snapchat and Instagram, watching feeds unspool the totally lit Saturday night, unforgettable vacation, or carefully chosen selfie. Among more casual observers, the widely held view is that girls log on to connect addictively with their friends. A parent's job, by this logic, is to teach their girls to be decent digital citizens.

But that's only one part of this swiftly moving story. In the last few years, social media has raised the ultimate catwalk in a girl's pursuit of perfection. It's the drive to achieve and project success, as much as a wish to connect, that draws girls like moths to the digital flame—and which can undermine their confidence and self-esteem.

Today, a girl's social media brand is yet another highly demanding platform where she is expected to perform, achieve, and compare herself to others. "Most girls I know use Instagram, Snapchat, and Facebook to be like, 'I'm beautiful, I'm awesome,'" Maya told me. "Social media is a way to show everyone what kind of person you are and what kind of girl you are. It creates a me I am in front of other people."

The problem is that the very bones of the Internet reflect and intensify the fruitless drive for perfection. Online, as in life, there will always be somebody thinner, more successful, in a better relationship, with more friends, and doing something more fun than you—and that truth cuts even deeper when images are so easily altered. There will never be enough "likes" if you always believe you should have one more. That's why too many girls turn away from their screens, believing they are not good enough at anything. The well can never be filled.

When I marveled at the gorgeous social media presence of Tala, a twenty-three-year-old former student of mine whose posts toggle between glamour shots to career highs to memory-making Saturday nights in New York, she rolled her eyes.

"I hate social media," she said.

"You *do*?" I asked.

"So I published a story [at my journalism job] that went viral, great. I feel great for two days, then I'm back at my desk and it's like, how can I match that? How can I get twice as many likes on Facebook?"

Social media rewards behaviors that girls have been long primed to express: pleasing others, seeking feedback, performing and looking good. Girls slide right into this world with nary a squeak. But bashing social media is the wrong strategy. If all the Internet had to offer girls was angst, it would have gone out of business long ago. "Social media shouldn't be seen as a positive or negative," writes educational consultant Ana Homayoun in her book *Social Media Wellness*. "Instead, it should be addressed as a new language and cultural shift that provides different opportunities to connect and communicate."

What girls learn online can open doors to a sense of purpose and political identity. Girls use social media every day to mobilize and inspire their peers to activism. The viral #PerfectlyMe campaign, launched by Instagram and *Seventeen* magazine in 2016, allowed users to tag posts promoting body positivity and self-confidence. When girls feel alone and that no one understands them, the Internet regularly offers what a hallway or classroom can't. What girls need from their parents is not a conversation about what's wrong with social media, but what's wrong with the way many of them use and value it.

Attempts to link general social media use to well-being or depression have been inconclusive in the research. What's more promising are the findings suggesting that *how* adolescents use social media, as well as the quality of the connections they create there, will influence their emotional health. This chapter will give you the tools to help your daughter navigate the increasing demands of her online presence with balance, self-respect, and critical awareness.

HOW SOCIAL MEDIA SEDUCES GIRLS: THE ILLUSION OF CONTROL

I'm in charge of how my life looks to others.

The last decade's new media explosion created a new kind of social "work" for girls, one their mothers never confronted. Hunched over a laptop on her bed or hallway carpet at school, vibrating phone to the side, a girl now constructs a duplicate persona with her fingers: expertly manipulating filters to lighten blemishes and narrow curves, agonizing over a caption that will seem equal parts witty and casual, as if dashed off with barely a thought. "There's pressure. You have to look perfect, and you have to be doing cool things, and eating pretty salads, and taking pictures of them," twenty-year-old Alexis told me. "All this is going into painting this facade that you're living this great life."

It is a virtual second shift for adolescent girls, who spend an average of six hours a day using new media. This is the generation psychologist Jean Twenge calls "iGen": born between 1995 and 2012, they have never known a life without the Internet. Twenge reports that twelfth graders in 2015 spent twice as much time online as twelfth graders in 2006; by 2017, a survey of over five thousand teens revealed that three out of four owned an iPhone. But where boys (who log the same hours) typically play games online, or post about a favorite team, girls pursue a different set of goals. A smartphone catapults her into a thriving marketplace of social capital, where she can amplify the features of her life to make herself appear prettier, sexier, smarter, more accomplished, closer with her friends, happier, and more popular than she really is. It takes no small amount of effort: "You have to Instagram everything that you do, you have to edit pictures, you have to make sure all the tags of pictures that you put up [look good] and you have to untag if you don't look good," Alexis said. "It's so much work."

But the payoff is hard to beat. Online, no one can see how little you've slept, how much you ate at 2:00 A.M., or the hookup that didn't work out. Girls become spin doctors of their own lives. Vivian, twenty, was born in the United States, grew up in Fiji, and returned to the United States to attend a large public university in the Northeast. Her new American friends had no clue she left behind a life in Fiji marked by abuse and years of body shame. Over the last year, Vivian had found feminism, a political consciousness, and the determination to succeed in America. The goal now was to become the badass woman she'd always wanted to be. This often meant shielding her vulnerability from others, whether they were friends or professors who might offer extra support. It also meant using social media to compete with peers. "I'll take a picture of this really nice view when in reality I'm just doing nothing," she told me.

> There's this need to take nice photos of what people think is the good life—to show people, "I'm better than you. Where I'm at [right now], I'm better than you." We go to incredible lengths to prove that our lives are somehow better than the other people's. The people we don't like, the people back in high school or at home.

She did this, she explained, "because I'm trying to keep up."

In the twentieth century, new appliances like dishwashers and washing machines freed women from some of the worst drudgery of housework. Technology refunded women the time they needed to take on new social roles, such as paid work outside the home. Today, technology helps girls manage a different, but equally limiting, challenge of being female: role overload. Social media enables them to curate an exhausting range of identities— jock, scholar, beauty queen, party girl, best friend, and on and on—demanded by the new rules of girl success, crammed into a twenty-four-hour day.

Maya strategically used Snapchat, an app that creates a montage of videos and pictures taken over the course of a day, to execute a dizzying, digital pirouette to show off her multiple selves: "If I'm working on a Saturday and it's six-thirty, I can post a picture of me and a paper I just wrote," she explained. "Then at 11:00 P.M., I can post a picture of me playing beer pong at a party. The next day at brunch, I can also show myself as a family girl. And for the next twenty-four hours everyone can see the nice juxtaposition of me be-ing very smart and me being very cool at the same time."

It was a daily collage that was made to appear as effortless as it was intentional. "So if it happens to be that you're meeting the stan-dards of cool girl, sexy girl, and smart girl at the same time, you have this amazing opportunity to have the combination of you perform-ing in those roles—in a sphere that everyone is on," she said. "It gives you a stage to perform on—and be all those different roles—good girl, bad girl, cute girl, sexy girl, smart girl."

This is the seductive offer social media makes to an overworked, underslept girl working to manage her reputation and brand: post different parts of yourself, in different places, and get the job done with a few clicks. "I have two thousand friends on Facebook," Maya told me. "Do I know two thousand people well enough that I'm homies with all of them? Definitely not. But at the same time it feels like that's a huge number of people, that's a world, and I get to choose pretty much what I want to put out into that world." At a developmental moment characterized by the feeling of being out of control, in swoops social media to the rescue. Control your avatar, and maybe you can control your life.

I control the way I physically appear to others.

Before the Internet, a girl learned to manipulate her body through makeup, exercise, fashion, haircuts, and diet. Now she is privy to a second set of lessons, this time while scrolling through a daily pageant of selfies in her own feed. She can alter her online appearance, improving the one she has in real life. All it takes is a handful of apps, a well-positioned camera lens, and time.

Vivian had a close friend who spent two hours photographing a new tattoo for Instagram. Her friend was overweight yet managed a selfie angle that made her look much thinner. "I don't know how she managed to bend her body that way," she told me. "It blew me away. We invest so much time trying to take that perfect picture that represents that perfect life we have." She hated the Instagram game because of what it did to her friends' self-esteem. "We are just sort of taught self-conscious ways of trying to compete with each other. Who's the prettier girl, who's the better person, who has the better body, who has the cuter boyfriend. You feel the need to exaggerate what you have to make the feeling of not being enough go out of your mind."

When girls are surrounded by a constant drumbeat of people who consistently alter their appearance, who post only the thinnest or most toned photos of themselves, it takes a toll on those who bear witness. It telegraphs a message to girls that there is something not right with how they look off-line, and that the Internet is a place to address that. It reminded me of something Maya told me: "I don't hate myself when I'm alone," she said. "I just hate myself in comparison to other people."

Maya ogled the "Instagram famous" girls she knew the way her mother might have idolized a magazine cover girl. "I can spend like hours looking at [an acquaintance's] Instagram, being like how can I replicate this. This is what people like. It's like what you do when you see someone walking down the street and you see them wearing something you like." Listening to her talk, I can't help but wonder what else girls like them might have done with those hours.

I can find out what others "really" think of me.

When I need an icebreaker for a group of girls, I ask them to name a superpower they wish they had. A startling number pick mind reading. Why? "So I can know what people really think," most say. Some add: ". . . of me."

It makes perfect sense: girls live in a social world where the unwritten rule is to hide your strongest thoughts and feelings. Enter social media, which beckons with an alluring promise: *I'll tell you what people really think of you.*

Let's say a girl wonders if one of her friends really likes her. All she has to do is open a photo-sharing app to see if that friend "liked" her picture. *Am I popular?* She can count the likes she gets on a new selfie, and time how quickly they pile up (the one-like-per-minute ratio is the goal). *Is she mad at me?* She can download an app to monitor who *unfollowed* her. *Am I pretty?* She can scan the comments on her most recent selfie to see how many of them say she's pretty or hot. For every question a girl has—and these are questions most any adolescent girl is plagued by, at one time or another—a like, follow, comment, or retweet is a public, tangible, reassuring response. A "like" can stand in for a host of meaningful statements that were never actually made to a girl—but which are interpreted by her in her own way.

Many girls quantify their own self-worth by the number of likes they receive on an image or post. They refresh their phones obsessively to track their progress. And some delete a post that hasn't received enough likes—"Instashame," one girl called it.

THE DOWNSIDE: THE EMOTIONAL ROLLER COASTER

Appliances may have simplified life for women in the 1950s, but they also transformed domesticity into a science where women judged themselves and one another. Likewise, the very tools that make girls feel more beautiful, successful, and social online are the same ones that exacerbate insecurity, low self-worth, even paranoia. If you interpret a like to mean anything from "you matter to me" to "you're beautiful," you will translate its absence to mean something much more than it really does. The same goes for feeling excluded; instead of seeing the situation for what it may actually be—you weren't invited—you jump to a big, fat conclusion.

"If I see people hanging out [online] and I wasn't invited," Maya told me, "I'm like, 'They must not want to be friends anymore.'" It's crazy, she went on, "that from just a ten-second video on Snapchat, you can feel so isolated and so hated." For many girls, social media is like a drama-heavy romance: when it's good, it's great; when it's bad, it's very bad.

Social media puts girls on a nonstop roller coaster of emotions, veering from surges of social adoration to stomach-clenching lows of exclusion and insecurity. The rush of control, optimism, and even power you get from producing social media can swiftly evaporate while you wait anxiously for a response, or, worse, don't get the one you're hoping for.

Twenge reports that teens who spend more time than average in front of a screen are more likely to be unhappy. Engaging in nonscreen activities, by contrast, is linked to more happiness. In her study of generational trends, 48 percent more girls said they often felt left out than in 2010 (compared with 27 percent more boys), a spike Twenge links to girls' outsize social media use. Twenge directly blames the arrival of the smartphone for the precipitous decline in teen wellness—and she finds it's girls who struggle the most. Sharon Thompson and Eric Lougheed found that, among first-year college students, more women than men say Facebook causes them stress, and that they felt anxious when off Facebook for long periods of time (though notably, more women also said that Facebook made them feel excited and energized). Twice as many women as men agreed or strongly agreed with the statement: "Sometimes I feel like I am addicted to Facebook." One quarter of the women said they had lost sleep because of the site.

SOCIAL COMPARISON: "WHY IS MY LIFE SO SHITTY AND EVERYONE ELSE'S SO AWESOME?"

Grace was a smiler. During my workshops, she looked straight at me, eyes crinkling, head cocked, brown hair in a long, high ponytail, hand at the ready to be raised. She was one of those students who would never leave you hanging in the brutal canyon of awkward classroom silence.

But don't let the sweetness fool you: in school and in her chosen sport, the seventeen-year-old was competitive to the bone. It ran in the family. Her dad, she told me, was "all about winning, winning, winning. I was always raised subconsciously that number one is best." He never said it out loud, but it was how he lived. "That seemed strong, and it was what I wanted to do," she said.

Grace funneled her drive into elite competitive dance, traveling regularly for meets. By junior year, her peers were at the top of their sport, scattered around the country as they trained for the next contest.

Grace slid her phone across the table at the café where we were sitting. Instagram, she explained, was the dancer's virtual stage, the place they could post their latest moves, or new outfits. It was a way for them to perform and compete while they were apart.

I picked up her phone and watched image after image of gorgeously filtered girls scroll by: one held an ankle aloft, flush to her ear; another was suspended over the shoulders of a partner. Then came a video of a gravity-defying twist on pointe, followed by a shot of a postworkout green juice.

Grace had a hard time staying away from the screen. The phone was in her hand so often she sometimes didn't feel it. But she wasn't pulled to it only by the promise of a gushing comment, follower to her account, or like. She looked so she could bear witness to everything her peers were accomplishing, and wallow in what she was certain she would never become.

"I will literally stalk them on Instagram and say to myself, 'This will never be you,'" she said. There was a video of an elaborate new choreography. "I can't do that," she'd say. A crazy expensive outfit. "Or that." A shot of a flawless split. "Or that."

For many girls, social media is a brutal beauty contest, a gallery of physical finery that functions like a fashion magazine, making girls feel unpretty. But for girls like Grace, social media plays a different role: it's the place where she feels less *capable*. In the looks department, Grace knew the score. "I'm not going to look like Beyoncé," she said drily, rolling her eyes. "It's fine." But dance was something else entirely. It was a skill. It could be improved. It was in her control.

Grace judged herself relentlessly online against the skill of her peers. There was one girl on Instagram who really dogged her. Jen was pretty and uber-rich; her parents bankrolled private dance coaches, international trips to compete, and "sick" outfits. Jen had become an ambassador for multiple clothing brands: in exchange for posting pictures of herself performing in their clothes, she got them for free (not that she needed the discount, Grace pointed out). Grace couldn't stop scouring the feed to track Jen's latest move.

Grace was engaged in what psychologists call "social comparison," comparing herself to others as a way to define her own abilities and opinions. The Internet is a giant, sprawling petri dish for social comparison: take a girl's feeling that she's not pretty, successful, or social enough, combine it with her inimitable drive to improve herself, then add a relentless stream of others' edited images. It's no wonder one young woman told me social media is "a way to establish that my life is so much better than yours."

Social comparison is a vital part of an adolescent's development. We build a sense of self as we make choices about which personal values we want to keep, and which we will throw away—and we often do this by watching our peers. In healthy doses, social comparison helps girls manage their feelings, get inspired, and make decisions.

But Grace is trafficking in a more pernicious kind of thinking—the kind of comparison-making that can lead to depression, self-criticism, and lower self-esteem. What Grace is doing is not about motivation but about shaming; as she compares herself to the illusion of that person-doing-more-than-I-am, she walks away defeated, not inspired. She spins her wheels and goes nowhere, driven mad by self-judgment.

People who make social comparisons on social media report greater depressive symptoms. They also say their "current self"—the person they believe they really are—is discrepant from their "ideal self," or the person they aspire to be, which is a recipe for unhappiness, if not outright shame.

WHEN SOCIAL COMPARISON MEETS SOCIAL MEDIA

Girls appear to be prone to what researchers call "social comparison and feedback seeking" online. There is a strong association between this behavior and depressive symptoms for girls, and the comparisons girls make online seem to be more threatening to their self-worth. In other words, social media exacerbates the tendency to compete and compare in girls.

Girls are more vulnerable to social comparison for several reasons. First, they are socialized to take care of others and be attuned to their needs. As a result, they spend a lot of time wondering what other people think of them. They think deeply about themselves in relation to others, which makes them more interested in comparisons. Second, girls are more likely to internalize stress from their relationships, especially when they become conflictual. Finally, in a culture where their appearance is linked to their social value, girls are pressured to spend lots of time comparing their appearance to others'.

But what is it about social media that sends social comparison into overdrive? Scholar danah boyd's groundbreaking work at Harvard revealed how social media inflects the emotional lives of adolescents. boyd argued that social media took information that used to be private and intangible—say, the number of friends you had, or where you went and what you did with them after school—and made it publicly visible online. Being able to see how many friends or followers someone had allowed you to measure those numbers against your own (*She has 546 followers, but I only have 400. Why?*).

When you could "see" what your friends were doing after school, you suddenly learned each time you'd been excluded. Now, you didn't have to wonder about how popular you were. You could actually see and quantify it. Social media thus introduced a painful new strain of TMI, or "too much information." It also launched a new set of metrics for social success.

Achievement has traveled the same private-to-public road; accomplishments that were once shared among a few people are, via screens, screaming headlines available for public consumption. You can hardly log on to Facebook in December or April without seeing a college admit announcement: "University of Maryland Class of '22!" "Penn!!!!!!!!!!!!!!!!!!!!!!!!" Girls bear forced witness to an ongoing crawl of triumphs large and small: internships, awards, championships, GPAs. Add to this the "everywhere" factor: you can broadcast your wins on a seemingly endless array of platforms, and all at once.

For the record, I'm all for girls promoting their achievements; it's an invaluable leadership skill that many girls fail to develop in a world that values their humility. The problem here is in the eyes of the online beholder—or should I say, scroller—and how she interprets what she reads. That is, if you struggle with a constant, nagging sense that you are less-than, it's nearly impossible not to compare your own life to whatever is on your Snapchat or Instagram feed.

For recent college grads, the digital highlights reel can be particularly crazy making. "When you see a peer get engaged, pregnant, or fall in love," Isabel said, "it makes you feel that there's something wrong with you. That you are the only person in your circle of acquaintances that hasn't found that." She knows, she assured me, that people struggle, too. Yet she still finds herself wondering: "Why is my life so shitty and everyone else's so awesome?"

Siblings complain about the comparisons their parents make. "Why can't you be more like your brother (or sister)?" Social media asks a similar question of its most vulnerable users. It speaks in the voice of the overbearing parent who is never happy. Haley, a twenty-six-year-old who grew up in rural Tennessee, whose peers are mostly young mothers and underemployed, remarkably found her way to a media job in midtown Manhattan. Yet when she goes online she sees only what she lacks. "You see what you should be doing through these social media platforms and it makes you feel like less of yourself," she told me glumly.

HELP HER UNDERSTAND THAT ANOTHER'S SUCCESS IS NOT HER FAILURE

It's not just the practice of social comparison that caused Grace pain. It's *how* she did it: Grace logged on when she was already feeling badly about herself. "I'm, like, in a sweatshirt and my hair is all gross and I'm eating raw cookie dough," she explained, "and [Jen's] pictures are so elegant and I'm like, 'Are you serious? Why does she get to do that?' And it's like, 'I will never get that because I will never have that much money.'"

I put down my coffee.

"Okay, I'm confused," I said. "Why go online to see other people looking amazing when you're already feeling bad? Why make yourself feel worse?"

She didn't hesitate. "You want to feel bad for yourself. If I'm having a bad day, I'll just be like, everything sucks. That's when I'll go on Instagram. I'll say, 'Are you serious, like why why why why why why why,' and then I'll get there and see what's actually happening." She wasn't the only one she knew who did this, she made sure to point out.

Research confirms that two kinds of social media use lead to unhappiness. The first is Grace's, and can be summed up by one of my favorite pieces of social media advice: "Don't compare your insides to someone else's outsides."

In 2012, a study by Joanne Davila found that college students who used Facebook often were convinced their online "friends" were happier and more successful than they were—especially when they didn't know the "friends" well. The students were also more likely to disagree with the statement "life is fair." "It appears," researchers concluded, "that people might be comparing their realistic off-line selves to the idealized online selves of others." That's

41

the eating-raw-cookie-dough-while-scrolling-through-fabulousness phenomenon—comparing how you feel on your worst day to what someone looks like on their best.

This is a rigged gamble that always leaves girls defeated. To walk away from the table, girls have to break the habit of turning to their phones without thinking in search of distraction from difficult feelings or thoughts. They have to—and yes, this can be a big ask—pause to think about their feelings first. But there is a payoff here: when a girl stops turning to social media to address feelings of insecurity, anxiety, or unhappiness, she controls how intense those feelings become.

The answer to loneliness is not necessarily to go online; if anything, that can only enhance her sense of isolation. Utah Valley University found that college students who spent time going out with friends were less likely to agree with the statement that others were having better lives and were happier. They were also more likely to agree with the statement "life is fair."

The second type of depressive media use is "passive profile viewing," more commonly known as "lurking." It's reading what others post, but not sharing anything yourself. In studies of young adults by the University of Michigan's Dr. Ethan Kross, lurking increased feelings of jealousy and envy among Facebook users. One study of nearly three hundred college students found that women spent twice as much time as men lurking. The solution here is to find balance: a mix of producing and consuming content, of sharing and lurking. The affirmation that comes with sharing will offset the envy that lurking may cause.

Back at the café, Grace was only lurking. She glanced down at a new post from Jen, then rolled her eyes. "Jen's not that great at dancing," she said. "I know that. When I travel to a competition and I dance with her, I know that I am technically better than she is."

"You do?" I asked.

"Yeah," she said. "But for me, when I look at it on Instagram, it's so real, and she's so much better and she's so amazing."

Again, I was confused. "Let me get this straight," I said. "You know Jen's social media game is smoke and mirrors, and you know deep down that you're a better dancer? Yet you're still driven crazy by what you see?"

"Okay." Grace was quieter. "I guess I feel very weak when I look at her on Instagram. But then I feel empowered when I'm with her. That sort of journey from weak to strong is empowering. It brings me up. It makes me feel better. It's like I go from zero to a hundred." Grace seemed embarrassed as she explained herself, and uncharacteristically glum. She called her zero-to-a-hundred practice "sad" and "so not brave."

Sad, yes, I told her, but also not uncommon. Social comparison is a two-way street: you can make "upward" comparisons, pitting yourself against someone you've deemed superior, or "downward" ones, holding yourself above someone you regard as inferior. "If I'm looking at someone who is *gorgeous* online and I feel awful," Hannah, nineteen, wrote me in an e-mail, "I'm like well, I'm definitely smarter than her ha-ha! Even though I know that's mean."

Both upward and downward comparisons converge at the same dead end: negative feelings and lower self-worth. Grace celebrated her superiority to make herself feel better, yet wound up feeling just as empty when she wallowed in what she lacked. When a feeling of accomplishment is driven more by what someone else has done—or hasn't—instead of something inside yourself, it cannot be sustained. It is a false confidence at best.

Dr. Julia Taylor, author of *The Body Image Workbook for Teens*, suggests asking girls what they get out of putting themselves down in relation to someone else. What's the reward? How does it make them feel and how long does the feeling last? Is there a long-term cost?

Taylor advises girls to reframe their comparisons by acknowledging that everyone is different, and that some comparisons might actually be true. Instead of saying, *My best friend is prettier than me*, Taylor advises, say, *My best friend is pretty*. "Try to see those people for what they are, not for what you're not." And even if a friend is, in fact, prettier than you, that doesn't make you *unpretty*. It's not a zero-sum game.

Self-esteem isn't the only casualty of comparisons. It's a short walk from comparing yourself to others' success to resenting them for it. Relationships suffer. Lily, sixteen, says posts of friends carrying designer bags or eating at nice restaurants remind her mostly of what she lacks. "It's like, okay, I don't have that," she told me. "I'm not good enough or I don't do those things or I don't have those things." The insecurity follows her to off-line hanging out, where she says she feels vulnerable and insecure.

If in its healthiest form social comparison should help girls develop a strong self, in its ugliest it drives wedges between them, becoming a tool to manage anxiety about performance and self-worth. Grace can only make herself feel better when she disparages her friend. *I feel okay*, Grace is saying, *because I'm better than you*. "Rampant and constant competition between peers," professor Suniya Luthar and her colleagues have written, can impair the intimacy that is vital for well-being in adolescence.

When I work with girls on how to use social media wisely, I share Theodore Roosevelt's quote: "Comparison is the thief of joy." After countless conversations with girls about the way social media makes them feel, this is what I've learned: we can tell girls all day, as many parents already do, that social media isn't a representation of reality—that it's an illusion crafted by shrewd magicians of their own lives—but until a girl decides that social media can't be the barometer of her own self-worth, very little will change.

She can do this by changing the way she uses social media and, in the process, controlling the influence it has on her life. Here's what this looks like in practice:

- Refusing to use social media to prove something about herself to others, and instead using it to say something about herself.

- Refraining from using social media as a tool to compete, and instead using it to connect.

- Not using social media to ask a question about what others think of her, but instead using it to make a statement about what she thinks: about the world, the issues she cares about, or herself.

- Choosing not to use social media to amplify herself, but to be part of something bigger than herself.

- Pausing to ask herself, before she posts content, a direct question: Why am I doing this? What is my intention? How am I feeling right now? And then, being willing to answer that question honestly. If I am looking to be filled up with affirmation from others, is this the right way to do it?

- Being willing to name and seek off-line avenues for support, connection, and affirmation. What resources exist, besides social media, to feel the connection she is seeking? Who can she call on for reassurance when she questions herself?

We know that teaching young women to train a critical eye on the culture's worship of a "thin ideal" helps them avoid unhealthful eating behaviors. Likewise, coaching girls in social media literacy can buffer them from the Internet's most toxic elements.

In my workshops, I place four cards in four corners of the room. They read EXCLUDED, INSECURE/ANXIOUS, CONFIDENT/HAPPY, and INCLUDED. I ask groups of girls to stand under each card and brainstorm the ways social media has made them feel these emotions. The discussion that follows is always powerful: many realize that—no matter what, and for every person in the room—there is something rigged about the very nature of social media. The cost of doing business, for every consumer, is some degree of happiness and sadness, and it is up to us to moderate how we use it.

Taylor challenges her students to list the top three social media accounts that make them feel less-than, and unfollow them for a week to see if they feel better. Most surprising, she told me, is how many girls respond by saying, "I can't unfollow my best friend." Now, Taylor asks them to unfollow the people they don't know personally.

There is a core conflict between the rules of success that girls are taught and the research about wellness online. For example, girls are expected to accumulate as many friends and followers as they can. Yet Hui-Tzu Grace Chou and Nicholas Edge found that spending time viewing the lives of people you don't know well makes you vulnerable to assuming they're living happier, better lives than you are. When you keep your social media circles smaller, and read posts from people you actually know, you are more likely to have a balanced view of them.

Ask your daughter to consider how the pressure to excel at all things can undermine her happiness online. This kind of parenting focuses on consciousness-raising: helping girls see beyond their own daily experiences and into the systems that help shape them. When you know why something bothers you, and see that it's not "just you," it's empowering, even life changing.

Social media breaks also help. I often ask girls: How would a day feel if you didn't see your friends hanging out without you, or the person you like with a new flame, or that girl who seems totally perfect? What would a day be like without the hurt feelings that social media generates? That day, a day where you open yourself up only to the people physically near you, is just a deleted app away.

LOGGING OFF AND LOOKING INSIDE

When Grace applied early action to a small college with no dance program, her friends and family were stunned. The nearest airport was ninety minutes away, making competitive dance all but impossible. "It was the easy way out," she told me. "I would have to stop dancing and be good at something else, instead of having to compare myself constantly. I truly think in a very sick way Instagram was part of the reason I wanted to put dancing on hold. At least [if I go to this college] you're all-out and not halfway in."

But the school rejected her, and the news came as a crushing blow. With her future up for grabs, Grace reconsidered her options. Did she want to focus on dance in college? What, and who, did she really want to be? She sat down with a pad and pencil and, as she puts it, "was calm and real with myself." She started asking herself tough questions. "I thought about where I wanted to go with the sport and where I wanted to go with life." Grace wrote and thought and wrote some more. She talked with a trusted teacher and shared her writing. "I stopped trying to trick myself out of things. It was the hardest conversation I ever had but it was also the most rewarding.

"And I realized," she continued, "that half in is okay. Loving dancing, competing sometimes, that's okay. You don't have to be Misty Copeland." She understood that she didn't want to devote her life to dance, or to rely on her parents to pay for it. Dance could be a hobby, and that was just fine. "I want to make my own career. I want to do something bigger than dance. I want to do things for the world, not just the dance world. I want to change things."

Now, she told me, she doesn't lurk or compare herself to Jen anymore. "I'm not making it up," she added impishly. "That actually happened."

Of course it did, I told her. Once she honed in on what *she* wanted, and what was true for her, she could stand behind it and plan accordingly. Grace was engaged in self-affirmation, or exploring diverse, positive aspects of herself. When teens are asked by researchers to reflect on their core values by writing about them, the findings are remarkable: the teens see negative events and information as less threatening. They become more capable of managing stress and more efficient in their lives. Their grades improve.

Grace was also connecting to a deeper sense of purpose, and it bolstered her in the face of uncertainty. "I want to do things for the world" and "change things," she said. When adolescents have a sense of purpose, they are known to be happier and more resilient. When girls have purpose, they feel more shielded from the intense pressure to perform and are less likely to say they are competitive with peers.

Grace no longer had to look at what someone else was doing in order to figure out what she thought of herself. Once she put down the phone, tuned out the noise, and looked inside, the answers were there waiting. But she had to ask herself the questions first.

LYING ONLINE TO COVER UP THE PAIN

The need to prove that your life or body or friends are better than someone else's can lead to an unspoken arms race, where girls doctor not only images, but also life events. For some girls, it's about the work of keeping up. For others, the skillful production of a sanitized online self may hide depression, anxiety, and helplessness. It's one thing to use social media to cosmetically enhance your life. But it is another thing, a dangerous thing, to use it to pretend outright.

Anna was not a partyer, and she never gave her early-to-bed ways much thought before college. A biracial (Chinese and white), nineteen-year-old sophomore at an elite urban college, she beat herself up for failing to go hard and party every weekend. Sitting in her room on weekend nights, she was convinced everyone was out doing something while she was alone. On the night of a big football game, she resolved to make the effort: she and a friend put on their superfan shirts, plastered on face tattoos, and pregamed in a friend's suite. They took a selfie, which she Instagrammed, then went to the stadium.

"It was the pinnacle of the thing I was supposed to be living for," Anna told me. But as she settled into the stands, in a sea of students wearing yellow T-shirts, she felt overwhelmed by sadness. She didn't love the people she was with, or where she was. "I was supposed to be drunk, having the time of my life. . . . I was feeling really alone, I was worried I wouldn't have a friend group at school." She began to tear up in the stands and finally left early. As she walked out of the stadium, her phone buzzed.

It was one of her high school friends. "She was like, oh my God, I love your Insta. You look so drunk and so college. Like you're having so much fun."

Anna wiped her eyes and texted back. "I'm not drunk. I'm miserable."

"Everyone lies on Insta," her friend texted back. "Lol no worries."

The friend's reply haunted me for a long time. It wasn't so much the "everyone lies" part. It was the "lol no worries": her casual indifference to Anna's split self, the easygoing acceptance of her lie and hidden misery.

The expectation that a girl should be happy no matter what only ramps up online. There, the dissonance between the emotions you project and the ones you actually feel can be painfully stark. This was never truer than in the story of Madison Holleran, a freshman track star at the University of Pennsylvania. On her Instagram account, she was a star athlete, adored friend, and beloved daughter and sister. Off-line, she hid brutal depression and a protracted struggle to adjust to college. In 2014, she leaped to her death from the ninth floor of a parking garage, leaving behind a small pile of gifts: necklaces for her mother, chocolate for her father, outfits for her newborn nephews, gingersnaps for her grandparents, and—most heartbreaking of all—a copy of the *The Happiness Project*. She was nineteen.

As friends and family tried to make sense of the tragedy, a friend of Madison's recalled the two of them scrolling through the Instagram feeds of their peers. "This is what college is supposed to be like; this is what we want our life to be like," they would say to each other. But it wasn't, and Madison felt defeated and insecure. As school vacation approached, Madison recoiled at the idea of facing her high school friends. "I feel like all my friends are having so much fun at school," Madison confided to her friend Ingrid.

Suicide cannot be reduced to a single cause, and Instagram did not kill Madison. Nor is it possible to know what might have been done to help her. But it's clear that she bought into the curated lives she saw there, then judged herself ruthlessly for not measuring up. A girl's social media account should never be used as a snapshot of how she's really faring. For parents concerned about a daughter's wellness, and even for those who just aren't sure, connecting with others in her life is vital. One way to do this is by following your daughter's friends on social media so that you can message them if you need to. In high school and college, a close friend is often eager to talk if she's worried about your daughter.

Parents can familiarize themselves with university resources like the counseling, wellness, and women's centers, and encourage their daughters to seek support when needed. In addition to individual counseling, these programs usually run extensive outreach campaigns throughout the year. They also offer stress management, mindfulness, and other support groups for students. Residence life staff can also be an excellent line in.

After college is trickier, especially when her network is new, but a Facebook message to a friend of hers can open a line of communication about how your daughter is really doing.

━━━━━━

I get some degree of eye rolling when I talk with young women about the false, curated selves they offer up and bear witness to online. *I know*, they say. *We get it.* Yet even as they give me the brush-off, they are quietly riveted to social media's message of perfection—and, even more concerning, often let it make or break their day.

This isn't the first time we've seen girls claim immunity to destructive media. In 2010, professor Susan Douglas noticed a strange phenomenon among her students: they'd begun bingeing on reality television that openly degraded women but insisted it was no big deal to tune in. They were fully aware, the women told Douglas, of how demeaning the shows were. They rolled their eyes as they watched, mocked and winked at the ridiculous characters. Doing that, Douglas argued, made the women feel superior and "above" the garbage.

But the students were far from immune to these images. What they were consuming, Douglas wrote, was "good old-fashioned grade-A patriarchy, just much better disguised . . . in seductive Manolo Blahniks and an IPEX bra." It was affecting what the women thought of themselves and each other. Douglas called this phenomenon "enlightened sexism": the belief that sexism was defeated and feminism was therefore unnecessary.

The same may now be true of social media, which—unlike television—girls not only consume but also create. Social media offers a world rife with false, often sexist representations of girls' selves. It is a virtual reality show of sorts, where girls perform the conventionally feminine parts of themselves, showing off their hyperfriended, party girl, materialistic, sexy sides. It is a world filled with illusions, and girls know it. They roll their eyes at it, complain about it, snark at hyperfiltered images that don't look anything like the girl who posted them.

And yet they cannot look away. They cannot stop. "You have no idea how many articles I read about how I shouldn't believe [what I see online] and how I shouldn't feel bad about that," Isabel told me. "I know it's not true. . . . But then I look at my phone and someone's sharing a romantic dinner. At that particular instance, I don't remember their lives aren't perfect. I just remember that I'm hungry and tired and they have a lovely significant other bringing them food."

Girls may adopt this posture toward social media—one that is blasé, ambivalent, and deeply vulnerable all at once—because they have never known a world without it. They have no choice but to tolerate it and adapt. "It's kind of like having a friend in your life," Maya explained, "and you like them, and you talk to them, and when someone's like, 'Why are you two friends?' you're like, 'I don't know, because we are.' People who have been in your life for so long—they're just in my life forever."

It's a wise analogy. Friendships must be carefully monitored to ensure they are meeting our needs. The same is true of social media. Sometimes, because no one friend can be everything to us, we need to take some space. Other times we have to speak up and challenge the parts of the relationship that aren't serving us, especially when they hurt our feelings. So, too, with social media.

3

Can We Fat Talk?

A day won't go by when I don't think about how I look.

—BIANCA, SEVENTEEN

Before they are old enough to carry a cafeteria tray, girls worry about getting fat. Weight anxiety can first surface in preschool. Between 40 and 60 percent of elementary school girls monitor their weight. By adolescence, up to half of all girls have engaged in "extreme" dieting, including fasting, vomiting, and the use of laxatives and diet pills. That's one out of every two girls riding in the back seat of your car.

I don't care how many women we've sent into space; girls still come of age in a world where, Lindy West writes in her memoir, *Shrill*, a fat female body is "lampooned, openly reviled, and associated with moral and intellectual failure." A girl's appearance affects her potential as much as how she thinks, learns, and relates to others. We have come far, yes, but not far enough.

For if a girl's mind has been freed from social restrictions—*you can be anything you want to be!*—her body still bears the long history of women's oppression: you cannot look any way you want to look. Girls' bodies remain a site where they are expected to serve throwback stereotypes about femininity, where they must still honor the bikini selfie, push-up bra, and low-rise skinny jeans. If a girl's mind can be big, her body is still expected to remain small.

In fact, if you want to know just how far we *haven't* come, ask a group of girls to talk about their bodies. You'll quickly learn that a body is never just a body, but a barometer of a girl's worthiness, likability, and potential. Our fat-hating, thin-worshipping culture has made thinness into the ultimate asset, suggesting a cascade of other treasures: wealth, intelligence, friends. Girls, especially those who are white or affluent, are programmed to assume thin people are successful in every way, and that the overweight are unlovable and lazy. The message, Courtney Martin writes in *Perfect Girls, Starving Daughters*, is that "if you are overweight—even if you are brilliant, dynamic, funny, and dedicated—you have no chance at the perfect life."

The thin ideal, pressure to have an idealized, conventionally thin body, distracts girls daily from their work and lives. Beginning in adolescence, destructive thoughts about the body are considered a main reason girls suffer depression at twice the rate of boys. College women are the most vulnerable of any group to developing an eating disorder. Yet we rarely talk about body image and body shame; they have become the white noise of girls' development, something we know is there but rarely discuss.

Indeed, the girls I interviewed for this book mostly saw the siege of their brains and bodies as unremarkable, merely part of being female. But when we interpret girls' suffering as a rite of passage—as we did, say, with "mean girl" bullying for generations—we rationalize inaction on the toughest parts of their lives. I learned long ago that girls' silence or shrug-off is rarely an all-clear signal. It almost always points to a hidden subculture of struggle.

But silence on this subject persists. We pay sincere attention to girls' bodies only when they get visibly sick. Intervention at the point of emergency allows troubling behaviors like meal restriction, body obsession, and body dysmorphia to be rebranded as side effects of girlhood. And as Claire Mysko, CEO of the National Eating Disorders Association, told me, we "make it that much easier for someone for whom food and weight and body image are a major disruptive factor in their lives, to look and say, that's not me. I'm not that sick."

That's why this chapter isn't about girls with eating disorders, or girls who starve, binge, or purge—far from it. It's about how to support the majority of young women who navigate the exhausting, daily challenges of their body image. They are the "normal" ones, the ones for whom body surveillance is an invisible, walking illness—a kind of cognitive virus—where questions of what to eat and when, when you will work out and what it will mean if you don't (or can't), disrupt the day's activities and relationships.

This chapter is about how the body is much more than a body. It is increasingly a tool for performing, striving, and winning—yet another site where girls' confidence, courage, and authenticity are undermined. In writing this chapter I learned that the work of empowering girls can't live only above the neck, and that parents must not only understand the mind-body connection in girls' lives, but also help them rework it. This chapter will show you how.

THE MEASURE OF A GIRL: THE BODY IN TRANSLATION

Girlhood and body image collide with explosive developmental consequences in adolescence. As puberty approaches, a girl's body changes radically. Weight gain can be sudden and confusing, giving her the impression she has lost control over her body. A slim-hipped, flat-chested body that once complied with the culture's demands of thinness now gives way to something wider, softer, and thicker. Body image—the way she sees herself when she looks in the mirror, or pictures herself in her mind—becomes distorted. Self-critical thoughts about the body—*Why did I wear that outfit? I am so fat right now. Everyone will think I'm fat if I don't order a salad. Did I eat too much? Should I run for ten more minutes?*—intensify in adolescence. So does the level of distraction: in class, some girls begin pulling shirts down to cover a perceived roll of flab. While they take notes and listen to a lecture, they cross and twist their legs to reduce the appearance of cellulite. They sit at the top of their chairs, raise their legs, and dangle their toes to the floor, so their legs don't touch the chair and they look "thinner." And as their screen time deepens, so does their exposure to an unremitting flood of images of impossibly toned, altered bodies.

Late adolescence is marked by transitions: to new schools, homes, and jobs. Stress runs high. Girls must construct new social networks and mine fresh sources of support. College is also the first time many girls choose their own meals without parental guidance, and decide how and when to exercise in a gym that may be open twenty-four hours a day. A girl's sleep and eating patterns change. Pubertal changes settle and she must begin to accept what her body has become.

During this period the rising pressure to excel in every domain is increasingly written on girls' bodies. The body is where the tension of conflicting roles—be both scholar and sexpot, world changer and skinny girl—crystallize and collide. No longer is it enough simply to be thin: the body now has its own résumé. The how-you-got-thin is as important as the are-you-thin-enough. Do you run? Spin? Lift? Are you gluten free, raw, plant-based, or paleo? Do you juice? Do you "waist train"? That's wearing a corset at night—yes, as in the one from the Victorian age—to shrink your waist ("It seems really weird but it won't damage your organs," one girl told me). Do you document all this on social media?

Many girls use their bodies the way they might an Instagram

feed: as a platform to project a carefully constructed image to others. Look good, and no one will know you're worried about failing chemistry. Look good, and people think you're competent. The "revenge body," a celebrity's self-imposed makeover to avenge being wronged by a friend or partner, went viral in 2017 with Khloé Kardashian's eponymous show. Changing your body after getting dumped is "a way to do *something* and still feel in control," said *Vanity Fair*. With her body, twenty-four-year-old Kaitlyn explained, "You can prove something. You can prove that you're established in one area of your life in order to make it seem like the rest of your life is in order." Thinness affords "not only confidence," says Amira, a seventeen-year-old cross-country runner, but approval "of me."

If, as Martin writes, "beauty is the first impression of total success," extra pounds will mean much more than a snug pair of pants. They are a storm cloud of looming, global decline. In *Life Doesn't Begin 5 Pounds from Now*, Jessica Weiner writes that to be labeled fat means "complete girl failure"—someone who was "undesirable, messy, ugly, out of control, stupid, lazy, unpopular." The body can be the most visible symbol of all that a girl thinks she has failed to become.

"If you're not able to achieve the body that you're trying to, and you fail at that, then it's like you'll fail at other areas of achievement in your life," Kaitlyn added. "If I'm not thin, how can I expect to be doing school right and being the student that I am, or financially in a position that I feel safe, or secure in my friendships? It makes you second-guess other things."

Amira put it more succinctly: "If you can't be like that on the outside, then you can't be like that on the inside."

Weight loss, on the other hand, is tangible progress for the hardworking soul who longs to know she is doing things right. As with the likes piling up on an Instagram post, or a spike in her GPA on the online grading platform, the body offers instant gratification:

A flat stomach before breakfast. A dropped jeans size. A flurry of adoring comments for your new, slimmer selfie. "It takes four long years to see 'summa cum laude' etched across our college diplomas," writes Martin, "but stepping on a scale can instantly tell us whether we have succeeded or flunked." The body reveals its success openly where other achievements may be harder to glean. You might not be able to see the grade that girl got on her exam, but you can see her perfect ass from across the quad.

The body also offers a rush of control. Unfair professors, dreary postcollege jobs, and boring Saturday nights may be largely out of your hands, but the body? That's indisputably, entirely yours. "I do have control over what I put in my body and what I do with my body," one college student told me. "If that's something that I can't control, then what else is out of my control?"

And yet: wherever a girl looks—at a meal, in the gym, or in class—there is a better, tighter, thinner body that she does not or cannot have. There is someone with a wider thigh gap, less prominent nose, rounder butt, smaller waist, straighter teeth, less arm hair. Someone you may resent and be jealous of. Someone who may even be your best friend.

The body is always there. There are no vacations from the sight of your upper arms, or the sinking feeling you get when you see a rounded belly in the mirror. "You wake up and it's yours," Kaitlyn told me. "It's not something you can put aside. You can leave the office at five and choose to take work home or not. But you can't leave your body." The body will not be compartmentalized.

Girls are well aware that how others see them will impact who they will become. Iyana, seventeen, told me no matter what your goals are—whether it's "the girl who does every club and activity and is going to be president someday" or "the housewife who has her hands in her lap," you better be skinny. "To be successful," she said, "you have to be a certain size no matter what, and no matter what identity."

There are two key points to keep in mind as you talk about body image with your daughter: first, what she sees in the mirror may bear little resemblance to what you think she looks like. Second, when you call attention to her body in a negative way, even to be helpful, she will almost always hear it as failing to live up to what a girl should look like, and what you expect of her. If girls infuse their bodies with ideas about success, likability, and self-worth, what you say about her body may be heard by her as a commentary on all three.

Even if you don't mean to be critical, she is likely to hear it as such. Think of it this way: girls are famously prone to hearing a critical voice as yelling, even when you aren't yelling at all. The same sensitivity kicks in when it comes to their bodies. The female ear is always pricked for hidden criticism. "Are you going to eat (or order) that?" is instantly read as "You can't afford those calories." "Don't you want to look good for your prom?" is heard as "Whatever you're about to eat will make you too fat to be seen as attractive by others." "Are you really still hungry?" means "You can't afford to eat that much and look good."

The conversation here is loaded. On the one hand, your daughter needs you to be clear that her looks are not the measure of her character, ability, or potential. Yet her world constantly tells her just the opposite: that social status and success, indeed all good things in life, are inextricably linked to appearance. You may be pushed into what feels like an impossible spot. Yes, your job is to offer shelter from toxic messages. But by doing so, you can become a target yourself. She may turn the same messages she is plagued by on you: *You think the world really cares how nice I am? You have no idea what you're talking about.* In the dressing room where she's having a meltdown, or as she stares in bitter silence out the window of your car, warm thanks won't be her first response. This is no small test of your parenting, and it is as exhausting as it is unrewarding.

In these moments, she needs you to remind her she is more than a number—more than her weight, jeans size, and BMI; more than how many calories she's eaten today or how many times she worked out. What do you love about her that has nothing to do with how she looks? Dr. Julia Taylor suggests helping girls connect with the things they love to do, the quirky qualities they have, or the important roles they play. What are three positive words her friends or family would use to describe her personality? If the culture has reduced a girl to her body, the parent must step in to affirm how much more to her there is. Remind her that someone else's "better" features don't cancel out her own value. Just because that other person is pretty, the saying goes, doesn't mean you're ugly.

If she is overweight, keep in mind that there is little refuge from the messages that shame her for it. Your criticism, well intentioned as it may be, deprives her of an oasis where she can feel loved for who she is. Attempts to inspire her by pitting her weight against something she values—"Your boyfriend may lose interest if you get bigger"—is the exact opposite of a safe motivator. If anything, it can lead to drastic, unhealthy choices that come from panic or anger, instead of a genuine desire for change.

With very few exceptions, body comments that dwell on appearance reinforce the message that a girl's first priority should be how she looks. And there is evidence that parents are far more vigilant about their daughters' appearance: in 2014, parents googled "Is my daughter overweight?" about 70 percent more often than "Is my son overweight?" That's despite the fact that boys tend to be slightly more overweight than girls.

The only comments adults ought to make about girls' bodies should call attention to what a body needs to be strong and do its many jobs, whether they be studying, playing a sport, or working at a job. Feeling good about your body—genuinely, sustainably good—will never come from an external source.

Instead of talking about your daughter's weight, consider changing focus. Weight ties directly to the ways her body is expected to comply with society's demands—it immediately raises the question *Do I weigh too much?* Focusing on the body, by contrast, casts a wider net. *What does your body need right now to be strong? In order for you to feel happy? What are you grateful that your body can do?* If talking about weight makes a girl an object focused on pleasing others, thinking about her body asks her to assert her own authority. The more focused she is on the noise of what others expect, the less she can hear her own thoughts and needs. We know a girl will develop a healthy body image when she can connect with her body as it serves her, not others. This is particularly true in organized sports. According to the Women's Sports Foundation, girl athletes have a more positive body image (and more confidence) than girls who do not play sports.

Let her know what you are grateful for about your own body. Maybe it's that your body lets you go on long walks or bike rides. Perhaps your body allows you to do important work or take care of people you love. What do you love about your body? What do you love about hers? What are you grateful for that your body allows you to do? Fathers' voices are just as crucial.

Your voice as a cultural critic is key. Call out unnatural thinness in advertisements and on-screen. Say things like, *You know no one really looks like that, right?* Or, *Can you imagine how many hours a day she has to work out, and how little she probably gets to eat, to look like that?* Or, *Well, maybe if I had a personal trainer I could have a butt like that, but right now I've got more important things to do.* We know that girls who are media literate—who are more aware of the ways media manipulate bodies and distort consumers' perceptions—have a healthier body image and eating habits. Besides, you can be sure that even if you say nothing, she is still thinking about it.

DRIVEN TO DISTRACTION: OVERTHINKING ABOUT THE BODY

The girls I met confided thoughts about their bodies that bordered on relentless. Body worry shunted cognitive resources away from studies, relationships, and activities, to say nothing of the spirit. Ever since sixth grade, seventeen-year-old Bianca told me, "There's not a day when I don't look at myself in the mirror and think, 'Today I look good, or today I look bad, or I look like this.' It's very, very present in my life. A day won't go by when I don't think about how I look."

"It's always an underlying thing," she went on. "If I'm playing sports with my friends, I think, 'How do I look in these sports clothes?' If I'm sitting a certain way with people, I wonder if I'm looking fat. I wish it wasn't that way." In high school, she sat in math class and tried flexing her stomach to tighten her abdominal muscles. "It's like, you're in math class!" she told me. "Focus on math! What are you doing?" In her bedroom, she often stopped her homework to do crunches. Her father would stick his head in and cheer her on.

On pasta night at her boarding school, Kavya, a high school junior, carefully filled half her plate with spaghetti. "If it were up to me, I'd have two plates," she told me, "but I feel like people are watching. [They're probably thinking] 'How's she going to eat all of that?' They might notice me now more often, like 'she's really heavy,' and they'll be like, 'oh, that's why.'" Her friend Lauren confided she'd spent most of her sophomore year focused on how big her thigh gap was. "I just spent so much time looking at myself, and kind of with so much criticism," she told me. "There were a lot of times I could have been with my friends or something, but I was in my room staring at myself."

In case you were wondering, these girls pass for A-OK on the outside. Inside, the anxious thoughts are so disruptive that I imagined their cognitive burden as the equivalent of going through life wearing a fifty-pound backpack. How could these girls be so productive in life (and they were) when they were weighed down by obsessive, single-minded thinking? How much less work is done in the library when, as one girl told me, she spent an hour there convincing herself not to eat a scone? The answer, psychologists say, is the minds of girls are exhausted: body surveillance in girls (not boys) can lead to overthinking and depression.

How often are girls distracted? I couldn't find any research that answered the question, so I decided to find out. Last year *Clover Letter*, an online newsletter for girls, and I surveyed nearly five hundred girls, ages fifteen to twenty-two. Almost 40 percent of the young women polled said they were distracted by thoughts of their appearance at least six times a day; nearly one in five admitted they thought about their looks ten times a day or more. Schoolwork was their number one worry, but appearance came in second. They worried more about what they were eating than their friendships, and more about how much they were exercising than their crushes. A majority of girls said that concern about their appearance has at times prevented them from doing activities they enjoy.

While boys face more pressure than ever about their looks, girls face exceptional barriers. It is girls, not boys, whose maturing bodies are swiftly marked as sexual objects as they enter puberty. During this period, they are leered at and objectified by peers and adults with unprecedented frequency. In the United States, over half of girls in grades seven through twelve say they have been sexually harassed at school, but only 9 percent report it. In a study by the UK's Girlguides (the U.S. version of the Girl Scouts), 60 percent of girls ages thirteen to twenty-one reported sexual harassment in school or college in 2014; 20 percent said they were touched against their will. And it is girls, not boys, who experience harassment online at disproportionately high levels: 26 percent of women ages eighteen to twenty-four have been stalked online, Pew surveys found, and 25 percent were the target of online sexual harassment.

Adolescence is when girls tune in to gender norms, the culture's unwritten rules that tell a girl how to look and act. It's the moment when their bodies and voices contract in an effort to take up less space, in order to be liked and seen as worthy and attractive by others.

The sum of these changes—sexual maturation, objectification by others, and the mandate to be liked above all—is what psychologists call self-objectification, the moment when a girl sees herself as an object whose primary value is based on appearance. Self-objectification is associated with academic and social problems, eating disorders, depression, and body shame, and it shows up in surveys with girls as young as eleven. Psychologists say the gender difference here is so large that the challenges faced by girls in this space are "substantially greater than those experienced by boys."

Differences among ethnic and racial groups of girls are less pronounced. On the one hand, Black girls and women appear to have a more positive body image than white girls and women, in part because Black women have been known to adopt a larger ideal body size. In one study, when Black and white adolescent girls were asked to define their beauty ideal, Black girls were more likely to name personality traits like pride and confidence; white girls talked about physical traits like blond hair and cheekbones. Black girls are also more likely to name positive parts of their bodies than white girls.

But Black girls have stereotypically been thought to be relatively immune to eating disorders and the thin ideal, leading many to assume these issues are a "rich white girl's problem." That's a dangerous myth. A meta-analysis by Shelly Grabe and Janet Hyde of almost a hundred studies revealed that women of color struggle just as much as white women. Hispanic and Asian American girls are known to have the lowest levels of body dissatisfaction. Researchers concluded that the issue "may not be the golden girl problem promoted in the literature."

That said, affluent girls appear to be somewhat more vulnerable to body image concerns. Researchers trace the problem to a closely linked, and self-reinforcing, set of factors: these girls are often raised by mothers who are anxious about body image, grow up in communities with high levels of stress, and possess a genetic predisposition for eating disorders. They also attend school with peers who share their struggle.

FAT TALK IS FRIEND TALK

In a single day, most girls will hear their peers degrade their own appearance more times than they can count. "'Oh my God, I look so ugly. I'm so fat,'" said Lauren, sixteen, quoting her friends. "Or when people take a picture for Snapchat they're like, 'Oh, I look so gross. I'm so fat.'"

Amy, sixteen, couldn't go to the bathroom at her public high school without hearing a chorus of self-criticism. "I look terrible. My face looks really pudgy today."

Martin calls this the "ritual language of self-hatred." Psychologists call it fat talk, or body-bashing, and it's one of the unspoken membership fees of girlhood.

Fat talk accomplishes three goals in short order: it offers an outlet for a girl to voice body shame, nets her some reassurance (*you're not fat, you look amazing!*), and provides a conversation starter to boot. Fat talk is nearly ubiquitous among girls. In 2011, a study by Rachel Salk and Renee Engeln-Maddox revealed that 90 percent of college women engaged in fat talk, even though only 9 percent were overweight. Fat talk is something that occurs almost exclusively among girls who are not actually overweight. This is hardly a shocker; obesity is rarely spoken about between friends.

The seduction of fat talk lies in its ability to bring girls together. It is many a girl's go-to icebreaker and friend maker. *Oh, you hate your thighs? Well, I can't stand my stomach.* It is a duet girls learn to sing at a young age. The put-down is always met with the compliment—the *No, you're not, you look amazing, you're just being crazy.* The *You don't look bad at all.* The *No, it's ME who's disgusting.*

Some fat talk starts with a compliment. "We'll say, 'I wish I looked like you, or had abs like you,'" one twenty-four-year-old woman explained. "Another friend will say, 'I wish I was thin like you.'" This establishes a faux intimacy, a point of connection that feels unique and even heartfelt. Fat talk builds up a relationship at the expense of the put-down individual. It also enlists girls as ego boosters who stand in to shore up their friends in a culture incessantly undermining their self-worth.

Oh come on, you might be thinking. It's a little banter about feeling fat; big deal. But this is far from harmless chatter: an analysis of several studies linked fat talk to body shame, body dissatisfaction, and even disordered eating. In one study, a majority of girls who fat talked told researchers it made them feel better about their bodies, yet they showed lower levels of body satisfaction.

Girls believe they'll be more likable when they fat talk, even though they privately say that they prefer girls who *like* their bodies. And all those nice compliments you get when you do confess your "fatness"? The women who say they feel good about body compliments tend to have higher body dissatisfaction and body surveillance.

The problem is that fat talk feels less like an option than an expectation. If your friend says she's fat, it's often not enough to tell her she looks great; the unspoken rule is that you've got to announce that you're feeling like a cow, too. Studies confirm fat talk is "contagious";

when one or two girls do it, the others follow. But here's a nice surprise from the research by Salk and Engeln-Maddox: girls tend to think others engage in fat talk much more often than they actually do. The more value girls place on being thin, the more likely they are to think this. Researchers call this an "injunctive norm"—you do something because you think your friends approve of it. (The same is often true of alcohol use in college: students wrongly assume the majority of their peers are drinking, which in turn eggs them on.)

When I hear a girl use fat talk, I imagine it as a muscle she is flexing. It's the same muscle she flexes when she says, "I totally failed that test," or introduces an idea in class by saying, "I'm not sure this is right, but . . ." It is the muscle of self-defeat. The more she uses these muscles, the less she works the ones that affirm herself. No matter how casual it seems, to use fat talk is to habitually insult yourself.

There is no better way to help your daughter stop fat talking than the power of your own example. Mothers are all recovering girls, and many of us import the habits we learned as adolescents into adulthood. A study by Engeln-Maddox of thousands of women ages sixteen to seventy revealed that fat talk continues throughout the female life span. Other research has found that men engage in fat talk, too, though on a lesser scale. The question to ask yourself now is how much you do it, and whether you have scripted your own daughter in this regard.

How often do you talk about how much or what you've eaten? How much or how little you've exercised? How "good" or "bad" you've been and deserve (or not) to eat something fattening? How much do you talk about other people's weight or appearance being "better" than yours? Do you make comments about what other people are eating (or not)? Seek connection over flawed body parts or through ogling someone's "better" body? All these fit the fat talk bill. Girls are watching and listening.

Parents, Iyana told me, "need to be more aware of how much

importance is in every little action they do." In a world where fat talk runs loud, silence can be a powerful strategy. One mom of girls remembers that her father never made a comment about her own beauty and body—or any other woman's. "As I got older, and experienced other 'father figures' make comments about women, even relatively innocuous things like, 'Oooh, nice body on that actress,' I realized how incredibly grateful I was to be spared this kind of commentary by the adult men in my life, growing up. It did wonders to protect my sense of self."

If you're not sure how much fat talk you engage in, ask the people closest to you, including your daughter. Be willing to face the answer, whatever it is. Then commit not to do it. Even better, have your daughter and your friends call you out when they hear you fat talk. It is a habit so ingrained it can be unconscious.

Experts believe that people use fat talk as a proxy for sharing difficult feelings. It's easier to say you "feel fat"—an actual status update on Facebook, until it was removed in 2015—than to tell a friend how scared or insecure you feel. Some girls use anxiety about their bodies as a reason to stand down from healthy risks and not pursue activities they love. A girl who wants to run for student government bows out because she fears she's not popular enough to win; she says she isn't popular because she doesn't have the right body or hair. A girl who wants to try out for a sports team decides she's not thin enough to play.

Taylor advises girls to dig beneath the fat talk and surface the feelings driving it. If a girl says, for example, "I look so fat in every pair of pants I put on," think about what she's really feeling. Is she self-conscious or nervous about going out? What does she need from you right now? Is it connection? Reassurance? Redirect with questions that help her get to the deeper source of the insecurity. The next time you feel the urge to fat talk, consider asking these same questions of yourself.

Getting girls to stop responding to fat talk is harder. Refusing to engage with fat talk, or changing the subject to avoid doing it, can seem uncaring to girls. Fat talk is one of the unwritten girl rules about humility (put yourself down when someone else does, or else be seen as conceited). That's why a direct conversation is best.

Girls can tell trusted friends that they've committed to ending their own fat talk and want to stop doing it with others, too. They can couch the change in their concern for someone they love: "It hurts me to hear you talk like this about yourself." They can also invoke their own politics: "I think fat talk hurts all of us."

Indeed, fat talk is cruel to the overweight girls who hear it. Embedded in the casual question "Do I look fat?" is genuine terror of being overweight. Weiner told me that fat talk is a reminder "that people are scared of being . . . YOU." Every time a girl uses fat talk in front of an overweight peer, she sends the message that she would rather "die than be fat," and that "having a body like a fat person is the worst fate imaginable." Choosing to stop fat talking is not just a matter of wellness. It is a moral choice and an act of conscience.

MIRROR, MIRROR ON THE SCREEN, WHO'S THE THINNEST IN THE FEED?

We have long understood that movies, magazines, and television damage teens' body image. Less known is the impact of new media. Most educators and parents assume that social media's most pressing threat is that it can be used as a vehicle for cruelty or crime, so they focus on "digital citizenship." But with the rapid aging down of smartphone ownership, the biggest liability of new media has changed.

Social media has become a toxic mirror: in 2016, psychologists found the first cross-cultural evidence linking social media use to body image concerns, dieting, body surveillance, and self-objectification in adolescents. The change for girls is radical: pre-Internet, you had to go to the grocery store to find a magazine featuring celebrity bodies, or at least swipe your mother's copy from the bathroom. Now the images are as endless as they are available. Girls can spend hours fixating on the toned arms or glutes of celebrities, who hawk their bodies as much as their talent.

Visual platforms like Facebook, Instagram, and Snapchat have also turned the spotlight onto girls themselves. If girls once compared their bodies to models they would never meet, social media now lets them measure themselves against someone in their dorm or homeroom. In one study, female first-year college students were more likely than male peers to say Facebook made them feel bad about their bodies. Another found that posting, tagging, and editing on Facebook was correlated with weight dissatisfaction, a drive for thinness, and self-objectification. The most vulnerable users are the ones who spend most of their time posting, commenting on, and comparing themselves to photos. Female college students who do this on Facebook are more likely to link their self-worth to their looks. In late 2016, researchers published the first look at the impact of Instagram on body image; their study of college women found that "acute exposure to thin and attractive female celebrity images has an immediate negative effect on women's mood and body image."

Thanks to an array of free applications, selfie-holics now have the power to alter their bodies in a way that's practically on par with makeup and other beauty products. If the Internet has been called a great democratizer, then what social media has done is let anyone enter the beauty pageant. All this provides an illusion of control: if I spend more time and really work at it, I can improve at being beautiful. "I don't get to choose how I'm going to leave my apartment today," one young woman told me. "If I could, my body would look different. But I can choose which picture makes my arms look thinner." Teens can cover up pimples, whiten teeth with the swipe of a finger, curating their own image to become prettier, thinner, and hotter. "Many of today's girls' greatest body icons are not household names," Weiner told me.

Indeed, as Dr. Jill Walsh, who studies social media and body image, told the *New York Times*, "Girls are not comparing themselves to media ideals as much as one would expect, but they are making microcomparisons to their peers. It's not me versus Gisele Bündchen in a bikini, it's me versus my good friend Amy in our bikinis."

This may make pursuit of the thin ideal feel more accessible, but it may also amplify competition among girls. The 2016 Instagram study found no difference between the negative impact of viewing celebrities and thin, attractive, unknown peers. Instagram "presents both on an equal platform," the researchers wrote, and because celebrities post pictures of their private lives, "viewers feel more personally connected to them." In my survey with *Clover Letter*, one-third of the girls said looking at social media made them feel worse about their appearance.

The news isn't all grim. Many girls are starting political conversations about the body online, often in ways that push back against the thin ideal. The movement, which is alternately known as "body positivity" or "fat acceptance," challenges fat phobia and weight bias, and advocates for body acceptance at any size. Fat isn't a moral failing, it argues, but often a by-product of slower metabolism, socioeconomic status, and a mix of factors that go beyond mere "willpower." Besides, some research has shown that dieting can damage the body's metabolism, while other studies suggest significant weight loss is rarely sustainable in the long term.

On Instagram, accounts like "MyNameIsJessamyn" feature photos of real-bodied, curvy girls and women. In one post, Jessamyn

Stanley wrote, "My body epitomizes strength. It's worthy of respect. But most importantly, my body only belongs to me. No matter what the haters say, #thisbody belongs to me. And I'm going to show it the respect it deserves." Stanley has 283,000 followers; the post garnered nearly ten thousand likes.

Weiner said these girls have leveraged social media to "make the invisible body, visible." The Internet has "allowed girls to form communities and connections never previously available to them in locations around the world. This is especially important for girls of color, who are often left out of mainstream conversations around body image." For girls feeling alone and misunderstood, "a stranger's blog or insta-feed can resonate more clearly with a girl in need of a healthy connection and body reality check."

Mainstream media have begun to pay attention. Reporting on the diet industry in 2017 for the *New York Times*, Taffy Brodesser-Akner wrote that magazine headlines began "acknowledging that perhaps a women's magazine doesn't know for sure what size your body should be, or what size it can be." Phrases like *Get fit! Be your healthiest! GET STRONG!* replaced diet language like *Get lean! Control your eating! Lose 10 pounds this month!* Dieting, she wrote, was by many "now considered tacky. It was anti-feminist. It was arcane."

Enter the "wellness" industry whose meteoric rise online has launched a legion of fitness celebrities on social media. Their posts are filled with daily BMI measurements, protein powder menus, and daily workout routines. Millions of followers embrace their regimens for diet and exercise, but increasingly, the drive for "wellness" and "clean eating" has become stealthy cover for more dieting and deprivation. This year, an analysis of fifty so-called fitspiration Web sites by L. Boepple and J. K. Thompson revealed messaging that was indistinguishable, at times, from pro-anorexia (pro-ana) or "thinspiration" Web sites. Both contained strong language inducing guilt about weight or the body, and promoted dieting, restraint, and fat and weight stigmatization.

As always, a balanced take on social media is the best way into a conversation. Be open to the good online. Ask your daughter what she loves about social media. What does she think about the ways people use it to modify their appearance? What do they gain, and from whom? How does she feel after looking at images of other people's bodies online? Sometimes just naming a feeling as normal can make a young adult feel less alone. And it never hurts to tell her she matters more than her looks or likes. As she peers into the mirror on the screen, a good old-fashioned "I love you exactly as you are" may be more timely than ever.

HOW ONE GIRL GOT HER GUT BACK

When a girl talks about a problem or challenge with unusual intensity, I try to understand what may be underlying it. I ask two questions about her problem. The first is, *What would happen if your worry became a reality? Say more.* The second: *What would that mean?* When you help girls surface the larger fear, they can begin to make meaning of it, and you can make real progress in a conversation.

These questions work because girls often assign the challenges of their lives with exaggerated meaning. Getting a bad grade on one test is rarely just about the grade; it means: *What if it ruins my final grade? What if I don't get into a good college/graduate school/job? What if I'm not successful? What if I don't have a good life?* The same is true of body shame: girls use concern about their bodies as a vehicle to express global worries about self-worth, likability, and success.

Katie was nineteen, just wrapping up her first year at a large state university in the Northeast. She hailed from the upper-middle-class suburbs of a large city nearby, though unlike many of her peers,

Katie paid half her tuition herself. Determined to be financially independent, she had worked long hours in retail and restaurants since she was sixteen. In high school, Katie often locked up the restaurant where she waited tables at 1:00 A.M., a shift that began just after the last school bell rang.

Katie declined to attend the private colleges where she had been accepted. She was adamant about avoiding debt. "I never want to have to rely on another person to take care of me," she told me. "I want to be able to support myself and be secure in my financial situation."

Waiting tables had given Katie people skills, responsibility, and respect for the dollar. She was proud. "I know how to be a good employee," she told me, looking me in the eye. Sure, life had been harder for her in some ways; she knew that. "But I really do value what I've learned and how hard I've worked, because you can't get that anywhere else."

The first year of college had been a breeze after the backbreaking schedule she'd kept to get into school. Here she could plan a double major in business and psychology, and still have time to watch TV and work out. "I'm not stressed out at all," she said gleefully, "and I love it." College was also a chance to experiment with new sides of herself. No longer would she wear a full face of makeup to class, a daily ritual she hated back home.

But there was one thing she couldn't leave behind: shame about her body. When Katie talked about her size, her sparkling confidence evaporated. She confided, "I've always had low self-esteem about how I look." She scrutinized her arms, her stomach, and her legs multiple times a day. She felt the jiggle of her arms and hated them. Her new friends talked endlessly about fear of the "freshman fifteen." The subject of fat was always in the air.

It was her "muffin top" that Katie most detested. There was, she practically growled, *no way* she could wear any shirt that called attention to it.

I decided to ask my two questions. "So if you wore a shirt that showed your muffin top," I asked Katie, "what would happen then? Say more."

"They wouldn't take the time to notice me," she said.

"Who?" I asked.

"Guys. They would think I was ugly or fat."

"What would that mean?"

"From a guy's point of view, I wouldn't be attractive? And they could find someone better at a party to look at."

Behold the next layer of the onion: Katie's love life.

"My love life doesn't exist," she went on. She couldn't get her head around the social hierarchy at the university. "These girls, they're just like really mean people, and they have boyfriends! And I'm like, 'What am I doing wrong?'" she told me.

Sometimes she put on a happy face and went to class when she wanted to cry in her room. But mostly, she kept her chin up and played the game. She worked out as much as she could. She went to basement frat parties, where she learned to read the signals of approaching guys. If one came up to dance, it meant he'd probably want to make out with her on the dance floor, sometimes without even talking to her. Just showing up to a party meant you were "up for it," *it* being hooking up.

But Katie was meh about the hookup scene. She felt "objectified." "Because like here's this guy dancing, grinding on me, and doesn't even want to know me for who I am. Like, I'm more than just a body. I'm a person," she said.

Not long after Katie and I met, a promising guy came into her life. They hooked up once, and it was fun. The guy said he'd been tested for STIs, and that he'd be at a party over the weekend. Katie tried to decode the message. Maybe, after the party, they would get more serious and define their relationship.

On the day of the party, Katie got in a minor but scary car accident. Suddenly, she felt something shift inside of her. She called a good friend. "I shouldn't hook up with him," she said. The friend chalked up her willies to the accident. But Katie sensed it was something more.

"I just got one of those bad gut feelings that I get every now and again," she told me. She opted to ignore it. That night, Katie lost her virginity. Not long after, she called him weeping from the emergency room. She had genital herpes. He cried, too, and said he'd gotten the positive test results after they had been together. There was nothing they could do. It was a virus; there was no cure. Katie had hoped he might still want to see her, but he wasn't interested in a relationship.

For four months, Katie hated herself and her body. She was despondent, then angry. She oozed shame. When she returned to school in the fall, her mind raced constantly. She started crying in her statistics class out of the blue. "I felt like shit overall. Just like in every way." Katie began seeing a therapist for anxiety and depression. She wondered if anyone would ever want to sleep with her again.

Now, nearly a year later, she cried to me on Skype, shame audible in her voice.

"So why," I asked gently, "did you go against your gut and sleep with him?"

"I think I honestly just wanted to have sex," she said. "I was going to be twenty and I hadn't slept with anyone. I was hard on myself about that."

"What would it mean if you were twenty and still a virgin? Say more."

"Just like that I was inexperienced and couldn't relate to it with my friends," she wept. "I never imagined I would be twenty and never have had a serious boyfriend or things like that. I just, the way my life has turned out, I never pictured that I would be in the position that I am today. I wanted to be like everyone else. I wanted to be a normal person as opposed to a weird person who hasn't had sex."

"What would happen if you were the normal person who had sex?"

To be twenty and sexually active, she explained, meant that she'd relate to what her friends talked about. "It means a guy wants you, like you're attractive. And if people view you positively you feel good about yourself."

Some of Katie's angst was a garden-variety desire to fit in, a drive that begins around puberty and pulses painfully throughout adolescence. Yet the choice Katie made was about more than not wanting to be weird. It was not hearing the sound of her own internal voice that told her to stop. It was feeling unable to set the boundaries that would protect her from harm. And it was feeling so physically inadequate, so less-than, and so ashamed of herself that she would settle for less than she deserved.

The way a girl feels about her body reverberates far beyond the realm of diet, exercise, and her reflection in the mirror. Body shame left Katie with a pervasive sense of being one-down among her peers. The belief that her appearance was flawed made her feel abnormal, as though she had defects in need of correction. Self-hating thoughts about her body propelled her to take dangerous action with it.

Katie refused the antidepressants her therapist recommended, so the doctor suggested exercise. She agreed to try yoga. Katie had run on more treadmills than a pet store hamster, but these workouts felt different. This exercise was decidedly *for her*: not to smooth the muffin top that bulged against her shirt, not for a guy she might meet at a party, and not to feel not-weird. "It made me feel good about myself," she said. "It was like an internal locus of control. It's just motivation to do better and make yourself better. It's just kind of like strength."

Katie began listening more to her body, opting to sleep more and eat more healthfully. "I made my body a priority for the first time," she said. "Just taking care of myself overall is more important than it was before." Once Katie began to do things for her body—and steered her body away from serving as an object for others to evaluate—she started to get well.

She had to stop looking at her body through the world's eyes. From that vantage point, her herpes made her disgusting and unlovable. When she connected with herself, she forged a more complex relationship with her body in which the herpes was but one small piece of who she was. It was part of her, but did not define her.

If she didn't look out for herself, she realized, no one would. "I just know I have to listen to myself, or else I'm going to be miserable," she told me. "Which is kind of weird. I just know how bad it can be. I never want to go back to how I was in the fall. I never want to feel that way ever again."

With her newfound connection to her body, Katie found herself able to act on her instincts more and more. Hookup culture, she decided, wasn't for her. "Emotionally, I can't do it," she told me. Real feelings rarely survived in the world of no strings attached. "I have feelings." She laughed. "I also know I want to be at 110 percent emotionally before I get myself into a relationship. I want to be ready."

Katie traded her muffin top obsession for the better kind of gut: the one that told her how she was feeling. The girls I interviewed for this chapter described relationships with their bodies that converged at a single question: *Who am I doing this for?* It was only when they started to eat and work out to satisfy their own needs, instead of depriving themselves and exercising to look a certain way for others, that they achieved their own personal bests. As with so many other domains in girls' lives, the moment these girls let go of pleasing others, they found their center. They began to feel like they were enough.

4

Overcoming Self-Doubt and Closing the Confidence Gap

Each time I did something that I was afraid or nervous about doing successfully, it made me more confident.

—JESSIE, NINETEEN

A few years before she came to my Courage Boot Camp, Jessie was afraid: of talking to people she didn't know, of public speaking, and of mistakes. At her state university in the Northwest, she kept up a high GPA but avoided clubs and activities, keeping to herself and commuting from home. In class, she rarely spoke up, even when she knew the answer. "If I say it out loud, I might say it wrong, or actually get it wrong, or mess up in some way, or somehow embarrass myself," she told me.

Jessie's parents had divorced a few years earlier, devastating her mother. Bearing witness to her pain galvanized Jessie. "I don't want to let my fear get in the way of doing something I want to do," she recalled deciding.

She began tackling her fear of meeting new people by going to cafés. Normally, she could barely utter an order because she feared the judgment of cooler-than-thou baristas. This time, she said, "I started making myself go alone. I would stumble, and drop the money, and make a fool of myself. I was forcing myself into a new situation."

Over and over again, as her internal voice hollered with anxiety, Jessie talked back to it and reassured herself. *No one cares how I order my coffee. It doesn't matter if I stumble.* When she felt overwhelmed, she reminded herself "that really, if I want to do anything in life, I have to be able to talk to people to get over it."

Jessie soon discovered her courage was a resource that replenished itself. "Each time I did something that I was afraid or nervous about doing successfully, it made me more confident," she said. When she faced down a new risk, she reminded herself, "I've done things like this before. I can do it again!" The rush of courage was addictive, and she wanted more. Jessie was afraid of needles, so she went and gave blood. Another fear conquered.

When she came to Courage Boot Camp, she was struggling to confront a roommate who stayed up late talking loudly on her phone. I asked her what the worst thing that could happen was if she took the risk (a great question to ask your own daughter when she's wavering). Jessie thought about it. Then she wrote down a script of what she would say and ask for. She role-played her conversation with a friend. Finally, she went to talk to her roommate. The following week, the roommate posted a QUIET HOURS SCHEDULE on their dorm room door, written in calligraphy.

What did Jessie learn that allowed her to leave her comfort zone? How did she summon the courage to take a risk? What inspires a girl to face her fear and take a first, intimidating step? In this chapter, I share what I've learned about cultivating confidence in girls.

Despite all the progress girls have made, a stubborn confidence gap persists. In a twenty-year review of the National College Health

Assessment, UCLA's Linda Sax found that male college freshmen consistently ranked themselves higher than their female peers in almost every category linked to confidence, often by double-digit margins. Men said they were stronger in academic ability, competitiveness, emotional health, leadership, math, physical health, popularity, public speaking, risk taking, intellectual confidence, social self-confidence, and self-understanding. In answering the question, "How smart am I in comparison to my friends—as smart? Smarter? Not as smart or capable?" Black women score lower than Black men, even though they outperform them academically. There is a notable exception: graduates of all-girls schools report feeling smarter, more confident, and more engaged on campus than female peers who graduated from coed private high schools.

Yet few schools explicitly teach students skills that increase their confidence. The good news is that there is plenty you can do to help, beginning with how you talk about it. There are three framing points to keep in mind as you begin working with your daughter:

1. *Ease up on the Girl Power talk.*

Since the 1970s, we believed telling girls they could do anything would translate to high confidence. But messages like these can actually undermine it. When we tell girls the sky's the limit, they become afraid to admit when they can't get there—and that, ultimately, makes them fearful of taking risks and being brave. Confidence is much more about how we handle our fears than about how good we are at concealing them.

Girls develop confidence when they face down the unknown and come out the other side—note that I didn't say *succeed* at the other side. The trying is just as important as the outcome. Put another way, it's when a girl attempts a feat that makes her *question* her ability to be and do anything that builds true confidence. When girls move through challenges and learn to appreciate their lessons, they come to understand that the outcome doesn't define themselves or their self-worth. They learn they are stronger than they thought. That, in turn, infuses them with motivation to try again.

This is why vulnerability, not invincibility, is crucial for confidence. As one new college graduate put it to me, learning to take risks and face the unknown was "a bit like putting yourself fully into an emotional relationship, risking getting hurt, risking losing what you built or worked for, but really putting your heart into it." If you don't leave your comfort zone and become vulnerable, she said, "you won't get the full experience . . . you won't fully feel the joy of getting into whatever job, school, or project you applied to, and the hope surrounding what that can be for you." Without risk and some fear, she was learning, there would be no real reward.

2. *Closing the confidence gap is not your daughter's job.*

The confidence gap is anything but her fault. It is a tax she pays for growing up in a society that still withholds full equality from women. To tell a girl that she can get braver if she only tries hard enough is to ignore this reality.

Let her know you understand it's not exclusively her responsibility to "fix" her confidence deficit. She may be under a different impression. In a so-called postfeminist world, write professors Shauna Pomerantz and Rebecca Raby in *Smart Girls*, girls are told they "can do, be, and have anything they want without fear of sexism or other inequalities in school or beyond to slow them down." In this world, gender inequality is seen as a thing of the past, putting success entirely in girls' control. Sexism is "framed as a personal, rather than a social defect."

But sexism is alive and well. Indeed, girls question their competence because they are often treated differently by teachers, who are more likely to critique their ability (leading to less intellectual confidence). Girls are less confident because they are ghettoized in certain fields of study and work, and see women occupy only tiny minorities at the highest levels of power. Girls doubt their worth because they are inundated with images of half-dressed models and celebrities selling the idea that stick-thin sexiness is the way to make friends, be attractive, and succeed in life. And they worry about failure in part because they are still expected—per the rules of "good girl" femininity that refuse to die—not to burden others with their mistakes. Let her know you understand all this.

3. *Confidence can be learned and practiced.*

Most students are well aware that practice improves performance when it comes to solving a math equation or playing a sonata. Athletes know they'd blow a game if they showed up cold. Yet many of these same students adopt a black-or-white attitude about confidence: they believe you're either brave or not, a risk taker or not. But practice and repetition are as crucial to success as the gifts or talents we bring to an experience. The more a girl does anything in life, the better she gets at it—and this is especially true when it comes to building her confidence.

Skills are like muscles: they must be flexed repeatedly to stay strong and agile. Risk taking is just such a muscle. My students are inspired by the TED Talk of Jia Jiang, the Chinese immigrant who decided to conquer his fear of rejection by purposely getting rejected for a hundred days in a row. Among his "rejection therapy" exploits: showing up at a stranger's house and asking to play soccer in the backyard. Asking a flight attendant to make the safety announcement on a plane. Asking a cop to let him sit in his patrol car. Students love Jiang's journey because it's funny, and because he shows how he learned over time to stay confident in the face of the word *no*.

Play his videos for your daughter. His journey is a fantastic teaching tool because it happens in small steps, not one big aha moment, and this is a crucial message for girls to hear. You can also explain it to her this way: just as most sane people wouldn't go to the gym for the first time ever and do squats with a fifty-pound bar—they would be hurt, overwhelmed, demoralized, or some combination of the three—it's equally foolish to attempt a huge act of courage straight out of the gate. The same is true of building confidence: it happens little by little, step by step, "no" by "no."

While it's true that confidence building is not entirely your daughter's responsibility, she will have to commit to building it like any other goal she's ever taken on. In the sections that follow, I'll introduce you to four questions that eat away at your daughter's confidence, and show you how to help respond when self-doubt overwhelms her.

WHAT IF I'M NOT SMART? UNDOING THE FIXED MINDSET

One of the most powerful predictors of a girl's confidence is her mindset about her intelligence. In her widely read book, *Mindset*, Stanford professor Carol Dweck showed people can adopt one of two mindsets. Those with a "fixed mindset" believe their basic intelligence cannot be improved. They interpret a tough challenge as a sign that they don't have the ability to succeed. They may then opt for a safer path, avoiding future risk or giving up altogether.

Morgan, twenty-two, spent years watching deadlines to apply for jobs, schools, and internships she wanted expire. "If I didn't get it, I thought it might mean that I wasn't good enough to go down that career path, but also more holistically that I had failed as a person." If Morgan did apply to something she loved, she would only put in partial effort, "so that if I didn't get in I didn't feel as hurt." For a girl like Morgan with a fixed mindset, every challenge felt like a defining judgment of her potential.

By contrast, people with a "growth mindset" think their abilities can be improved with effort, strategy, and mentoring. Drawn to challenge, they persist despite setbacks, or even because of them. Allison, seventeen, refused to give up when she struggled in math. "I don't get it and then I move on and I say, 'I think I'll get it later,'" she told me. "I don't do tests in order. I save the hard stuff for later so I'm already feeling good." She is exhilarated by the success that comes after struggle. "The one time I get it, it's like, this is the best feeling. I feel my brain working. I imagine it, all these connections touching each other and there are sparkles and it's great!" Allison is bewildered by her mother, who gives up quickly in the face of a challenge. "She has that mentality," she told me, "[and says] 'I don't get it, I'm stupid.'"

Dweck has long believed that girls and women may be more likely to have a fixed mindset. In one study, fifth-grade students were given a task that intentionally confused them at first. It was girls, especially those with high IQs, who struggled the most and were unable to learn the material.

In a bombshell 2017 study, more evidence emerged: researchers announced that by the age of six, girls were more likely than boys to say they were not interested in an activity because they weren't smart enough. When told that a game was for "really smart" children, five-year-old girls dove in, but the six-year-old girls demurred—a sign that girls acquired but were not born with the belief. Girls were also significantly less likely than boys to view their own gender as "brilliant."

The psychologists concluded that cultural stereotypes were in part to blame, as were parents, who in 2014 googled "Is my son a genius?" more than twice as often as they typed the same question about their daughters—even though girls tend to do better in school.

The consequences of these beliefs can last a lifetime. In 2015, the same team of researchers found that women were underrepresented in fields thought to require *brilliance*, including science and engineering. Indeed, in adulthood Dweck has found that women are more likely to avoid working in academic disciplines that require a growth mindset, such as economics, math, and computer science.

Here's what this looks like in college: Harvard economist Claudia Goldin noticed that undergraduate women were electing not to major in economics at Harvard, and she wanted to know why. She discovered the women typically left when they failed to get A's in the intro class. The guys, meanwhile, hung in even when they struggled. They played the long game, telling Goldin they were hoping for a job in finance later on. Their desire to make money was more compelling than the fear of screwing up.

"You can hit the guys over the head with a baseball bat, and they would still major in econ," Goldin told me. "Whereas the women, if they don't get an A-, they're far, far less likely to major." Goldin is the first woman to be tenured as an economist at Harvard, Princeton, Cal Tech, and the University of Pennsylvania, and the third woman ever to be president of the American Economics Association. After forty years of teaching undergraduate women, she has concluded this: "Women tend to go to a comfort zone. They want to be in the field that gives them comfort and gives them the sense of the pat on the back that says, you're really doing well."

Mindset can be traced, in part, to the types of praise we receive from parents and teachers. Telling a girl how smart, or "amazing at soccer," or "brilliant at poetry" she is can instill a fixed mindset. This is called "person praise," and it's detrimental to motivation as girls move through adolescence. It works like this: if you frequently praise your daughter for having a particular trait, she'll be motivated to prove that trait every time she faces a challenge. If she fails, she'll interpret the setback not just as a mistake, but as a sign that she's not smart, not good at soccer, and a bad poet. In other words, the failure confirms that she doesn't have the trait.

To be clear, a girl's ability is not the issue here. It is what girls *believe* about their ability. The good news is that parents can move the dial on this, just by changing the way they talk to their daughters about their achievements and setbacks.

When your daughter does something praiseworthy, focus your attention on her effort: "You worked really hard at that," or "I'm so impressed by how you stuck with this, even when it was hard." Try asking her about the strategies she used to achieve her goal, and if she had to change course along the way. This is called "process praise." When used in response to a success, process praise reminds a girl that she can improve herself through practice and that nothing is "fixed." Change is possible, always.

When process praise is used in response to a setback—"Okay, you haven't figured it out *yet*, but I know you will," "Look how far you've gotten already," or "Let's talk about which strategies worked for you in this process, and which ones didn't"—it reminds girls of the value (and necessity) of a journey where they learn along the way. Process praise tells girls that setbacks are a meaningful part of any learning process. It also lets girls know that Mom and Dad don't need them to crush it on the first try. Research shows these kinds of conversations are unusually successful in motivating girls after a setback.

How you respond to failure in front of your daughter is perhaps most critical. In 2016, a Stanford graduate student found that parents who believe failure is a debilitating experience, and who react to their children's failure with worry about their ability or performance, are more likely to have children with a fixed mindset. In a groundbreaking paper published with Carol Dweck, Kyla Haimovitz found parents' beliefs and behaviors in the face of failure were most visible to their children, and thus played a powerful role in shaping their children's mindset.

That's not to say you're not entitled to criticize her performance. Just be sure to ask yourself first how much that strategy may serve to comfort you in an anxious moment, rather than to motivate her.

One way to illustrate the journey of a setback is to write a "Failure Résumé" with your daughter. A Failure Résumé is a mock résumé of a loss, instead of a win. My students love to make them. Each setback is followed by a lesson learned, like this:

THE SETBACK: I failed a psych midterm and then didn't know what to do.

THE LESSON: I can lean on people like my adviser and teammates for advice about what to do next, and just to vent.

THE SETBACK: I dropped out of school after my first semester, certain college wasn't for me. A year later, I applied for readmission and got in.

THE LESSON: Sometimes you need time away from a situation to figure out what you want. No matter the pace, you will get to where you need to go.

At Smith, we asked faculty and staff to create Failure Résumés to show students that the adults they admire have screwed up, too. The college president even participated. What Failure Résumé would you create? Consider doing one with your daughter.

For girls of color, girls from low-income families, and first-generation college students, the fear of "doing it wrong" while trying to fit in can be particularly keen. Lee is African American, was assigned female at birth, identifies as nonbinary (not exclusively male or female), and uses they/their pronouns. Lee comes from a high-achieving family in a suburb in the Northeast, and was one of the only Black girls at their private middle school. Like many Black girls in predominantly white environments, Lee struggled to connect with their peers and educators. "People saw me as a problem child," they told me. "I was temperamental. I had a lot of feelings." African American girls are often coded as too loud or volatile by educators and peers. They are six times more likely to be suspended from school than white girls. In predominantly white environments, Dr. Charlotte Jacobs writes, they often become "hypervisible or invisible."

The challenge of belonging followed Lee to an elite, more diverse public high school, where they struggled to connect with Black peers. "Because I'd gone to this all-white middle school, I decided it meant I didn't belong with other Black people," they told me. "I knew," Lee said, "how to be Black around white people."

At home, Lee felt pressure to be the "exceptional Black girl" and make their race proud. "I didn't have confidence for myself," Lee said. "It's like, be good for Black people." Meanwhile, at school, Lee used their Blackness to gain social capital with white peers. "I definitely played into the sassy Black friend, socially," Lee told me. Yet Lee remained out of place, whether they were with the white kids they felt most comfortable with, or the Black students they most resembled. Lee was sure Black students resented them for having a lighter skin tone and "talking white." "I was clearly a Black person, but I wasn't part of the Black community," Lee said. Their evolving gender identity further complicated their efforts to feel safe at school.

Lee toggled between the pressure to do right by their parents and race, and the desire to achieve social status with their peers. Lee's motivation was largely extrinsic: driven more by outside rewards than by internal desire. All that pressure to perform, and the need to please others, came together in a fixed mindset where Lee avoided risk and made choices that guaranteed success.

Lee hated to fail and interpreted all challenges as ability based. "Failure, to me, was always about me personally failing, like on a basic human level I must have messed up," they told me. When Lee struggled in math in eighth grade, they thought, "Other kids are doing better in math because they're better people than me." Maybe, Lee thought, if I "wasn't damaged at a core level I would do better in math."

Fear of failure kept Lee away from situations where they might falter. "I only really spent my time on things that I was good at," Lee told me.

I used to love science. My dad would buy me science books for my birthday. Then I took environmental science and wasn't that good at it and I stopped. I did that with a lot of things. I was really into track for a while because I was winning a lot of medals. When I stopped winning I was like, I don't really like running, it's not my thing. I loved playing basketball. I went to basketball camp, I got MVP, I'm like, it's lit, I'm a star, I'm going to be in the WNBA. I got to my high school and I didn't start on JV. I traveled when I dribbled. I didn't have a great jump shot. I [dropped out].

Praise fed Lee so much that they gave up activities they genuinely loved in favor of praise, and let feedback completely influence every choice.

Early on someone told me I was a good singer. Early on someone told me I was a good writer. Someone along the way said I was good at it so I kept going. I didn't have a lot of internal motivation to do things. My motivation to do things was other people recognizing me for being good at something. . . . I was like, "As long as I'm particularly good at this I'm fine with it."

This worked well until college, where Lee was overwhelmed by the workload, writing a ten-page paper in the four hours before it was due, sobbing on the phone to their mother. They continued to struggle socially, falling in with a friend group they didn't much like. Partway through first semester, Lee crumbled, stopped going to class, and rarely left the dorm.

Lee's turnaround would come with two realizations. The first was that you couldn't depend on praise to drive you forward; there was a whole lot less of that in college. It was clear Lee needed to find their own reason to get up every day. "When you're by yourself there's no one to tell you that you're awesome." Lee turned to Tumblr, a social media platform, where they would write affirmations. No one seemed to notice. That's when they realized, "Oh, I can make myself feel better about myself. And I have to because no one is doing it for me."

The second epiphany was discovering what they really desired in life: Lee wanted—needed—to make college work. But, Lee told me, "I didn't know how to be a person." Lee still struggled socially and was afraid of risks. So, second semester, Lee went to class more, went to meals on time, and tried going to professors' office hours. They joined the a cappella group. They tried to make new friends.

The summer after their first year of college, Lee spent time alone, on purpose. They took walks and had fun, "just hanging out with myself." And, Lee told me, "I had this realization: 'I care so much about what other people think and I don't really know how to dig me. I don't know how to tell myself that I'm killing it.' I realized I don't have that skill and I have to get it as soon as possible." Lee spent their summer "dating" themself, figuring out who they were.

The change in Lee has been remarkable. Risk taking isn't terrifying anymore because, they said, "I realize that if I'm not particularly good at it, the world isn't going to shun me. It's fine." Lee also understood that most people didn't care what they did or how they did it. Lee was taking German and was "terrible" at it, they said proudly.

The change in Lee's friendships is also notable. "I'm not like, 'I hope this person at all levels of who I am only has good things to say about me.' It's like, 'I hope this person likes me but I really like me.'"

Slowly, Lee's mindset is changing. Part of this change is about context: they couldn't thrive in a predominantly white, cisgendered environment. But Lee also realized that the only weapon powerful enough to vanquish Lee's need to perform for others was . . . Lee. They understood that when you discover what truly matters to you, you're willing to get into the muck with it. You can stick out the clumsy moments, like falling into the wrong friend group, or getting run over by the workload in college, and keep going for you and no one else.

WHAT IF I CAN'T DO THIS? LEARNING TO SET REALISTIC GOALS

Girls with fixed mindsets approach challenges with a strange logic: the more they fear failure, the more they expect of themselves. But outsize goals rarely equal success; in fact, they typically thwart it. Perfectionism makes for unrealistic expectations in the face of a challenge.

How your daughter pursues her goals matters just as much as, perhaps even more than, what those goals are. The good news is that she can learn to manage self-doubt by changing the way she thinks about achievement.

You want your daughter to understand that real-life successes come in small increments, not in a single, epic moment of glory. In my workshops I suggest, "Do something that makes you slightly nervous every day." Jessie, for example, practiced microbravery:

small, local opportunities to try out a big new skill. She went to one café, then another and another. Lee decided to start going to professors' office hours. They committed not to skip any meals. Small steps, one day at a time.

To put this into practice, I use a system of three stages to plot out a goal: the comfort zone, low-risk zone, and high-risk zone. Hadia was a college sophomore whose goal was to speak up in class. Her comfort zone—what came easily to her right now—was keeping quiet in class. Occasionally, she told me, she volunteered to read aloud. I asked what her low-risk zone was: one small step she could take toward her goal of speaking up. The low-risk zone should make you nervous but not terrify you. In other words, it involves some degree of manageable risk.

Hadia decided she would speak up three times in every single one of her classes. This from a girl who barely spoke in class at all! No, I said. Try again. Go smaller.

Hadia rolled her eyes at me but thought about it. She said she could e-mail the professor about her anxiety about speaking up, and ask to meet with her to discuss it. What was her high-risk zone? This would be a step she could take toward her goal that felt too scary *right now*. For Hadia, it was moving her seat from the back of the class to the front, where speaking up might be unavoidable, and her professor would be more likely to call on her.

Two great things happen with this exercise: first, as girls nail their low risks and feel braver, the high risk looks a lot less scary. Over time, practice morphs into habit. "The confidence you get from mastery is contagious," write Katty Kay and Claire Shipman in their book, *The Confidence Code*. "It spreads. It doesn't even really matter what you master: for a child, it can be as simple as tying a shoe. What matters is that mastering one thing gives you the confidence to try something else." So when girls realize they want to switch friend groups or try out for a play, they don't think in terms of a single, terrifying moment they have to overcome, but of a ladder of steps they will climb gradually to reach their goal.

This was especially true for seventeen-year-old Joanna. At Courage Boot Camp, her goal was to become more physically flexible as a dancer. Before our workshop, she told me, she would not have thought twice about expecting herself to stretch for an hour every day, five days a week. That's probably why she sat in our classroom and gave me the fisheye for the first few sessions.

Over time, though, she began to see that setting the bar too high made her feel defeated, and she stopped stretching altogether. She decided to stretch during homework or random downtime at school instead. No, it wasn't ideal. "It's a compromise," she said, and it felt weird at first.

A few days into her new plan, Joanna realized she loved living without the burden of an "expectation I'm never going to fulfill." She saw that setting a goal of stretching for an hour every day, then falling short, would have made her feel crummy. "When you do things in smaller steps you feel better about yourself. You know you're accomplishing something . . . [like] the sense of happiness you get when you check things off a list." But, she said, "When you have these high standards, I think there's less focus on the joy of learning and living through the process, as there is in just trying to perform for the best result."

"Confidence," write Kay and Shipman, "is linked to doing." Perhaps the single biggest threat to a girl's confidence isn't failure. It is inaction. Not doing. Not trying. Not practicing. And this is what girls tend to do: to look down and keep their hands in their laps instead of raising them, to demur instead of dive in.

Over and over again, as I work with girls on goal setting, I give my big-dreaming, overachieving students one piece of advice: *lower your standards*. They laugh, every time. But I'm serious, and they soon figure out how effective it can be. I use a little trick: after they pick a small risk to take, I ask them what they think of it. If they roll their eyes, mutter that it's pathetically small, or say it's "kind of dumb," bingo! They have found a suitable goal. And they are ready to act.

WHAT IF I DON'T BELONG HERE?
IMPOSTER PHENOMENON

The first months of a new opportunity—high school, college, or a first job—are often an exhilarating, long-awaited chance to enjoy a hard-won accomplishment. For others, a new anxiety may reveal itself: becoming a little fish in a big sea.

Anu was twenty-seven and in her first year of a Ph.D. in bio-medical science at one of the most selective schools in the country. A native Sri Lankan who attended college in the United States, she excelled in the Boston lab of a prominent stem cell biologist. On this day, we were video chatting at 5:30 A.M. in her time zone; it was the only window she had free to speak with me.

At first, Anu found grad school thrilling. She spoke up in class and lab often. Then, a few months in, she was flooded with anxiety. "In Boston, I worked with really smart people who told me I was an integral component of the lab," she said. A few months into her program, she recalled, "I didn't believe any of it."

Anu was steeped in imposter phenomenon: the belief that you don't belong where you are, that you are a fraud who will be shortly discovered and booted out, or that a mistake was made by admitting you to your position. Impostor phenomenon is firmly in place by adolescence. It is strikingly common in the transition to college and other high-achieving environments, and particularly for those individuals breaking barriers in their field. Some researchers believe women are more vulnerable to it, but at Harvard Business School, about two-thirds of incoming first-year students raise their hands when asked, "How many of you think you are the one mistake the admissions committee made?"

IP is prevalent in STEM (science, technology, engineering, and mathematics) for two reasons: First, because women and people of color (Anu is both) are small minorities in these fields. A sense of belonging diminishes in a world where few people resemble you or share your experience. Second, as Anu taught me, most of the time scientific experiments fail. "It's really hard to distance yourself from that," she explained.

Anu felt herself shrinking. Her motivation waned as she questioned her fitness for science. Asked to propose future projects, she was now hesitant to pursue higher-risk experiments that would almost certainly fail.

Preparing for her qualifying exam, Anu sat in front of her computer wondering why she was in grad school at all. Was it worth spending the next four years trying when she felt so insecure?

She typed out an honest, vulnerable e-mail to her class, about thirty-five people, asking if anyone wanted to get together and talk about the stress of the program. Nearly half responded. As they drank coffee and unloaded their fears, her colleagues were astonished that Anu, who to them appeared fierce and confident, felt insecure. "I never would have thought that you, of all people, would be dealing with this stuff," a man told her. Anu was stunned. That first meeting evolved into a peer-mentoring group that continues today.

Imposter phenomenon thrives on the (wrong) belief that you're the only one struggling to belong. That's why sharing your story with others and finding compatriots can be so powerful. If you are working hard to conceal important parts of yourself from others, and your inner self is at odds with the self you show to others, that can only intensify feelings of fraudulence. "Fake it till you make it" can work well, too, but it's a strategy that only works for some of us.

Being real about IP can be especially healing for first-generation college students, who are frequently burdened by the fear they don't belong in college at all. "It's a thing where you're scared of being found out," said Nicole, a hispanic junior. "You shouldn't be here." For some, IP can become a kind of self-fulfilling prophecy: if you assume you don't belong, you may not take advantage of the resources that could alter your perspective. Nicole avoided asking for help during her first year of college, at times because she didn't know where to go, at others because she felt embarrassed not to know the answer. She never went to professors' office hours because, she recalled, "I didn't feel like I was at the same level as other people." The sense of not feeling at home in college made it harder to find the inner anchor that grounded her conviction that she deserved to be there.

Silvia, a first-gen sophomore, decided to stop pouring her energy into assimilating into the mostly privileged student body at her college. Instead, she began openly celebrating her Mexican heritage, and she began to feel stronger. She learned, she told me, to "embrace who you are and where you come from, so no one can tell you who you are. No one can ever tell you you're not good enough to do this. You find purpose in that."

Jordan heard friends talk about unfamiliar college traditions and kept quiet out of fear. Today she is a senior who tells friends and acquaintances about being first-gen so they can learn about her and support her. "If you tell your story, you own that," she said. "Talking about it gets people to understand." To be sure, this isn't her responsibility; it's the job of Jordan's more privileged peers and educators to learn about and respect the experience of others. But Jordan turned a lonely burden into a value by educating others about first-generation lives.

Girls can also take on their fears more directly. In my workshops on IP, I ask students to complete this sentence on an index card: "I sometimes worry that I'm not as _____ as other people think I am" (overwhelmingly, girls write in the word *smart*). Then I ask students to reflect on these questions:

> *What evidence do you have that this isn't true?* I am taking two AP classes; I get good grades; I won a poetry contest.

> *When are you most likely to feel this way?* When I'm feeling tired or am spending a lot of time alone.

> *Who are one to three people you can talk to about your feelings?* My mom; my therapist; my friend Cathie.

The exercise asks girls to reflect on three powerful weapons against IP. First, it asks them to consider evidence that would challenge their beliefs. Second, it nudges them beneath the surface of how they are feeling to dig into its root cause: when we feel like a fraud, it's often because of a deeper triggering circumstance or emotion. Finally, it asks girls to resist the destructive tendency to isolation by naming sources of support.

You don't have to ask your daughter to write anything down. This can be a conversation, too. It's absolutely crucial, though, to empathize first. Avoid minimizing or denying her feelings by saying things like, "But that's silly, you know that's not true!" She needs you to know you take her imposter phenomenon seriously. Then, have at it.

Anu works on her IP by redefining what success might look like. She tries to appreciate the small victories of her experiments, even when the end result isn't what she expected. "If certain aspects work out, I've learned to sort of rejoice in that," she told me. She reminds herself that she cares a lot more about her own work than do the people around her. She rejects the Imaginary Audience, the adolescent belief that others are watching her with the same intensity she trains on herself. "It's important not to take yourself too seriously and realize your performance isn't being judged every step of the way," she explained.

Finally, she avoids comparing herself to others. Anu reminds herself that there will always be peers who are more skillful in certain areas—"someone who knows more than you, who's more vocal and critical thinking than you." But, she told me, "It's not a personal failure if you don't match up to other people in your same cohort." Instead of expecting herself to be the best in every domain, she tries instead to focus on herself and her own efforts.

Notably, when Anu gives herself credit for her success, she has found she is far less distracted by others. "The biggest self-preservation mechanism," she has concluded, "is just to think that this is a continuous process of improvement." This balance is crucial to her wellness.

In fact, people who manage their imposter phenomenon well (I'm not sure it ever goes away entirely) can occupy the complicated middle ground of their own ambition: they respect their limits without questioning their worthiness, *and* they are comfortable owning a success.

There are many ways you can help your daughter work toward this balance. When she needs to acknowledge a deficit, she can practice the three steps of self-compassion in the face of a setback (in chapter six). Self-compassion will help her be accountable in a healthful, mindful way that doesn't erode her self-worth. To affirm her success, she can practice gratitude, the work of appreciating every day what she *does* have. When she gets a compliment, encourage her to say "thank you" instead of putting herself down and giving the credit to someone else.

We all need a reserve of our own assets in order to offset the insecurity that inevitably dogs us. Girls who traffic in self-deprecating speech—who reflexively say, "I failed that test," "I'm so stupid," "I'll never get in"—and who are quick to deflect anything good, make themselves more vulnerable to IP. Let your daughter know that affirming her accomplishments isn't being conceited or full of herself: it's stockpiling defenses for the moments she falls short.

Finally, just realizing she is not alone makes a difference. Check in with yourself: Do you accept compliments and take pride in your accomplishments? There's zero shame in owning what you may have modeled as you talk with her; in fact, it only ups your credibility with an adolescent when you acknowledge the double standards they so often encounter with adults. To see that everyone has doubts about themselves—even the highest achievers and the peers she most admires, and yes, even her parents—will normalize something that may have been making her feel a little crazy.

WHAT IF THIS IS ALL MY FAULT? MAKING BALANCED ATTRIBUTIONS FOR MISTAKES

Not long ago, I offended a new friend over e-mail. She made her feelings known, and I immediately apologized. A few days later, I tried to smooth things over by inviting her to my house (again, via e-mail). She responded but was noncommittal. A few days after that, I messaged again to say I was anxious that she might still be upset. Could we talk by phone? I got crickets.

I was undone. *What did I do? Why is she so upset?* I called a friend—okay, two—okay, and also saw my therapist—to perseverate. There was middle-of-the-night waking and wondering. *Should I have called her and not e-mailed anything at all?* I didn't know her number, but I could have asked for it. *Was I rude and insensitive?*

The story we tell ourselves about our setbacks has a powerful impact on our confidence. Psychologists call it "attribution." If I blame myself for my friend's radio silence, I make an *internal* attribution: the cause is me. I then spiral into self-criticism, even shame. If I also consider the circumstances—wonder, for a moment, if maybe she's busy this week, or stressed-out at work or home—I make an *external* attribution: the cause may also be something outside of me. I then might feel guilty—perhaps I made a poor choice—but I don't get thumped by taking all the blame.

Your gender will play a key role in the kinds of attributions you make. You can explain this to your daughter with a story like this: Let's say a man and a woman interview for a job, but neither of them gets it. Research shows the man is more likely to decide it's a tough time to apply for a job, or think his application wasn't reviewed closely enough. He makes an *external* attribution. The woman? She thinks it's because she wasn't qualified or capable enough, or because she wore the wrong dress, or said something stupid. She makes an *internal* attribution.

Who's more likely to put themselves out there and try again? The man. Who's more likely to sit around dissecting every moment of the interview: what they wore, whether it was right, what they said or didn't say, how they shook hands? Yep.

Two weeks after I e-mailed this friend, she replied. She'd been "swamped." I put myself through a lot of unnecessary agita to get to that.

Ask your daughter if she's done this before, and let her know if you have, too. If something comes up, and you find yourself wondering about what attribution to make, share the story aloud with your daughter and work through it together. I ask my students to take their "mistake stories" and reframe the way they interpret them. Girls bring up everything from "My friend said she had no plans this weekend, and it's clear from her Snapchat that she went out this weekend" (internal attribution: I'm too boring to hang out with; external attribution: something came up for her last minute and she didn't tell me) to "My boss didn't give me an extra unpaid vacation day" (internal: I'm not a good-enough employee; external: my boss is under pressure and may need all hands on deck). When possible, I encourage girls to ask why something happened instead of assuming they already know the reason.

The meaning we make of our mistakes, or even of the way people treat us, is like standing at a fork in the road and deciding which way to go. The point is, we do get to decide. Our choice directly affects our confidence: when we take all the blame, we rewrite the story of what happened with ourselves as the antagonist. In my own example, had I made a conscious choice to try an external attribution, it would have saved me a lot of self-blame and overthinking. I would have considered the possibility that this woman was the kind of person who reacts to small slights with big feelings, a person for whom an immediate apology isn't quite enough. I would have realized this kind of friend might be safer at arm's length, anyway. It's not that this would have erased my guilt, or my anxiety. But it would have cut it down to a much more reasonable size, and it wouldn't have cost me my self-respect or sleep.

Changing the story we tell ourselves about setbacks takes practice. It requires undoing habits of mind: yanking ourselves away from the deep tread of self-blame we so easily slide into.

There's another kind of attribution women make that can be equally destructive to their confidence. When women and girls succeed, we tend to think it's because we worked hard. We attribute our success to effort. When we fail, we think it's because we're not smart. We attribute our failure to ability.

Here's the problem with this: we get ourselves coming and going. If you attribute a failure to your lack of ability, you're more likely to think, "Well, I guess I'm inherently not that smart or capable." It's that much harder to recover and try again. If you credit your success to hard work, the same might be true: this mentality implies there's not a core talent within you, and that circumstance is everything. That's not true, either.

How do you tend to explain your successes and failures? Look inside before you begin coaching her. As you move through a setback, take note of your patterns. Do you quickly fault your own lack of ability, consider an outside circumstance, or speculate about both? When you succeed, do you credit only your hard work? If you need to shift your script, spend time practicing before you begin working with your daughter. As always, be ready to own your own need to change course as you begin talking with her.

The next time your daughter screws up, steer clear of faulting her ability, and stop her from doing the same. Look instead at the choices she made, and the larger context. Ask her: What could she *do* differently instead of how could she *be* different?

Praising effort can cultivate a growth mindset, but it's still important to remind your daughter of her gifts. The next time she succeeds, train your praise on a combination of her ability and circumstance. What gifts does she have that brought this success to fruition? Was it the internal resources she used? Did she talk to herself in positive ways, refuse to give up, maintain discipline, and handle constructive feedback well? Was it her talent in a particular subject? It's fine to include the circumstances like hard work and aptitude, but don't let her credit them entirely.

Kay and Shipman have written about a study in which five hundred college students were asked to solve a series of spatial puzzles. The women scored measurably worse than the men, not because they weren't capable, but because they skipped over the puzzles where they doubted their ability. Professor Zachary Estes decided to repeat this experiment, and this time told the students to try to solve each puzzle. The women's scores soared. They pulled even with the men.

I am haunted by this study. It always leaves me wondering: How many exam points have girls lost because they didn't guess? How many answers went unshared in a class or meeting because they didn't raise their hands? What have we lost because girls doubted themselves and didn't act?

Risk taking—*doing*—can open up exhilarating change in a girl's life. In college, Jasmine took what she called "safe and predictable" risks, anything "that wouldn't impact me seriously and I could hide it if it didn't work out." After finishing my Leadership for Rebels course, Jasmine took the little money she had and bought a plane ticket to South Africa. She turned down a couple of internships to do it, and didn't even tell her parents until the plans were made. "They thought I was crazy," she remembered.

The leap changed her life. "I was literally on the bottom of the world exploring a beautiful country that I later learned I have ancestry in. I fell in love for the first time. I learned about living a life of my own, stopping to enjoy the beauty and doing something age appropriate for once in my life." What she proved to herself on that trip has sustained her through an insecure job market today.

When I work with girls on taking healthy risks, there are three questions I ask them:

1. What's the worst that can happen?

2. Can you live with that?

3. Do you have the resources to deal with it?

Their answers to the first question range from "I wouldn't get the job" and "I'd get a bad grade on the test" to "I'd get rejected" to "They wouldn't text me back."

When she set out to become more assertive, Lindy West worried constantly about the worst that could happen. Along the path "from quiet to loud," she writes in *Shrill*, "[I remember] the moments when I died inside, and then realized that I wasn't actually dead, and then died inside a little bit less the next time." She advises young women to ask themselves after taking a risk: "Am I dead? Did I die? Is the world different? Has my soul splintered into a thousand shards and scattered to the winds?" Older adults may find West's language of "death" a tad dramatic, but West is speaking Girl 100 percent.

Maybe one of my students, out of hundreds of girls I have worked with, told me that the "worst that can happen" if she took a risk would be truly catastrophic. Most of the time, though, their answers are fairly mundane, followed by a somewhat surprised, "Yeah, actually, I could deal with that."

They are even more surprised when they do.

5

Mental Treadmills: Expecting the Worst and Overthinking

I'm that person who when I go to bed I relive every single thing I said during the day and kick myself for more than half of it.

—HARPER, SIXTEEN

THE NEGATIVE PROPELS ME FORWARD: DEFENSIVE PESSIMISM

Sit around with a group of girls before an exam, and you'll hear a chorus of voices angling to predict the worst:

"I'm going to fail that test."

"This is going to destroy my GPA."

"I'm never going to graduate."

Psychologists call it "defensive pessimism," or planning to fail. It works like this: When you face a challenge, imagine a negative outcome. If things go your way, you're pleasantly surprised. If they don't, you've prepared yourself for the letdown. It's the mental equivalent of packing a go bag. You do it just in case.

"I just tell myself the worst all the time, so even if I don't do all that well, I'll feel better," sixteen-year-old Avesha told me. Morgan, a twenty-two-year-old college graduate, described hitting the "submit" button on job applications. "I say, 'Well, they have this huge applicant pool, and most people are more qualified, and you've only done this and this, so you're not going to get it.'"

"You go into a test and say, 'I'm going to fail. I'm not going to pass this class,'" Phoebe, twenty-one, said. "Or 'I'm going to have to use the pass/fail option.' Or 'I'm not going to graduate. Or find a job. I have to prime myself for failure.'" Anticipating rejection, she added, let her numb herself to any potential pain in advance.

Research by Wellesley College professor Julie Norem has found that about 30 percent of people use defensive pessimism, primarily to redirect anxiety, and that defensive pessimists are often more effective in their work. Harper, sixteen, put it simply: "The negative propels me forward." In other words, it's not necessarily a bad thing.

But when I hear girls sound off about how royally they're going to bomb, I'm skeptical. Defensive pessimism means you're inviting negative energy into your life just so you can cope. Psychologists argue it's a useful way to manage anxiety, but studies show that defensive pessimists often have negative thoughts about themselves. *I'm going to fail* is followed shortly by *I'm probably not that smart* or *What if I fail and don't get into the school I want to attend, and disappoint my parents?*

This kind of negative thinking lowers self-esteem and elevates depressive symptoms. The drop in self-esteem may motivate a girl to work harder, perhaps as a kind of self-inflicted punishment. So she applies herself, succeeds, and hikes up her self-esteem. If she does predict a failure, she gets the small victory of being right about her shortcomings. She can tell herself, "I told you so." When the next challenge arrives, the cycle begins anew. Lather, rinse, repeat.

Is this how we want girls to learn? To be motivated more by fear of failure than by the hope for success? To think about what they want *not* to do than to think big about what they might? Research has shown that people motivated by performance avoidance goals, the desire to avoid doing worse than others, are more likely to struggle to accomplish their goals. They are less intrinsically motivated, too: they worry more about damage to their image than learning (and enjoying it). A 2003 study found that significantly more college women than men worried about performing worse than others.

Girls may be more likely to engage in defensive pessimism for several reasons. Girls take failures especially hard, interpreting them as a sign that they lack ability. They report substantially more anxiety than boys. And girls discount their talents when they succeed more than boys, which means success doesn't make them more confident (as it does for boys). If the threat of failure looms larger for girls, it may force them to adopt a stance of self-protection, rather than an aggressive, *I'm going to crush this* stance.

Let's not forget, too, that Girl World loves a defensive pessimist. To expect the worst is to practice socially approved modesty. *I blew that test* is also girl code for *I'm not that smart, or successful, or skillful.* Humility in girls has long been rewarded by peers and adults. Who better to illustrate this than comedian Amy Schumer, whose viral sketch "Compliments" showed young women demeaning themselves in response to kind words. "I tried to look like Kate Hudson," says one woman, shrugging, with newly dyed hair, "but ended up looking like a golden retriever's dingleberry." When told how pretty she looks, Amy responds, "I'm a fucking cow. . . . I sleep standing up in a field."

The I'm-ugly-no-I'm-the-ugliest dialogue is a close cousin of defensive pessimism. A girl worries aloud about her career dreams no longer coming true, and her friend reassures her. *Are you kidding, I'm sure you killed it, plus I did way worse than you anyway.* Both girls get a shot of peer approval and a tension release. They're let out of their own heads to externalize their fear. And they're instantly more likable to each other, having passed the Girl World modesty test.

"It's this twisted sense of community," seventeen-year-old Joanna told me. "It's reassuring to know you're not alone. You've done everything together and prepared together and stuck through it all, so afterward it's only natural to be a community in your failure."

Dig a little deeper, though, and you find something less sisterly unfolding beneath the surface. As girls share their fears, competition begins to bud. "You compare yourself with other people," Joanna said.

> Even when you listen to someone say "I screwed this up," you're reassuring them, but on the inside you might be saying, "Oh, she screwed up this but I didn't." Therefore it puts me on a little bit of a higher level. There's a little bit of . . . putting others down to raise yourself up.

Girls quietly turn from allies into competitors. Dwelling on their shortcomings together, girls feel inadequate and less-than. It's a recipe for toxic comparisons. To be truly reassured, they may need to know another person has fallen short. As Gore Vidal once said, "It's not enough to succeed. Others must fail."

More troubling, though, is how this behavior becomes a habit, a crutch girls lean on every time they face a challenge with an unknown, potentially disappointing outcome. How can girls remain fully open to new possibilities if they're planning on them not actually happening? Defensive pessimism may make girls feel better, sure, but it inevitably puts a ceiling on curiosity and growth. It's not a thoughtful consideration of their chances at success. It just coats every big question with "I'll probably fail, anyway." It also may affect confidence. As we've seen, when women underestimate their ability, they are less likely to take risks and explore new opportunities.

There is a joy shortage when it comes to growth and learning for girls, especially the highest performers. Too many seem to think suffering equals success. If it doesn't hurt you, scare you, give you nightmares about failure, or stress you to your breaking point, you must not have worked hard enough. Nor do you deserve to succeed.

Defensive pessimism is part of this subculture of suffering. It is a tool to minimize anxiety and maximize humility, but it comes at the expense of girls' courage. After all, girls won't get sturdy in the face of risk by boarding up the windows of their minds and souls, praying for protection from a failure that has not even occurred. No, they'll get stronger when they can think realistically about what failure might mean and look like, instead of turning to cartoonish images of catastrophe in their minds.

Helping girls visualize not just a setback but also their response to it can be a confidence-boosting alternative to defensive pessimism. For decades, sports psychologists have trained elite athletes to do just this, by visualizing an event before they compete. Athletic "imaging" is a training tool that lets competitors strategize responses to unpredictable situations before they occur. "You try to keep it fresh in your head, so when you do get there, you are not just starting at square one," an Olympic bobsledder told the *New York Times*. "It's amazing how much you can do in your mind." The results are so powerful that almost every athlete images before a competition.

At New York University, Gabriele Oettingen's work on "mental contrasting" asks people to imagine both the barriers to a goal and what it would be like to overcome them. Across age groups, ethnicities, and professions, people who can see both sides of the potential outcome are much more likely to succeed than those who imagine *only* failing or *only* succeeding. The exercise only lets you imagine a setback if you're willing to see it through to a productive response. It's dramatically different from exclusively imagining failure. Try it with your daughter sometime.

If your daughter is worried about a potential rejection, whether from a job or school, talk through together what it would be like to hear the "no." How does she imagine she will feel? What might she think to herself? How could she take care of herself in the immediate aftermath? What might she do next to move herself forward?

Now, imagine together what getting a "yes" would feel like. What will she feel and think? Why does this win matter to her? How would she celebrate? Owning both scenarios will help remind her of why she cares about this (or, in some cases, maybe doesn't) in the first place. It helps her remember she has choices about how to handle what comes her way, and affirms that you stand with her no matter what.

When I began teaching girls about defensive pessimism, expecting the worst had been my secret strategy. I'd never given it much thought. Then I started hearing myself in my students' words. Listening to these bright, hardworking girls, who had their futures before them, tell me how much they were going to fail galvanized me—by which I mean it pissed me off.

I started confronting my own bad habits. I had been submitting op-eds to the *New York Times* every couple of months or so. Each time I pressed the "send" button, I'd whisper to myself, "They'll reject it." And I did get rejected: once, twice, a third time. A fourth time. It was disappointing, of course. Then something weird happened. An image popped into my head. It was me, holding the *New York Times*, and seeing my byline on the printed page.

A fantasy of success was utterly foreign to me. But I had gotten rejected so many times that the experience of hearing "no" was no longer unfamiliar. Not only did I know it well, but I also knew it wasn't going to kill me.

Without realizing it, I had pulled the curtain back on the Great and Powerful Oz (which was, for the record, failure and not the *New York Times*), only to find that failure was a scrawny little dude working the controls. Developing a muscle for failure, for "no," for rejection, for the letdown: that was key to letting go of my defensive pessimism. Once my fear of failing subsided, I had nothing to protect myself from. I could focus more on the joys of the risk I was taking than on building cognitive barriers to protect myself from it.

Let me repeat that: I could actually enjoy what I was doing. I could have fun taking a chance, and learning from the challenge.

If you are a defensive pessimist, it's likely that you've transmitted some of that to your daughter. We script our children and students in how they approach risk. As one undergraduate told researchers, "My parents have always said, 'Don't set your goals too high because you'll only get disappointed.' . . . They're always careful not to raise my hopes so I don't get disappointed." Spend some time reflecting on your own habits before you talk to your daughter about hers. Norem has published a questionnaire designed to measure defensive pessimism. Questions include:

- I often start out expecting the worst, even though I will probably do OK.

- I spend lots of time imagining what could go wrong.

- I'm careful not to become overconfident in these situations.

- In these situations, sometimes I worry more about looking like a fool than doing really well.

- Considering what can go wrong helps me to prepare.

Most of us don't tell our kids to expect the worst in order to knock them down. We think we're protecting our girls when we advise them not to get too excited about a goal. But it's safe to say society's working hard on that front already, and what girls need from parents is help visualizing resilience and success, too.

OVERTHINKING

The other day a very pregnant friend of mine came over to hang out after we put our kids to bed. Danielle heaved her swollen feet onto an ottoman, plunked her spoon into a dish of sorbet I'd brought her, and worried aloud about how this third child would affect her other two. She looked close to tears.

"Oh, they'll be fine," I told her cheerfully. "Remember, right after your second was born, you were so scared about it? But it all turned out okay, and this will, too."

As I watched Danielle's car back out of the driveway, a small bud of anxiety sprouted inside of me. *Had I been too callous? Should I have empathized more? Was she mad but not saying anything? Maybe she didn't say anything because she just expects that kind of brush-off from me? Does everyone see me this way?*

I texted her and apologized, then waited. No reply. The anxiety began to take root as I replayed the conversation: once, as I put on my pajamas, a second time as I brushed my teeth. I checked my phone and got into bed. Nothing. *I'm sure she hugged me genuinely when she left . . . right?*

This kind of overthinking has a name: rumination. Ruminating, or compulsively worrying about the causes and consequences of a problem, interferes with people's ability and motivation to solve problems. First identified by the late Yale professor Susan Nolen-Hoeksema, rumination is disproportionately seen in women and adolescent girls as young as twelve. When over six hundred young teens were asked to tell researchers how often they worried about things like physical appearance, friendships, safety, and family problems, girls scored as more anxious than boys on every measure except succeeding at sports.

Ruminating peaks in young adulthood, but I have yet to meet an adolescent girl who knows what it is. Instead most girls think they just can't stop thinking at best, and feel slightly crazy at worst. Ruminating is serious, and your daughter needs to know what it is and be able to name it. It is associated with depression, anxiety, binge eating, and binge drinking. By adulthood, ruminators are four times more likely to develop major depression than nonruminators. They are also intensely self-critical.

"I'm definitely my own worst critic. I nitpick absolutely everything I do," Harper told me. "I'm that person who when I go to bed I relive every single thing I said during the day and kick myself for more than half of it." Nighttime is ripe for ruminating. So is hanging out in your dorm or bedroom alone (Netflix does not count as companionship). Katie, a nineteen-year-old freshman at a public university, performed her internal monologue for me. "Why didn't I work harder? Why didn't I do this instead of that? If I went out to a party one night and I should have studied for a test, I'm like, that was so stupid of you, you should know better." Kayla, nineteen, said it was hardest when she made a mistake. "You return to the things you did wrong, not the things you did right. You're upset with yourself, you're disappointed with yourself, and they just keep coming back." Ruminating is self-criticism disguised as self-reflection.

Social media has introduced a new, virtual kind of ruminating. Maya, eighteen, spent hours looking at texts from her ex-boyfriend. "Do you know there are actual playlists for looking through pictures of your ex?" she asked me (I did not). Texts, chats, e-mails, and even photos bring life to much of what we think and say; online interactions leave a record we can scrutinize as much as the conversations we replay in our minds. "I went back and read all the moments when he was apparently still in love with me," Maya told me.

I was like, "What changed? How are you still not in love with me?" I looked at the good night texts he sent me, what he sent me when I was upset, how many times he said "nah" or "okay," as opposed to full sentences.

After her self-described "really scary virtual journey," Maya deleted all the texts.

Girls tend to think ruminating means you care a lot about a problem, and that you're closer to solving it, too. But Nolen-Hoeksema found overthinking amplifies the stresses we already experience. Describing it as a "yeast effect," she argues that the more you overthink, the bigger the problems begin to seem. Ruminating causes people to ignore positive memories of the past, skewing their perspective toward anything negative. Overthinking "doesn't give you clarity and insight into your past or solutions to your current problems," she writes. "Instead, it pollutes your thinking with negativity to the point where you are defeated before you begin."

There's a fine, often invisible line between perseverating about a problem and blaming yourself for it. Claire, twenty-two, put it this way: "If I'm not hard on myself, who will be? But the more I do that, the less I actually get things done. Because I'm so in my head." When Stanford University students were asked to solve a series of fictional personal problems, the students who were ruminators were both less motivated and less skillful problem solvers. They were slower decision makers, less confident about their choices, and often failed to enact solutions.

Nolen-Hoeksema believes the gender difference in rumination

is largely cultural. Parents of girls are more likely to pay attention to and support the expression of sadness and anxiety in girls, while discouraging it in boys. Parents of girls favor sharing their own negative feelings with daughters more than sons, laying a foundation for negative thinking. By adulthood, studies show that people who think feelings like sadness and anxiety are uncontrollable are likely to ruminate, and that women are significantly more likely to believe this.

Girls are also more likely to define themselves in terms of their relationships, think about them more than boys, and put greater weight on them, making their self-esteem vulnerable to how stable or troubled their relationships are. This "excessive relational focus" makes girls chronically anxious about small changes in connections with others, and overly concerned with why people act the way they do.

Rumination is also a culturally approved way for girls to manage sadness. If you dwell quietly on your negative feelings, you can still maintain your persona as a likable caregiver for others. And if you struggle to assert yourself, which many women do, ruminating becomes a tool to handle the thoughts that can't find an outlet. Linguist Deborah Tannen found that women engaged in "trouble talk" as a form of connection: they would respond to a friend's problem by sharing their own challenge, a kind of "tit-for-tat overthinking," as Nolen-Hoeksema calls it.

Ruminating can have its benefits. "Thinking about things long and hard is what women bring to the equation in the workplace," Claire Shipman, coauthor of *The Confidence Code*, told me. "We're not jumping off the cliff with all the guys. You want that brain on the team." But ruminating isn't a way to think things through. It is when the thoughtful part of your brain turns on itself.

Ruminators tend to think they face "chronic, uncontrollable stressors" and exhibit personality characteristics like perfectionism and neuroticism. These last characteristics fit the bill for the many aspirational young women I meet.

Phoebe was a senior who was hosting my visit to her university. While home on a break from school, she scheduled calls with me from her West Coast bedroom at 6:00 A.M. her time. As we got to know each other, she described what her home life was like downstairs. A self-described "show pony" born to older parents who emigrated from China, she said, "Chinese culture is very hierarchical. I am always performing. . . . I was always expected to be pretty and cute and nice, and play a nice concerto on the piano, and talk about all the things I am involved with, and be a size zero by Christmas." At school, she organized union workers, ran the women's leadership mentoring program, and worked with the administration to increase economic diversity on campus. Then, she said, "I go hard on weekends," meaning she partied, too.

When I arrived on campus, Phoebe met me in a café nearby, wearing a colorful wrap dress and boots. She had the poise of a woman twice her age. But when we sat down to talk, another voice emerged. It was the one in her head.

Phoebe described the late-night ritual she performed in her modest single room in her dorm. "I'm answering e-mails for the twenty minutes before I fall asleep and I'll kind of replay my day," she said. If something didn't go well, she asks herself what she could have done better. If, say, she'd spoken honestly to a friend, she'll fret that she came on too strong. Lying in bed, in the light of her laptop, she worried and wondered. "I'll ask myself a lot of unfair questions that I really don't have the answer to," she said slowly, as if understanding this for the first time as she said it.

Did she ask a stupid question in class today? Should she have done more research before she spoke? What did other people think of what she said? "Uncertainty really kills me," Phoebe told me. "I always feel like the ball needs to be in my court." One appeal of overthinking is that it offers girls a sense of control over situations where they have little. If you can't change something that already happened, rumination is the perfect place to take your anxious, whirring mind. It provides a mental treadmill that never moves toward a solution but is exhausting enough to give you a sense of having tried.

Phoebe took furious notes while I taught the lunchtime workshop her school had organized. Just learning the word *rumination* was liberating for her. She suddenly understood that her repetitive thinking wasn't some random behavior only she was struggling with. It had a name, a cause, and a solution.

Now, late at night, when her mental gears start to grind, Phoebe tries some of these strategies:

- Pictures a big red stop sign, a physical image that tells her to stop what she's doing in her tracks, cold turkey, and move on to something else.

- Schedules her ruminating. She says, "I'm letting myself obsess about this until eleven thirty. Then I have to stop and commit to doing something else."

- Focuses on her breathing to slow her thoughts down, and tries to count up to ten and back down to one.

- Asks herself questions that push her to stick with the evidence of what she knows to be true, instead of speculating about what she doesn't know but might ruminate about. If she's worried about a friend being mad at her, she'll ask, "Does this friend have a habit of not telling me how she really feels?" or "Did she seem genuinely cold or withdrawn when she left?" Other questions Phoebe has asked herself include, "Does this incident or action really affect my graduation status?" and "Will the people who love me stop doing so if I make this choice?"

- Asks herself how a friend she admires might think about the situation: "How would my best friend tell me to evaluate this?"

These tools let Phoebe shift away from wallowing in her flaws and toward concrete next steps she can work on in the morning.

Anu kept a notebook where she wrote down the lessons learned from the mistakes she obsessed about. "When I go back and read it," she told me, "I'm more likely to think about the things that I want to be doing next."

After taking one of my workshops, Casey, twenty, wrote down obsessive thoughts and deposited them into a "thought box" she made by her dorm room bed. The box had wooden letters spelling her name, a velvet leopard-print lining, and a poem about courage pasted inside. "The idea is that when I am overthinking something over which I have no control, I can write it down on a piece of paper, stick it in the box, and let it go (turn it over, surrender)," she wrote to me in an e-mail. "The physical act of doing this somehow makes the letting go more concrete and real."

It didn't always work. Sometimes she wrote down the same thought for several days in a row and stuck it in the box. "It's not a magic pill," she told me. "But the box makes me feel like I can free myself of responsibility for the things I can't control. I am not the most powerful force in the universe. There is something operating out there that has far more power than I do. Things tend to go far more smoothly in my life when I stop trying to control everything, put the stupid shit in the box, and let go of the things that drag me down." Casey's box shifts her from being consumed by her thoughts to putting them outside of herself. It allows her to understand that her ruminating doesn't define her.

CO-RUMINATING

Professor Amanda Rose at the University of Missouri was studying adolescents on campus and she was puzzled. On the one hand, she knew that girls' intense, connected friendships nourished them in singular ways. "The literature really highlights how sensitive girls are in friendship, and how supportive they are," she told me. One of the biggest social gender differences is disclosure: girls open up to each other a lot more than boys. These factors, she explained, should protect girls from some of their emotional problems.

But they didn't. Studies consistently find that girls are at greater risk than boys for emotional problems, and develop anxiety and depression at twice the rate.

Rose set out to make sense of the paradox. After years of observational studies, she began noticing how much time girls spent talking one-on-one about their problems (boys, by contrast, spent more time in groups). Confiding problems to each other was compelling for girls. They seemed to do it to feel better, and grow closer to each other. But maybe, Rose began thinking, it was making them feel worse.

"That's how I got interested in the idea that there may be things girls do with friends that might undermine some of their emotional well-being," she told me. In 2002, Rose published her first paper on "co-rumination," which she described as extensive talking about problems among friends, worrying about the causes of problems, focusing on negative feelings, and encouraging each other to keep doing it.

"Does he like me?" "Is she mad at me?" "What will I do if I don't get that job?" These are questions girls will spend hours delving into. They are the ones I remember relishing with friends throughout high school and college (and, if I'm honest, last week).

In her study of adolescent girls and boys, Rose found that girls were the group most likely to co-ruminate with friends. They were also the only group whose behavior predicted depressive symptoms, and for whom co-ruminating increased with age.

Rose realized that it was indeed possible that girls could have close, loving friendships, yet also be undermined emotionally by those very connections. In a study of college students by Christine Calmes and John Roberts, women were more likely than men to co-ruminate with friends (perhaps because men are socialized to avoid showing weakness to one another). This behavior predicated "elevated depressive symptomatology" *and* greater friendship satisfaction, but only for women.

I wondered if this happened because girls believe "trouble talk" is the foundation of a close friendship. Reading Rose's work, I was reminded of countless conversations I've had with girls about what they value in a close friend. Most said they cherished having someone to confide in. And this is what Rose saw, too: all the whispering and secret telling on the playground turned into conversations in dorm rooms and student centers. They yielded more intimacy and higher friendship quality, but at a cost: the conversations were also depressing.

Co-ruminating can happen in any relationship, but there are two where it appears to be most harmful for adolescents: with friends and parents. In the Calmes and Roberts study, researchers speculated that these conversations may be more "passive, repetitive and negative" compared to worries shared with others. In 2013, Rose published findings that suggested adolescents who co-ruminated with their mothers were also more likely to do it with friends, and to develop "internalizing symptoms" like depression and anxiety. In her study's conclusion, Rose advised that "mothers who co-ruminate with their adolescent children should be aware that they may be modeling a communication style that, if replicated with friends, could have negative emotional consequences."

What's the best way to handle your daughter when she comes to you with a problem? The answer is not to stop answering her texts or avoid talking about her problems. You can, however, think about whether you are co-ruminating with your daughter, about her problems or your own. Consider some of these questions from Rose:

- Do you spend most of your quality time together talking about her problems, and for a long time? Does this tend to happen every time you see each other or talk?

- Do you spend a lot of time talking about how bad she feels as a result of her problems?

- Do you spend a lot of time trying to figure out parts of her problem that you can't understand, the reasons why the problem has occurred, and every bad thing that might happen because of the problem?

- Do you encourage her to keep talking about her problems even when she isn't bringing them up?

- Do you do this instead of doing other activities together?

Whether we do it on our own or with others, ruminating runs on a circular track: we go around and around as we wonder, speculate, and emote. What we don't do is problem solve, make a decision, or simply find some joy together. Shifting away from co-ruminating with your daughter will mean letting go of what she doesn't (or can't) know the answer to, and embracing what is in her control to change. It will also demand empathizing with her feelings rather than dwelling on them.

TALKING WITHOUT RUMINATING

One sign that your daughter might prefer co-ruminating is that she blows you off when you urge her to act instead of talk. This is where you might hear, *It's hopeless. There's nothing I can do. I can't believe she left her dirty laundry on my bed!* Or: *I knew I should have gone to another school.*

There are few parenting maxims more resonant than the one that says we're only as happy as our least happy child. To help your daughter move away from ruminating, you will need to summon reserves of strength and energy so you can stay present, warm, and empathic when your heart may be breaking for your child.

Here's what you might say in response: "I know you're upset. I get it, and I would be, too. But at some point, we have to move forward, try to address what's happening, and make this better for you. The best way for us to move forward is to figure out your next steps. Let's do that together." Empathy is crucial in helping her shift away from ruminating. When she believes you really understand what she's feeling, and that you're making the effort to attune to her experience, she will be much more likely to listen to you.

ORID (Objective, Reflective, Interpretive, Decisional) is a problem-solving method that was developed to help individuals and groups break free of indecision and problem solve with clarity. I have found it a useful tool in redirecting conversations that are becoming too ruminative.

Say your daughter is talking with you about a roommate she doesn't like. The roommate is inconsiderate and unfriendly and, on top of that, doesn't seem to realize she's a royal slob. Your daughter sounds despondent. It's only the second week of school. How will she survive this for an entire academic year?

Your first line of questions should be *objective*: ask your daughter what she actually knows to be true. What events have occurred? What has the roommate said and done? What did she say or do in reply? Stick with the who, what, where, when, and how. No whys. Don't let your daughter start editorializing (*Can you believe how rude she is? How am I going to study when she's so insanely loud?!*). Remain on the solid ground of evidence, and what she knows to be true right now.

Your next set of questions are *reflective*: How does your daughter feel about this? Is she angry? Betrayed? Disappointed? Let her vent a bit about how the roommate assignment process is rigged, and whether pitching a tent on the quad is legal.

Now, move to *interpretive* questions: What does this mean for her? What is the impact of having an inconsiderate, unfriendly roommate? How will that affect her emotionally, socially, and academically?

Finally, move to *decisional* questions: What is she going to do about this, and how can you help her? What are the campus resources available to her, and what is the best next step here? To confront her roommate, talk to a residence life staff person, or try to switch rooms? What's the residence life policy and protocol? Identify one next step that is concrete and doable in a day.

Ruminating is, at its core, a negative thought pattern. It's not genetic, nor is it unavoidable. It can help to imagine ruminating (and co-ruminating) as a track your mind is chugging along. We have to shift onto a more positive cognitive track to start generating better thoughts.

People who ruminate are often beating themselves up about something. That's why learning to stop ruminating is not as simple as "thinking other thoughts." There is a crucial intermediary step: you have to forgive yourself, too. Only then can you get off the track and say, "Enough. It is not so bad. I am not so bad." That's where we're headed next.

6

Turning Self-Criticism
into Self-Compassion

You're saying that I should be *nice* to myself. Doesn't that mean I'd just sit in my room in my pajamas all day and watch Netflix?

—JENNIE, TWENTY

At a workshop for new college grads in Washington, DC, I scanned a dead quiet room for a bottle of wine that might warm the place up. No dice. The women sat quietly in folding chairs, balancing plates of crudités and smartphones in their laps, looking squarely at the podium.

"Okay," I began. "Imagine a toddler just learning to walk." They stared at me quizzically. These were twentysomethings. They did not hang out with toddlers.

I pressed on.

"You know how they always fall on their faces when they're first starting out?" There had to be some babysitters in this room. Finally, a few nods.

"So when she falls down, what do you say to her?" I asked.

"It's okay!" one volunteered.

"Let me help you up," another woman suggested.

"Do you tell her what an idiot she is?" I asked them. Their eyes widened. Then they laughed.

"Of course you don't," I went on. "Because being mean to the baby would make her cry and not want to try anymore."

And yet, the women slowly realize, they often talk to themselves in the same way.

Many of us buy into a compelling myth that self-criticism is the most efficient path to discipline. Is your alarm going off, but you don't want to get up? Tell yourself how lazy you're being, and haul your butt out of bed. Really want that third slice of pizza? You can't, fatso. Look away and have a carrot. How about that text begging you to come watch a movie at a friend's place? You'll be a loser if you don't get into the right grad school. Park it in the library for another two hours.

Gender differences in self-criticism intensify in adolescence. Girls tend to be more self-conscious, harder on themselves, and more prone to negative self-talk than boys. They overthink their setbacks and spend too much time wondering what they could have done differently. Many interpret "no pain, no gain" as something to actively inflict on themselves, feeling certain that beating themselves up will motivate them to change, and that without self-criticism, they will be immobilized and unable to perform.

This was never made more clear to me than at a workshop I gave at an Ivy League university. I was challenging a group of women leaders to be less self-critical. The students listened politely. Then one raised her hand, head cocked, and looked at me as if I'd asked them to attend class in mermaid suits. "So you're saying," she said slowly, "that I should be *nice* to myself." It wasn't a question.

"Yes," I said.

"But doesn't that mean I'd just sit in my room in my pajamas all day and watch Netflix?"

Her classmates laughed, and I couldn't blame them. Self-criticism was their secret Red Bull, and they were unapologetic. It had served them this long, and they weren't about to let it go.

It's time to help your daughter retire the myth that self-criticism will make her work harder and better. Research consistently finds that self-criticism saps her motivation. It undermines self-efficacy, her belief that she can succeed at any given task, which is a key component of confidence. In college, a self-critical student is less likely to make progress toward her goals and will report more procrastination. Self-criticism also makes her unhappy: it is linked in research to the higher prevalence of depression among adolescent girls. Among adolescents and adults, self-criticism is associated with low confidence in social and athletic skills, eating disorders, dissatisfaction in life, and difficulty maintaining relationships.

Negative self-talk also puts a ceiling on healthy risk taking. After all, if we don't think that much of ourselves, we're not going to put ourselves out there. That's why a self-critical person will generally shun the kind of leaps that lead to transformative growth. Being hard on yourself "can motivate you to be a meticulous worker-bee," writes Tara Mohr in her book *Playing Big: Find Your Voice, Your Mission, Your Message*, "but it can't motivate you to be a game changer." It makes sure we hew to a narrow, safe path.

It's unlikely that self-criticism actually makes girls work hard. More likely it is fear that fuels their effort: fear of failing, of being exposed as incompetent, of letting others down. Fear doesn't motivate girls toward a goal they cherish so much as make them run from a host of things that scare them.

Every day I teach girls that they don't have to beat themselves up as a tool to manage anxiety, burnout, or remorse. There are other ways to handle challenges, and this chapter will teach them to you. First, I'll translate your daughter's relationship to self-criticism. Then I'll introduce you to two simple, powerful practices designed to help her manage it.

WHY GIRLS ARE SELF-CRITICAL

Three main risk factors make girls more vulnerable to self-criticism. Puberty is the first. As their bodies change, girls become more self-conscious. They worry about how their physical appearance measures up against media, parental, and peer pressure to pursue the thin ideal. During this period, they also metabolize the culture's expectation to be the "good girl" and be liked above all, please others at the expense of themselves, and not make others angry or sad. This makes them more vulnerable to depression and anxiety, as well as overthinking; all these factors heighten a girl's tendency to turn on herself.

Second, girls and women report feeling shame more, and more intensely, than men. Shame is basically self-criticism on steroids. Research professor Brené Brown defines shame as the "intensely painful feeling or experience of believing that we are flawed and therefore unworthy of love and belonging." What this looks like in practice is your daughter making a mistake, then deciding she's a horrible or incapable person because of it. It's her speeding right past the more moderate feeling of guilt—the sense that she's done a bad *thing*, and an emotion much easier to bounce back from—and heading right for the jugular of blaming her *self*. Call it overachieving in the remorse department.

Once consumed by shame, she is more likely to isolate herself from others, especially the people who might help her move forward. It is nearly impossible to feel genuinely driven or inspired to change when she is in the grip of shame.

Finally, there is perfectionism, the relentless striving for often unattainable standards of performance while letting failure or success define her self-worth. Perfectionism is practically oxygenated by self-criticism. If no amount of success will suffice, she will always think she hasn't done enough. If no amount of effort will ever satisfy her, she will feel eternally lazy. And on and on.

It's worth noting that self-criticism has some benefits, at least in girls' minds. Blaming yourself gives you a hearty, if delusional, sense of control over your life. If your problem is you, the assumption is that you had control over it all to begin with. You're just not trying hard enough. For the ambitious woman who sees each day as a series of accomplishments to check off the list, this is hypnotic stuff. It's also a self-reinforcing cycle.

And it is of course totally false. Despite what girls may have been told about running the world, they can't control everything. Thinking they can traps them in an endless cycle of false hope, fleeting triumph, and self-judgment. That mentality is the opposite of girl power. It's girl poison.

Some girls are drawn to self-criticism because it lets them judge themselves before someone else can do it first. In a culture where they are penalized for taking up too much space, be it with their voices, ideas, or bodies, self-criticism may be an act of *self-defense*. Julia, a twenty-one-year-old junior, says she often jokes about how "totally fat" she is while eating ice cream. "I just say it before someone else gets the chance to think it and judge me," she explained. "If I say it, it's me who said it and not someone else."

All this unfolds under the all-seeing eye of the College Application Industrial Complex. Every day, the Complex pulses a message to its students, including those who have gone on to college still under its spell: you are never, ever enough as you are. In this "amazing race"—that is, the race to be as amazing as you can possibly be, according to standards defined by someone else—girls chase a way of being that is impossible to attain. They live in a persistent state of self-criticism, beating themselves up for failing to achieve some mythical state of achievement. No matter what they do, they feel like they've fallen short.

THE PROMISE OF SELF-COMPASSION

"There's almost no one whom we treat as badly as ourselves," Dr. Kristin Neff told me. The University of Texas at Austin professor would know. In her final year of graduate school, she slogged through a messy divorce, exhausting dissertation, and intimidating job applications. In despair, awash in self-loathing, she enrolled in a weekly Buddhism class.

There Neff learned about *metta*, the practice of loving-kindness, or showing selfless love and compassion toward others. One day the teacher made a simple point: if you can't be compassionate toward yourself, you'll never be able to share it with others. Neff knew the teacher was talking about her. She began exploring the practice of self-compassion in her own life.

At the time, Neff had been studying self-esteem. Yet she was skeptical about its value: her colleagues were discovering that high self-esteem was linked to narcissism, which includes selfishness, grandiosity, and a hunger for approval. It made a person feel good, yes, but it also seemed to depend on the need to feel better than others. In fact, many individuals with high self-esteem needed to feel better than or superior to others, just to feel good about themselves.

How could you raise yourself up without needing to put someone else down? It was a problem when we needed to feel "special and above average to feel worthy," she wrote, and when "anything less seemed like a failure." Neff predicted self-compassion could offer something better: protection from toxic self-criticism without needing to be perfect or superior to others.

Over the last decade, Neff and her colleagues have seen stunning results. Self-compassion has been linked to happiness, optimism, motivation, and emotional intelligence. A meta-analysis of over twenty studies found that the practice significantly reduced anxiety, depression, rumination, and stress. In 2011, Neff published *Self-Compassion: The Proven Power of Being Kind to Yourself.*

I have spent my career converting research that few laypeople read into original curricula that reaches thousands of girls. Finding self-compassion was like digging for oil and stumbling on a geyser. I have watched it instantly transform the way girls relate to themselves. The practice has changed my students' lives, and my own.

If I had to boil the gift of self-compassion down to a single sentence, I'd say it has helped me and my students understand that, no matter what happens on the other side of a risk we take or setback we experience, we know that we are enough. We know we are still worthy, even if we stumble. We realize we matter more than our successes or failures: we have something inside of us that transcends a GPA or test score, number of pounds lost or miles run. We don't have to trade our self-worth as ransom for our setbacks.

In 2007, a study by Mark Leary and colleagues found that self-compassionate people had "less extreme reactions, less negative emotions, more accepting thoughts, and a greater tendency to put their problems in perspective." The practice was a powerful tool to moderate the impact of negative events. The message of self-compassion, Brown wrote, is "you are imperfect, you are wired for struggle, but you are worthy of love and belonging."

Neff found that adult women are less self-compassionate than men overall, though the differences are small. In the last few years, researchers have begun studying this quality in adolescents. In a 2015 study of middle school and high school students, Karen Bluth showed that high school girls had significantly lower self-compassion than any other group of youth surveyed. In 2017, Bluth expanded her study, this time finding that while boys' self-compassion remained constant across all ages, older girls saw a decline between middle school and high school. Nearly 40 percent of her 765 subjects were not white.

An unpublished analysis of seventeen studies of adolescents, led by Imogen Marsh, found that self-compassion had a significant impact on psychological distress. Notably, though, self-compassion became somewhat less effective as teens of both sexes got older, a finding echoed by Bluth: by late adolescence, she writes, highly anxious girls "may have a harder time believing in the 'self-compassion message' that they are deserving of kindness" and that they are not alone.

Still, there are few things more promising in the research on girls than self-compassion. Bluth has written a curriculum called "Making Friends with Yourself." High school students who completed the program showed higher levels of resilience, life satisfaction, and social connectedness than the control group. After I suspected self-compassion might help girls take more healthy risks, I asked Bluth to include this question in her research. Not only did her students show more curiosity and exploration when they learned self-compassion, but they also reported *higher* levels of these traits as time passed beyond the program. I found similar results in a survey of over three hundred high school girls with Vassar College's Michele Tugade and Abbi Hiller: the more self-compassion the girls had, the more inclined they were to take healthy risks.

For the record, I never thought I'd write about, much less teach and practice, something called self-compassion. It is precisely the kind of New Age thing my dad likes to call "piffle." To my immigrant grandmother, who worked in a grocery store meat freezer to support her two kids as a single mom, self-compassion would have seemed useless. If she were alive today, she'd no doubt use a different word. Even five years ago, I might have rolled my eyes. I would have said self-compassion was a bunch of excuse making, a slick way to rationalize mistakes instead of owning them.

Research proves otherwise. Forgiving yourself for your mistakes and maintaining high standards of excellence can actually coexist. Neff and her colleagues have found that self-compassionate people are just as likely to have high personal standards as people without it; they are just less likely to beat themselves up when they fall short. They are more likely to be oriented to personal growth than their self-critical peers. They procrastinate less, formulate specific plans to reach their goals, and establish more balance in their lives.

Even more important, self-compassion tends to be found in people who have mastery goals, or an intrinsic drive to learn (the best kind of drive, and the one most strongly associated with well-being and lasting success). This makes sense: If you don't beat yourself up when you fail, failure becomes a lot less scary. It's easier to take intellectual risks, and go where your curiosity takes you. Self-compassion invigorates the desire to make important changes in your life. The drive to learn rather than perform makes self-compassionate people more motivated, more resilient in the face of failure, and more comfortable taking healthy chances.

When self-compassionate people fail, they are less likely to revert to feelings of shame and worthlessness. Their self-efficacy beliefs don't take a hit. "Far from being a form of self-indulgence," Neff writes, "self-compassion and real achievement go hand in hand."

TEACHING SELF-COMPASSION TO GIRLS

Self-compassion involves three steps:

1. Mindfulness, or observing what you're thinking and feeling without judgment.

2. Self-kindness, or saying something kind to yourself.

3. Common humanity, or thinking about others who share your experience.

Self-compassion is an uncanny fit with the woes of the adolescent psyche.

Mindfulness requires paying attention to the breath and present moment; this helps limit the rumination that plagues young adults. Self-kindness asks girls to disengage from the self-criticism they rely so heavily on as a motivator. Finally, common humanity, write Bluth and her colleagues, challenges the "personal fable": a teen's developmental belief that her struggles are unique and novel compared to others.

Help your daughter develop self-compassion by modeling the practice with a story from your own life. One caveat here: Avoid a big display of feeling or vulnerability in front of her, especially if she's not used to seeing it from you. If you come on too strong, you'll make her so uncomfortable she'll want to let herself out of a moving vehicle. Pick a situation where you can show self-compassion in ways that make her feel secure. That way, she can focus on learning, not on feeling awkward.

I do this by telling my students a story about a particularly tough breakup I endured years ago. I was riven by self-criticism during that time. I vacillated wildly between exaggeration—*Obviously this means there's something terribly wrong with me, and I'm going to be alone forever*—and denial—*Who cares, whatever, I'll just date someone else.* The former sent me into a tailspin of sadness and anxiety. The latter fortified me with anger but moved me no closer to healing.

To practice the first step, mindfulness, I had to zero in on what I was feeling and thinking at the time, without judgment. I had to sweep aside all my melodramatic predictions of what I was sure my breakup meant in the larger scheme of my life (*I'm going to die alone, clearly*), of what I believed would now happen to me (*many, many cats*), of what I thought it said about me as a person (*broken, obviously*), and so on.

Mindfulness is particularly key for girls prone to denying a problem or exaggerating it. While most of them know that denial is not an effective way to cope, plenty believe exaggerating a problem means you care about it. It's key to point out that getting really upset is often the opposite of dealing. It's hijacking your thoughts and feelings to a place of predicting the worst. It's catastrophizing so you can't focus, much less start solving a problem.

After I stopped exaggerating, I could ask myself one question: What did I genuinely think and feel in this moment? As I listened to my own thoughts, I heard: *This hurts, a lot. I feel sad and rejected.*

The second step was self-kindness, or being nice to myself. If you're starting to picture Stuart Smalley from *Saturday Night Live* (the guy standing in front of the mirror saying, "*Because I'm good enough, I'm smart enough, and doggone it . . . people like me*"), you are forgiven. Stay with me, though.

It's amazing to me how much girls struggle with this step, how hard it is for them to access a gentle word for themselves. When a girl I'm working with flounders, I ask her to imagine how a close friend or parent might respond to her if they heard her being self-critical. What would they say? I often channel my friend Daniella. In my situation, her voice sounded like this: *You did the best you could in this relationship. You learned a lot about yourself, too.* It's what I would have told a friend in the same situation, too, and it was the truth.

The third and final step of self-compassion is common humanity: connecting with others who have had similar or worse experiences. This step silences the destructive "I'm-the-only-one-who" disease that afflicts so many adolescents. To practice common humanity, I told myself this: *I know I'm not the only one suffering a heartbreak at this moment. I am not the only single person in the world, either.* True confession: I had googled "heartbreak advice" and gotten 1.5 million hits. Clearly I was not alone. For good measure, I reminded myself that my daughter and I had our health. That doesn't mean I

was telling myself that my feelings were trivial. It did, however, give me some perspective on my own suffering.

Another way to cultivate self-compassion in your daughter is to integrate these steps into daily conversation. For example, I might say to my daughter, "I'm really disappointed that I didn't get what I wanted today [mindfulness]. But I did my best, and there were other stressful things I was dealing with at the time [self-kindness]." Or, I might say, "I'm embarrassed that I screwed up the recipe and that dinner didn't taste great [mindfulness]. Turns out my friend did the same thing last week [common humanity]. We'll figure out something else to eat instead." By demonstrating a healthy way to respond to difficulty, you offer a vital script to a girl that she'll use in countless ways, throughout her life. And she is more likely to sustain a practice of self-compassion if she is a beneficiary of your compassion, too.

Transforming a negative inner voice into a kinder one is that much easier with loved ones who echo the gentle messages that you're trying to cultivate within yourself.

Learning to calmly name your thoughts and feelings by practicing mindfulness means leaving behind the exaggeration mentality so many girls revert to when they're insecure. Instead, mindfulness lets you connect to the situation as it is, not to what you're terrified it might be or become. It sits your pain right down next to you on the couch and makes you look it in the face. The upshot is that you soon realize your troubles won't drown you after all. The more you do this, the easier it gets to sit with real feelings, rather than try to run away from them. And that, ironically, is what helps you move forward and be stronger.

How we learn to interpret our setbacks is a skill, and it's one we learn in part by watching our parents. If we grow up with a father who handles a defeat at work by numbly going to bed every night at seven thirty, or a mother who circles the kitchen saying what an idiot

she is for losing a grocery list, we get a clear message about just how powerful a single mistake can be. If we want girls to stop taking all the responsibility and then some, the change will lie as much with us as with our girls.

TALKING BACK TO THE INNER CRITIC

Girls often think their self-criticism defines them. They don't just entertain their most painful thoughts; they swallow their self-criticism whole and convert negative, even delusional, thoughts into personal truths they hold about themselves. These are the girls who tell me, *I know I'm not cut out to succeed in this class (or school, or job), so it must be true.*

Some experts argue that to dull the roar of the inner demon, you have to face it first. Mohr urges her clients to head straight toward their self-criticism, even personify it, and turn it into a living thing inside of themselves they can label and confront directly. Writes Mohr:

> You are not the critical voice. You are the person *aware* of the critical voice. You are the person feeling perplexed by it or bummed out by it or believing it. You are the person trying to understand it and work with it and get rid of it. . . . The critic is not the core of you. The core of you is the you of your aspirations, of your inner wisdom. The critic is a kind of intruder. It's a voice that happens to play in your mind, but it is not who you really are.

Seeing your inner critic as a separate entity, Mohr writes, helps you understand that your inner critic is *part* of you, but not you as a person.

Kelsey's inner critic was at its most vicious when she saw her first LSAT score. "I was devastated," she told me. She sat sobbing at her dining room table while her mother tried to comfort her. Kelsey was a first-generation college student, and as she held her head in her hands on the table, her thoughts began to spin. *You're not good enough for law school. This is where the arrogance to think you could do more than go to college gets you.*

Some years ago, my strategy with Kelsey would have centered on talking her out of her self-criticism. I would have told her she was brilliant, and qualified, and destined for greatness. Even cognitive behavioral therapists, who practice a proven method for making people feel better, would urge Kelsey to consider the evidence: her high GPA, presidency of the law club, and outspoken voice on campus all made her a fine candidate for law school.

But in the distorted mindset of insecurity and self-defeat, facts matter little. Mohr suggests a different way to help, something akin to walking right into the belly of the beast. Kelsey needed to label, not turn away from, what was happening inside her. "That's the voice of your inner critic," her mother might say. Labeling tells Kelsey that her thoughts have a name and that they are not her; they are part of her. It tells Kelsey her experience isn't unique; others have an inner critic, too. It reassures her that she's not alone in her suffering, which will help anchor her in a sense of common humanity, pulling her away from the throes of shame.

Kelsey's mom could also help her daughter understand the purpose of self-criticism: Evolutionary psychologists believe it's an adaptive mechanism we developed millions of years ago to prevent complacency and protect us from physical harm. Today, self-criticism functions similarly. We still use it to protect ourselves from something we fear; it's just not a woolly mammoth.

Mom could ask Kelsey why her inner critic is screaming at her to give up her law school dreams. What might it be trying to spare herself from? Humiliation? Defeat? Fear of not fitting in with students whose parents attended college? Mohr suggests we ask the inner critic what it most fears and name its motives. We can then respond with, "Thank you so much for your input, but I've got this one covered."

Instead of trying to stamp the toxic voice out of her, her mother could help Kelsey see it as one voice of many that will always live inside her. The fact is, when we tell ourselves not to think or feel something, it almost always has the opposite effect.

Self-compassion doesn't make bad feelings disappear, but it does diminish them. In the middle of the night, when life can sometimes seem unbearably bleak, self-compassion is calming. But perhaps the true gift of the practice is perspective: when a girl connects with the experience of others, she begins to understand that others have faced the same situation and moved past it. This can give her a sense of hope, and gratitude for what she does have. It can also buffer her from feelings of shame.

Facing down a difficult challenge isn't just about what she does in a big, scary moment. What she does *after* that moment—say, when things don't go as planned—matters just as much. If girls don't know how to talk to themselves in the face of a setback, and if mistakes fill them with shame, overthinking, and a desire to isolate . . . well, who would want to bother ever trying to be brave?

That's why I ask students one question at the end of my workshops and classes. It is a question directed especially to the woman who was up on the elliptical at 5:30 A.M., and the one reading by a cell phone light in her dorm room past midnight. It is for the high school junior who has been in Sunday SAT prep since eighth grade, and the sophomore who is on her second bottle of 5-hour ENERGY. For these girls who struggle under the relentless pressure to do and be everything, I have one question: *Why are you enough as you are?* I do it every time I work with a group, and I never leave the classroom without a lump in my throat.

I tell the students that I am enough because I am my daughter's mother. Because I am a caring friend. Because I remember birthdays.

At my most recent college orientation, a group of very nervous eighteen-year-old girls answered the following question:

I am enough because . . .

I have friends who love me.

I try to face the challenges I have.

Learning new things fills my spirit with joy.

I try.

I make my family proud.

I love and am loved.

I care about everything I do and about how the people around me feel.

My students and I touch this knowledge all the time. It's given us access to a hidden well of courage that allows us to stand up, speak up, step forward, and take a chance—because we do it on our own meaningful terms, and with the knowledge that we are worthy, no matter what happens on the other end.

7

The Cult of Effortless Perfection and the Rise of Stress Olympics

I feel like my life is like all of the expectations bundled into one person, and I don't know how I'm doing it.

—ZOE, SIXTEEN

In the early 2000s, Dr. Donna Lisker surfaced a troubling trend among college women at Duke: a phenomenon where female students experienced "pressure [not only] to succeed academically, but be physically fit, fashionably dressed, perfectly coiffed, with the right group of friends and the right summer job, to say nothing of partying and hooking up after hours"—all without visible effort. One of Lisker's students called it a drive for "effortless perfection."

Perfectionism in girls is hardly breaking news. But Duke's Women's Initiative, chaired by then-president Nannerl O. Keohane, was witnessing a new mutation, a kind of perfectionism 2.0, where it was no longer enough merely to excel in school. Now, students said, you had to have every base covered, from looks to activities to grades, while acting as if, in Beyoncé's words, you "woke up like this." As if you nailed those fresh looks, killer grades, well-rounded résumé, and fabulous social life without help or effort.

Today, the cult of EP is in full effect by high school and has been observed in boys as well as girls. Sociologist Shamus Khan observed that among students at St. Paul's boarding school, "achievements seemed to passively 'happen'—as if the students themselves hadn't done it or that doing it was not really very hard for them." The idea is "to try hard but not look like you're trying so hard," a junior at an all-girls high school explained to me. Her classmate added, "Like it comes easily, naturally to you." At the very schools where discipline and achievement are everything, students are increasingly expected to appear as if they're not really trying.

"I put a lot of pressure on myself to appear like I have it all together," said Nora, a nineteen-year-old originally from Oklahoma who is attending a large public university in the Northeast. "I work out every single day because I don't want to have any physical flaws. Girls in my sorority look good on the outside and make it seem like we have it all together, even if we don't."

In this world, trying too hard codes as a sign that you are uncool, even incompetent. The logic goes something like this: *You must not be that smart if you're so worried about failing. You must not be that pretty if you had to work that hard on your hair. You must not be that confident if you're so stressed out about your grades.* If a girl gets too upset about the parts of her life that challenge her, it makes others uncomfortable. Because if *her* perfection isn't effortless, it implies that yours might not be, either.

The other day at lunch, Nora and her fellow sorority sisters made fun of a girl at the table next to them. The girl was dressed in a crop top and tight jeans, hair and makeup to the nines, and she was loud. "We were like, she was trying really hard to get attention. You can tell she likes herself a lot."

Nora and her sorority sisters called girls like this the "try hards," who irk their peers with one part wannabe (*she wants attention*) and one part self-possession (*who does she think she is?*). People tend to "get mad," she told me, at girls like them. In a dorm at another New England college, students gave the "Most Freshman" award to the person who tried just a little too hard to be best friends with everyone.

The cult of EP is more than a troubling side effect of a peer culture bent on excellence. It travels the razor-thin fault lines that run through modern femininity: look good, but act like you don't care that much or don't think you deserve to. Indeed, girls slot a little too easily into the rules of effortless perfection: EP reveres humility (make your gifts seem like they just came "naturally" to you) and self-sufficiency (you achieved all this on your own, so you won't need to put anyone out by asking for help). EP worships the thin ideal, a goal disproportionately sought by girls. And EP is marketed extensively on social media—through endless images of bikini bodies, memory-making late-night parties, and pretty vacation backdrops—where girls also dominate.

None of this comes cheaply. As professors Elizabeth Armstrong and Laura Hamilton write in *Paying for the Party,* a study of inequality at a midwestern university, competition is highly classed among young women: you need money to look good, go out, and eat well. If you have a campus job or take care of someone at home, you have a lot less time to go to the gym and do your hair. In the authors' study of a sorority rush, often the most public nomination of the effortlessly perfect, "failure to present a 'cute' appearance effectively screened out most of the less privileged women." Because women never knew who was chosen to rush or why, they saw their exclusion as a personal failure, "rather than a systematic sorting on social class and other characteristics."

But plenty of women on campus actively reject the cult of effortless perfection, especially underrepresented students. When I have asked groups of first-generation girls and students of color about the idea of making their struggle "look easy," many seem bewildered. These women have been raised to leverage their struggle proudly as a source of purpose and drive. Pretending it doesn't exist strikes them as absurd.

EP is a side effect of our culture's ambivalence about girls' growing potential. It continues the drumbeat of what I described in *The Curse of the Good Girl* as our "yes, but" mentality about female authority: Yes, society tells girls, be successful, but say nothing about it. Yes, be strong, but be sexy. Yes, be confident, just do it quietly. Effortless perfection has refashioned these impossible tensions into a goal of modern young womanhood.

ROLE OVERLOAD

The pursuit of EP sets girls on a never-ending slog toward a standard of achievement that will always sit out of reach. It undermines girls' confidence, pits girls against one another, and thwarts their ability to seek support. In other words, it makes self-harm a prerequisite of self-empowerment.

EP asks girls to embrace an obscene number of obligations in a single twenty-four-hour day. This is not just a lot of work for girls to do; it's a lot of different *kinds* of work. Zoe was a ponytailed three-sports-a-year high school junior in leggings, passionate about environmental studies and the outdoors. She sat eating pizza with a group of friends I was interviewing, rattling off a list of daily requirements the world was expecting her to meet.

"You have to have perfect grades, you have to excel at all areas of interest," Zoe said, her long legs crossed in her chair.

And while you're doing everything on the planet, you also have to be strong but be skinny, have a big butt and be sexually appealing. But at the same time, it's complicated, there's kind of the pressure to be a party girl and join hookup culture. But if you hook up too much you're a slut, and if you're in a steady relationship it gets boring. Then where do academics and sports fall in?

Zoe barely had time to see her boyfriend. She felt like a "bad girlfriend" for missing his lacrosse games. Her friends felt neglected, too, and she only saw her family "over dinner, when I'm running in the door." Zoe was not depressed, or anxious, or struggling; in fact, she was the opposite. "I think I'm generally an optimistic person," she told us. "I have a sunny disposition. But if I were any more emotionally unstable I don't think I could handle this. I feel like my life is like all of the expectations bundled into one person, and I don't know how I'm doing it." Suddenly her phone alarm went off.

"I have to go," she said abruptly. "I have to buy my mom milk before I go home."

This is "role overload" in action. As Lisker puts it, "Effortless perfection combined the brains of the 'geek' stereotype with the beauty of the 'dumb blonde' and told women to do both." The dissonance can tax a single person's capacity. It's no coincidence that in 2014, the American Psychological Association reported that adolescent girls slept the fewest hours of any group of Americans. Sleep deficits are linked to behavioral and mental health problems in adolescents, including depression, anxiety, risk taking, and emotional fragility.

In the 1990s, I showed up to college classes in sweats. Today, the roll-out-of-bed look has gone the way of the overhead projector. In Anna's classes at a Boston college, the unwritten rule was to dress up. Workout clothes were the only exception, so students wore them to class even if they hadn't been to the gym, just to hack the dress code. One of Anna's friends confided that if she ever felt badly about herself, she went to the grocery store down the street "to remember what people look like outside of school."

Weekends, Anna told me, brought a "whole different kind of work than you do during the week." After a day in the library, she explained, "You figure out where you're going and you make plans with people, and you're forever getting ready for a party and then you stay up really late." Where to go, who to go with, and what to do were anxiously debated, heavily tinged with FOMO, fear of missing out on the "right" weekend experience.

God forbid you wanted to stay in and watch Netflix. "There's kind of a script for what you do on the weekends," Anna told me. "There's a set of activities you're *supposed to* be doing in order to fulfill this norm and this ideal of what we're supposed to be." Then, she said, "On Monday, you're *supposed to* be doing really well in your classes." Weekends, ostensibly a time to decompress, were now as full of "supposed to" as the weekdays.

The multitasking required to stay on top of it all is staggering. Kayla, nineteen, a student in the honors college at a public university, told me, "I'm constantly thinking about what I'm doing later, what I'm doing next month, what I have to do, and why I have to do it. My mind doesn't really rest." Kayla had long brown hair and wore glasses. Serious and somewhat guarded as she spoke, she had been ranked fourteenth in her public school class and wanted desperately to be in the top ten. Her mom, she told me pointedly, had been number nine. It was hard for her to be in the present moment, she confided, because the next obligation on the horizon would begin haunting her. "I'll even be writing a paper and thinking about the next paper I have to write, the next thing I have to study for," she said. "It's like a hamster on a wheel and it just doesn't end."

When I talk with mothers about the drive for effortless perfection in their girls, there is instant recognition. Mothers are no strangers to the pressure to master a staggering array of roles: nurturer, disciplinarian, breadwinner, home manager, and schedule co-ordinator. If they are affluent, they are also expected to be thin, dress competitively, and post regularly on social media. Mothers are called the "primary socialization agents" of their children. Girls, in other words, are taking notes.

Yet few are talking about it. In a 2016 study of over 1,200 college students, three-quarters of whom were women, students who strove for effortless perfection felt more isolated from their peers. Keeping up the image of ease required extreme "self-concealment," the researchers wrote. You couldn't complain about how hard everything was, nor could you seek support. You had to keep quiet about insecurity and fear.

Lisker penetrated the silence in her interviews with Duke undergraduates. She found that as girls strive for effortless perfection, they harbor two concerns: they won't be able to maintain it, and someone out there is more effortlessly perfect than they are. The endless drive for more, more, more is a cruel cycle with no resolution: no matter how thin or smart the girls are, they still envy the even flatter stomachs and straighter A's of their peers. "Everyone here is so much smarter and better and more accomplished and harder working than me and I hate it and myself because I'll never match up," went one typical anonymous post on an elite college's "confessions" site. Effortless perfection is futile, a victory that can never be savored. It leaves girls with a constant sense of their own inadequacy.

"I just spent so much energy worrying about why I wasn't going out on weekends, and that, in and of itself, was a type of work, to be saying everyone else is doing this thing and I'm not doing it, what's wrong with me," Anna told me. She spent hours of emotional energy managing this anxiety during her freshman year. "I felt like I was the only one not doing the right thing or the cool thing."

Alcohol arrives for many as the escape hatch. For girls, drinking quiets the blare of self-judgment and allows them to shrug off the pressure. "We needed the wine to shut out the jackhammers of our own perfectionism and unlock the secrets we kept within," Sarah Hepola writes in her powerful memoir, *Blackout: Remembering the Things I Drank to Forget*. "Alcohol helped. Oh my God, it helped. Behind my fortress of empty beer cans, I was safe from fear and judgment. Alcohol loosened my hips, and pried open my fists, and after years of anxious hem-tugging, the freedom was incredible." A drink provides efficient release: it goes down quickly, and is easily worked into an overscheduled life.

Alcohol also offers quick relief from the role conflict plaguing girls. If femininity collars a girl's truest thoughts, alcohol could unleash them, along with her wildest impulses. Writes Hepola:

Booze gave me permission to do whatever I wanted. So much of my life had been an endless loop of: "Where do you want to go to dinner?"/ "I don't know, where do *you* want to go to dinner?" But if I poured some of that gasoline in my tank, I was all mouth. *I want Taco Bell* now. *I want cigarettes* now. *I want Mateo* now.

Breaking the good girl shackles was exhilarating. "How exciting to barge through the world, never apologizing for your place in it but demanding everyone else's license and registration," Hepola writes.

And there is no arena more powerful or popular for alcohol than hookup culture, which poses the keenest conflict of roles. It demands girls display uncharacteristic boldness for no-strings-attached sexual contact, while hewing to the self-control that circumscribes the rest of their lives. Alcohol eases the tension monumentally. As Peggy Orenstein writes in *Girls & Sex*, booze gives girls "license to be sexual, loosening inhibitions while anesthetizing against intimacy, embarrassment, or accountability."

But alcohol also lays bares the tensions it tries to ease. "What did it mean that I hid when I was sober, and I stripped off all my clothes when I was blind drunk?" Hepola asks. "What did it mean that I adored my roommate, but I lashed out at her after seven drinks?"

Last year, Suniya Luthar and her colleagues published findings documenting frequent binge drinking and marijuana use in high-achieving communities, and among girls especially. The researchers followed two groups of affluent New England youth for a decade. At the group's final assessment, when the subjects were twenty-six years old, women were diagnosed with drug or alcohol addiction at three times the national rate (men's diagnoses were twice the national rate). Overall, this group's use of cocaine and stimulants like Adderall were more than twice as high as a comparative sample of young adults.

There was, however, some notable good news: the study showed that when their parents adopted a strict (but not draconian) policy toward substance use in their adolescents—focused on mutually agreed upon rules that were consistently enforced—use levels were significantly lower.

PERFECT GIRLS, IMPERFECT FRIENDSHIPS

Self-concealment and insecurity are a toxic cocktail for girl relationships. Nora, the first-year college student in a sorority at a large public university, often compared herself to her best friend, who was also her roommate. "We're constantly sort of competing against each other, like unspoken," she told me. At the gym, they tried to outlift each other and be better on the mats. When her friend complained about her appearance, it drove Nora crazy. "I'm so mad at her," she told me. When Nora complained, her friend got angry, too. In the silence of their dorm room insecurity turned quickly to competition and resentment.

In 1986, psychologist Catherine Steiner-Adair observed that high-achieving young women are "constantly comparing their own size and shape to others [and] resent an 'obscenely skinny' woman unless they can classify her as abnormal by virtue of an eating disorder." Nearly two decades later, a sorority sister at Duke confided to Lisker a mix of "jealousy and superiority" when she saw an anorexic peer:

> It's almost like—oh thank God she has an eating disorder, like, she's not perfect. . . . Sometimes you rationalize, like when you walk by someone who's like obscenely skinny and you don't even know who she is and . . . you hear people are like, "oh my God she's so anorexic." . . . You don't really care that she's anorexic, it's more to the point, like, she makes me look fat so there's something wrong with her.

I'm not sure which is more troubling: that insecurity keeps girls from supporting each other, or that the sight of an anorexic girl "makes me look fat."

It's often said that the best way to get rid of jealousy is to admit it. But owning envy isn't easy for girls. It goes against the norms they have been raised to obey: good girls are supposed to be generous, not covet what other people have. They are supposed to celebrate the successes of their peers, not be threatened by them. Plus, in the land of effortless perfection, envy looks like too much caring about a thing you're supposed to make look easy.

Girls internalize their feelings instead. After a beloved senior at her high school won a prestigious college scholarship, school psychologist Marisa LaDuca Crandall saw two of the winner's friends separately in her office. "She's so amazing and I love her so much," one told her. "But how come I'm not that great? I should have worked harder." It's okay to feel jealous, Crandall suggested gently. This girl had accomplished something extraordinary. "I'm not saying she doesn't deserve it," another girl said. "She deserves every minute."

"They can't admit to how badly they want it themselves," Crandall told me. "That's not what a nice girl is supposed to feel. They turn it around to I'm a terrible person, I'm never getting into college, there's something wrong with me." If depression is anger turned inward, then this is what it looks like when girls swallow their envy. "You turn it on yourself and use it to beat yourself up, which is horrible to watch," Crandall said. By turning on themselves, and by extension, one another, girls don't turn their outrage toward a culture that pits them against each other in the first place.

In Emma Cline's novel *The Girls*, teenaged Evie begins quietly competing with her close friend Connie, whom she quickly grows to resent: "I remember noticing for the first time how loud she was, her voice hard with silly aggressiveness," Cline writes. "A space opened up between us as soon as I started to notice these things, to catalog her shortcomings the way a boy would. I regret how ungenerous I was. As if by putting distance between us, I could cure myself of the same disease."

It's downright depressing to hear overwhelmed girls blame themselves for toxic cultural messages. They downplay the stress as "just the way things are." They fault themselves for being "too perfectionistic." The tendency to blame the self, writes Brené Brown, is how perfectionism thrives. "Rather than questioning the faulty logic of perfectionism," she writes, "we become even more entrenched in our quest to look and do everything right." We question ourselves, not the system.

Too many of these girls are, to quote sociologist Sherry Turkle, "alone together": the more they put up a front to others, the more alone they perceive themselves to be, even if they are surrounded by adults and peers who want to help them. Notably, the students in the 2016 EP study told researchers they believed they had low levels of social support. The isolation of these girls is cause for special concern because relationships are uniquely important for girls' resilience. According to the 2017 Girls' Index, one in three high school girls report that they are sad or depressed four or more days per week. But girls who say that they get along well with other girls and trust other girls register the lowest levels of sadness and depression. They serve a key function of support, offering guidance, emotional strength, and opportunities for self-disclosure and self-validation. They also protect girls against problems like depression, loneliness, and lower self-esteem.

Until I researched this book, I thought stress was the malady of an individual. I worried about how stress would affect the way a girl sleeps, eats, and feels. I soon realized that stress was corroding her relationships just as much.

THE NEW RULES OF STRESS CULTURE

There are five unwritten rules girls carefully follow to manage their stress and relate to others. The rules let them appear busy but invulnerable, which prevents them from developing close, nurturing connections with others when they most need them.

1. *Being overwhelmed is the new normal.* If you're not constantly busy studying or attending meetings, something must be wrong with you, your schedule, or your work ethic. The rise in constant busyness means much less downtime for girls to hang out and connect. As one college sophomore told me, "I can't have downtime. I feel like I'm doing something wrong if I'm not doing anything."

2. *Stress is equated with worthiness and productivity.* The more stressed you are, the more successful you must be. As twenty-

one-year-old Nicole told me, "I like being the person who's always busy. I want people to notice it. I define myself as that person who was constantly working. When somebody walks by, they think, 'How is she *doing* all this?'" By this logic, socializing is a form of laziness.

3. *If you're happy, it must mean you're not working hard enough.* If suffering is equated with worthiness, then happiness is a selfish pursuit. As one student told me, "I have a hobby. I guess I'm doing college wrong."

4. *Don't share your good news with peers.* You don't want to sound like you're bragging, plus it might make your peers feel bad. As one college student told me, "I feel like I can't talk about doing really well without sounding like an asshole. Sometimes I feel like I have to drop my mood down a couple notches when I'm around other people." Her words reminded me of something Bette Midler said about her own career: "The worst part of success is trying to find someone who will be happy for you."

5. *Don't burden your peers with your own stress because that might stress them out.* Being a drag on others is a no-no. A college student overheard a classmate snap at her lab partner, "Don't start with your shit today, I've had the worst day of my life."

To sum up the mindset: Your work matters more than anything. Don't be too happy, and don't be too sad, or your friendships will pay the price. If you're happy you're not working hard enough. If you're not busy right now, you're basically lazy. These rules take direct aim at the relationships that might otherwise shore girls up in times of difficulty. They make it hard to justify even basic self-care, like sleeping, showering, and cleaning your room.

STRESS OLYMPICS

At high schools and colleges across America, a secret game is played in hallways, libraries, and text threads. "Stress Olympics" is competitive complaining: about how little you have slept or eaten during marathon work sessions, and about how much more work you have than everyone else. It sounds something like this:

STUDENT ONE: "Ughhhhhh I'm so tired, I only slept five hours last night because I had a paper due at nine and I started it at two A.M."

STUDENT TWO: "I know, ugh, I only slept three hours and I had cross-country practice this morning at six."

STUDENT THREE: "I have three papers due tomorrow? And I've only started one? I'm going to be mainlining coffee for the next twenty-four hours."

Columbia University's student blog published a "Stress Olympics Bingo" card. Options included: "My eight finals are all at 9:00 A.M.," "I pee in water bottles to save time," and "I haven't eaten anything but 5-hour energy bars in days."

Stress Olympics are a test of mental and physical ballast, and of bootstrap success. "Phrases such as 'I only got four hours of sleep last night!' are spoken with pride rather than regret," wrote junior Caroline Vanderlee in the Johns Hopkins University student newspaper. Stress Olympians thumb their caffeinated noses at self-care. Anna, nineteen, told me, "I wasn't getting a lot out of it, but I still had this sick, twisted pride that I was doing it all," she told me.

At first blush, Stress Olympics seem like innocent, bunker mentality bonding. But the ritual offers faux bonhomie at best. The conversations don't end in compassion, a hug, or offers of support. They aren't about listening or connecting with a peer's struggle. Stress Olympics are, at their core, about one-upping a peer's suffering. The contest to be "most stressed-out" invariably leaves others feeling like they're not stressed-out or working hard enough.

The work of Stress Olympians is hardly "effortless," of course. Yet they appear to manage their stress bloodlessly, and under the wire. Stress Olympics explicitly shun being vulnerable and reaching out for help. "Students who have two tests and an essay due the next day boast how stressed they are for the hellish task ahead, rather than e-mailing their teachers for an extension in order to alleviate the workload," Vanderlee wrote. And if you start that paper at 2:00 A.M. and hand it in at nine, you look pretty chill. You certainly don't look like the Anxious Annie who started the paper a month ago. Things must be really hard for her if she has to spend that much time and effort getting it done.

Stress Olympics are a sign of our culture's continuing worship of busyness. Researchers have uncovered a shift in how people talk about their lives, including a spike in the phrases "crazy schedule" or "I have no life" everywhere from Twitter to holiday cards. Advertisements that used to feature the wealthy relaxing have been replaced by images of the overworked and leisure deprived. In 2016, researchers from Columbia, Georgetown, and Harvard found that signaling how busy you are makes other people think you have high status. Being busy "is implicitly telling you that 'I am very important, and my human capital is sought after, which is why I'm so busy,'" author Silvia Bellezza told a reporter. Notably, it was only Americans who felt this way. Italians felt exactly the opposite. Leisure, they said, is what made you cool.

Talking about Stress Olympics, and even giving it a name, can help change the way students talk to one another. At Smith, students are dropping the competition and rewriting the conversation. In my workshops, we practice three strategies of active listening instead of turning the conversation back to ourselves. We empathize with the listener, paraphrase what we have heard, or ask a question.

When a peer says, "I have two papers and an exam tomorrow," the empathic response is, "You must be really stressed-out." The paraphrase: "It sounds like you've got a ton on your plate right now." The question: "Can I do anything?" or "Do you want to take a study break later?" When a peer announces how little they've slept or how many papers they have to write by tomorrow, the new reply is a word of encouragement. "You got this." "You'll be great." "I know you'll crush it." Or, a little compassion. "You have fourteen exams tomorrow? Dude, I'm so sorry." Or: "That struggle is real." There is also the offer of support: "Do you want to talk to someone about this?"

We've hosted several nights of Stress Olympics Bingo at Smith. We gave away winter hats and temporary tattoos that read RETIRED STRESS OLYMPIAN. Now students tell me they know it when they hear it, and they try to disengage.

But it's the internal scripts, and what they tell themselves about their peers, that also have to change. Stress Olympics are driven by the distorted fear that you're not keeping up with your peers. When you look around and recognize that everyone struggles in their own way, it's a lot easier to stop competing.

It took until her senior year for Phoebe to realize, "Okay, you're not the only one without a job. You're not the only one who's completely stressed and barely treading water." She went on, "It's not like I'm not going to have a roof over my head. It's not the end of the world. Are the people who love me going to stop loving me? I have all these irrational thoughts. You go into a test and say I'm going to fail or I'm not going to pass this class or I'm not going to graduate or find a job. But things do pan out."

CHILL GIRLS DON'T NEED HELP

Effortless perfection isn't just about looking competent. It's also about looking *happy*. In 2016, high school girls told researchers they felt under pressure not only to be nice to everyone, but also to be enthusiastic about every activity as a way to stand out. In college, men and women alike talk about the frozen-in-place smiles of invulnerability they see while walking to and from class. The phenomenon has been nicknamed on campuses across the country: at Stanford it's called "Duck Syndrome": the duck glides elegantly across the surface, paddling like hell invisibly underneath. There is "Penn Face" at the University of Pennsylvania and "BC Perfect" at Boston College.

More recently, the "chill" girl persona is on the rise. To be chill, wrote Wesleyan student Camila Recalde in her senior thesis, is to be "easygoing, independent, happy and unbothered" around sexual contact. In hookup culture, where the unwritten rule is no strings attached, chillness "is a state of being amiable yet indifferent" around sexual contact, lest you be deemed crazy or undesirable. Recalde called chillness an "achievement of invulnerability," in which success is measured by how well you tamp down your emotions and act fine, no matter what.

Chill culture is the product of an overscheduled generation that struggles to make time for relationships. To be chill is to have an undefined "relationship" that is only as meaningful as the moment, and is stripped of real obligation to another person. Chill sanitizes emotions and responsibility from connection. It creates closeness without dependence, and sharing without obligation.

Besides her sexual exploits, the chill girl is also fun. She's a "guy's girl" who eats burritos with impunity, who looks thin and toned but never goes to the gym. Gillian Flynn wrote about her in her bestselling *Gone Girl*: the "hot, brilliant, funny woman who adores football, poker, dirty jokes, and burping, who plays video games, drinks cheap beer, loves threesomes and anal sex." Girls have annointed Oscar-winning actress Jennifer Lawrence as the ultimate chill girl. She refuses to diet for a role and says she hates to work out but has a long-running love affair with nachos. She is not merely effortlessly perfect; she's effortlessly cool.

The new archetype looks appealingly feminist on the surface, but there's a troubling sexism here. The chill girl tamps down unseemly (read: aggressive) opinions and emotions. Girls sometimes assert their chill by saying, "I'm not like other girls." Unchill, writes Recalde, is "being affectionate, highly opinionated, angry, needy and vulnerable." The new chill girl, in fact, may be a doppelgänger to the compliant "good girl."

No matter what you call it, the pressure to hide vulnerability forces girls to conceal and disconnect from their most powerful feelings. In my 2015 survey with Vassar College of high school girls, we found that girls who met the criteria for perfectionism were more likely to say they had trouble seeking support. Students who didn't ask for help said they preferred to "hide their feelings," "act like they have everything under control," or "try to figure things out on their own."

Many girls confide a fear that others will judge them for needing help. This is almost always the voice of a girl's inner critic. "I don't want to be a burden," Maggie, twenty-two, told me.

It's like, I should know how to do this, I feel stupid. All the judgments I have about myself, I project onto others and what they think about me. I worry, am I asking too much? Is there a quota on the number of questions I can ask without being seen as stupid or a freeloader? At least for me, it comes from my own lack of self-worth and thinking, okay, I'm so sorry, I don't want to waste your time, and pretty much thinking my time is not as important as everyone else's time.

Shame dominates Maggie's reasoning. She beats herself up for needing help, so she is less likely to ask for it. She doesn't just think her struggle is less worthy of support; she thinks *she* is less worthy. For this reason, I now ask girls this: *Do you feel certain that others will judge you for needing help, or is it possible that you're judging yourself for needing help?*

Seeking support requires believing you are entitled to having someone in your corner to help you out. Sometimes, that person has to be you. But self-care, the practice of maintaining your own well-being and health, quickly disappears in a world where girls feel nothing they do is enough. Stress culture has demoted self-care from a right to a privilege, something you earn only once you've done enough work to deserve it.

"I should have done my work yesterday, but I didn't do it," a twenty-year-old college student told me. "So now I don't deserve to take a shower until the test is done."

Her housemates nodded in agreement. "It's a cycle," one said. "I need to sleep so I can do this better, but I don't have time to sleep so I can't do this better." These students talked about the most basic self-care as luxuries. One spoke of how long it took to brush her hair. "It takes me thirty minutes because I haven't done it in a while. You can do work in that thirty minutes." They simply didn't give themselves permission to relax.

Of course, at some point they would hit a wall in their workday, yet many still hung on and refused to leave their rooms or the library. "You feel like you should be going out and doing something fun, but you feel like you should be working. But you're too stressed-out to work and you don't go out." Like purgatory? I asked. The women nodded.

It breaks my heart to hear so many young women tell me they don't "deserve" self-care. Self-care is not a privilege. Self-care should never be optional. You don't "get" to clean your room, take a nap, shower, take a walk, or call a friend. You do these things because your body and soul need them to thrive. You do them as everyday acts of self-respect. Make sure your daughter knows this. And make sure you model it, whenever and wherever you can.

The ability to seek support is a muscle that will atrophy when girls lose the opportunity to flex it. Some girls never have. "Someone has always asked for help for them," the dean of students at a women's college told me. "We find that most of our students haven't yet had the opportunity to do that without their parents' support system under them." Parents who have been passionate advocates for their daughters may not realize that they have neglected to teach them how to advocate for themselves.

This isn't true of all girls: some ask for help constantly, and often for problems they should have the tools to resolve on their own. Educators have described this to me as a kind of "learned helplessness," where girls seek support more for personal validation or a self-esteem boost than as a way to obtain the resource they need to help them accomplish a goal.

IT'S OKAY NOT TO BE OKAY

The number of adolescents who say they are lonely is unprecedented. Most painful is how many see their loneliness as a personal failing. This doesn't surprise me: girls, whose social status is shaped by the number of friends they have, must have a crew of friends in order to excel at the game of girlhood. It is now considered de rigueur to roll with a "squad," or, as it's known online, #squad.

Remind your daughter that everyone gets lonely sometimes, even the people she can't imagine would be. Some of the most popular people on college campuses, including student government and dorm presidents, confide in me that they feel lonely. It happens to everyone. The point is not never to feel lonely, but to know what she needs when it happens. The inconvenient truth is that sometimes we need to feel lonely. It can be a signal that tells us something is not right, and that can help us change our lives for the better.

Loneliness isn't her fault. Remind her of the systems in play that contribute to a nationwide epidemic of quiet isolation: the staggering rise of smartphone use that keeps more youth online, and disconnected in person, than ever. The pressure to work constantly, and the sense among students that no amount of work completed is ever truly enough.

Tell your daughter to resist the system, not fix herself. Encourage her to cast critical eye on the College Application Industrial Complex, and on the cult of effortless perfection, both of which make hanging out seem lazy instead of restorative. Push her to own her right to self-care, and affirm the importance of live, rich, off-screen connections with friends. Ask her what she is doing this weekend. Encourage her to go out.

Above all, discourage her from remaining silent about feeling lonely. Loneliness thrives on secrecy, and that means shame is close behind. Shame will amplify her loneliness and gut her of motivation to make her life better. When we surface and share the thing we feel afraid of, we take away much of its power. We also find that others are feeling the same way. Urge her to tell someone, anyone, about how she is feeling. Even writing about it can help.

Staying busy all the time won't make her feel less lonely. Loneliness happens in part because students are too afraid to leave their laptops or walk out of the library. They feel certain that "everyone is working harder than I am" and "I can't stop," both erroneous beliefs that fuel their isolation. Loneliness will only begin to abate when they take a break, take a walk, or call a friend.

When a girl seeks support, it makes her smarter and braver. She can circle the wagons and invite encouragement that will help her face down her fears. I always tell my students that the five worst words they can say to themselves are: "I'm the only one who . . ." Because it's almost never true. And support gives her in-the-flesh proof that she's not alone: actual people who can dust her off and buy her some mint chocolate chip ice cream if things don't go her way. It offers her a perspective different from her own and can shine a light on a blind spot she didn't know she had.

After taking my Courage Boot Camp, Grace decided to ask for help on the day she was going to hear from her first-choice college. She gave an adviser at school and her friends a heads-up, with a clear request: "If it's a yes, that's great," she told them. "If it's no, I need you to support me through it and tell me it's okay."

The answer was no. Grace was heartbroken, but the support system she'd built ahead of time was a game changer. "Beforehand I would have read the letter, had a meltdown, and continued to wallow in a pool of tears," she told me. "I would have put myself down and said, 'You're not good enough, that's why they said no. If you had said this or done that, you would have gotten in.'" Instead, through a conscious choice, Grace circumvented the shame that can sometimes accompany facing failure by yourself. She was able to be real with people she trusted, and feel respected and loved despite her setback.

In my workshops, I often ask groups of girls to tell me what they would do if they were asked to drive a distressed friend several hours to see her parents. Almost all say yes, they would drive the friend because, they say, "she needs me." Or: "That's what friends do."

When I turn the tables and ask if they would ask a friend for the same favor—for themselves—there is silence. "I don't want to be needy," one usually says.

"Or annoying."

"Or impose."

Many of these girls would do almost anything for a friend, yet they recoil at the prospect of making even minor requests of others. In part that's because they've learned that good girls only give. But some girls avoid asking for help because they don't feel worthy of receiving it.

Jahleese is a child psychology major at her small, largely commuter women's college. She interns at a day treatment center, earns money for tuition working at a law firm, is captain of the step team, and works as an RA on her hall. At twenty-one, she will be the first in her family to graduate from college. Since she started college, her mother and sister enrolled in classes at the local technical community college.

Jahleese's father is African American and her mother is Puerto Rican, though Jahleese spends most of her time with the Latino side of her family, which lives nearby. In eighth grade, her parents put her in a college prep charter school. Her job, they told her, was to get into college and find something she loved to do in the world. They didn't care what that thing was, or how many A's she got along the way. "It took a lot of the pressure off," Jahleese said.

Jahleese thrived in college, though she often felt anxious and overwhelmed. She got so busy at school that she stopped taking care of herself. At times her back would seize up in pain. She overate. Exercise felt out of the question. "Why would I go to the gym if I could be doing a [dorm] event for my floor?" she said.

As a rule, Jahleese said, she rarely relied on others. As busy as she was? I asked.

"I'd rather struggle," she replied. She wasn't sure why. "I'm hardheaded," she mused. "I won't even let someone help me bring books to my car."

She learned some of these habits from her mother, who was the youngest of nine siblings and tended not to stand up for herself. "It's the submissive role" of women in her Puerto Rican culture, Jahleese said. "My mom makes sure everyone else is taken care of and then takes care of herself." It's where she gets a lot of her self-worth, Jahleese added. Research shows that in traditional African American and Latino homes, girls are more likely to have caretaking responsibilities at home.

In African American homes, girls may experience pressure from adult women to shoulder responsibility in silence. Alice Walker has written that Black women were called "'the mule of the world' [a term originating in Zora Neale Hurston's *Their Eyes Were Watching God*] because we have been handed the burdens that everyone else—everyone else—refused to carry." Under duress first in slavery, and then often as head of household, the "strong Black woman" became an ideal that came to include a veneer of invulnerability.

When I asked Jahleese to evaluate her work, rather than only describe how much of it she had, I began to see why she, and so many high-achieving girls like her, avoid seeking support. Jahleese was intensely self-critical. "I always feel like I'm not doing enough for the people I take care of," she told me. Nothing she did ever seemed to be enough in her own eyes, and she was frequently hard on herself. When I asked her to take a self-compassion test, she scored high in isolation and low in connection with others.

Girls who grow up being told they must be both caregivers and rainmakers face a special struggle. For Sadia, a first-generation Bangladeshi American attending an Ivy League university, giving help was no problem: at home on school vacations, she cooked and cleaned in her family's small New York City apartment. She contributed a portion of the wages from her campus job to her parents. And she loved to tutor on campus.

Asking for support was another matter. When she broke her ankle, Sadia couldn't bring herself to ask a friend to help her walk to the door. "I don't know, I feel very unworthy of asking for help," she told me. "If I was sick, I wouldn't ask a friend to get me soup. I wouldn't want someone else to have to feel burdened because they had to help me. It's like, who am I? I don't want me to have to be on their minds. It's like, I'd rather help them."

Parents need to be sure their daughters understand that a strange thing happens when you get in the habit of not asking for help. You start to think others are not interested in offering it. "I feel like people mean more to me than I mean to them," Sadia told me quietly, when I pressed her on why she doesn't ask for help, "and that's a hard thing to deal with." Was there evidence of this "care disparity"? I asked her. She shook her head.

The less you ask for help, the less you receive and the more you make up stories about what the silence of others means.

Support seeking has a PR problem. Reframing the concept will help girls see it in a fresh light. First, we can make the connection to self-worth: asking for help is an act of self-respect and confidence. In order to fight for your happiness, Kant wrote, you must first feel worthy of being happy (you also need to believe that happiness is not a sign of sloth). When you tell someone what you need, you are saying that you are *deserving* of it. That kind of self-worth is the raw material that makes you braver and more confident in the world. When we believe we matter fundamentally, the challenge of taking risks and falling short becomes easier to bear.

Telling girls it's okay to not be okay won't turn them into fragile ninnies. It will give them permission to reassert balance in their lives, engage in self-care, and maximize the resources around them. It will also give them the opportunity to practice vulnerability. As Joanna, the high school ballerina who took my Courage Boot Camp workshop, put it: "We're in a school that tells us all the time to use our voice. I thought I already had some of the skills I needed to be confident or at least appear confident. But it was this whole shift when you told us that being brave is about showing that you're vulnerable and asking people for help, and it's more about finding a mentor than trying to do it all alone."

Stanford professor Kelly McGonigal has found that connecting with others while you're under stress can make you recover faster. Stress causes the release of oxytocin, the so-called bonding hormone, which increases the desire to connect. "When life is difficult," she said in her TED Talk, "your stress response wants you to be surrounded by people who care about you." Connection, in other words, makes you resilient.

Girls need to understand that support seeking isn't just something we do in crisis. It's also a powerful leadership skill. The ability to leverage the resources around you to accomplish your goals makes you more effective at what you do. In an information economy that increasingly relies on project-based teamwork, knowing how to call in reinforcements or sound an alarm are vital skills. In 2015, researchers at Harvard Business School found that people who seek advice are seen by others as more competent than those who don't; particularly when the task is difficult, you ask someone personally, and you consult an expert on your topic.

Talk with your daughter about the benefits of collaboration in your life and hers. Challenge the assumption that self-made success is somehow better or more worthy. What do we gain when we make ourselves vulnerable enough to say we can't do something alone? Remind her that connections forged in vulnerability, in her personal life and at work, are often the most real and lasting.

Finally, if we want girls to seek support, we have to do it, too. I know how hard this can be to learn as an adult. I grew up with a mother who worked full-time and did almost all the housework. My brother and I had a single chore: bring the dishes to the sink after a meal, a job that took approximately thirty seconds. My mom did everything else, refusing to let us help her in the kitchen, or anywhere else.

I didn't become an overindulged brat. I became just like her: fiercely independent, declining help most of the time. Perhaps not coincidentally, I found myself single at thirty-six, and I decided to have a baby on my own. I got pregnant easily and went about my life as if little had changed. When Hurricane Irene knocked down the trees on my block, cutting my power and heat, I wore a head-lamp, shivering under a comforter in maternity long underwear. I was scared, and I called no one. I told myself I could manage. I always had.

When I went into labor several months later, I spent six hours tracking contractions on a smartphone app while a male friend slept on the couch. My elderly terrier sat at my feet, watching me intently. I didn't wake my friend up, even though I was scared. I didn't want to burden anyone until I absolutely needed to. Today, when I imagine my own daughter making that decision, I feel tears in my eyes. I want her to be a girl who invites the support she needs in her life, and who feels entitled to the love and generosity she showers on others. To do that, I have had to go on my own journey and learn how to model it myself.

8

Control + Alt + Delete:
The Merits of Changing
Course

I felt so trapped. I would wake up in the morning and be like, "Oh my God, I can't believe I'm here . . ."

—EMMA, EIGHTEEN

I won the prestigious Rhodes Scholarship two years after graduating from college. The Rhodes is one of the highest profile awards a new college grad can win, and there's a voodoo surrounding it: people who get the Rhodes have gone on to become presidents, pro athletes, and Nobel Prize winners. When you win a Rhodes, the vibe is rarefied. People are reverent.

The mayor of New York, my boss at the time, feted me at a packed press conference. The *Daily News* proclaimed a "genius" in City Hall. My college anointed me their admissions literature cover girl, and I traveled to Oxford University for two years of grad school, all expenses paid. I was flush with pride, determined to be the best Rhodes Scholar of the bunch.

Not long after arriving, I sat down at my desk, looked out at the foggy courtyard, and felt a tight pit of dread expand in my gut. I didn't like this place, not at all. My class readings were as outdated as the professors, and I wasn't making friends. As the weeks wore on, I found graduate school searingly lonely. I spent most of my time in the cavernous Bodleian Library, or running Oxford's misty roads, wondering what was wrong with me. Why couldn't I be happy like my classmates seemed to be?

But I could not fathom leaving. Who quit the Rhodes Scholarship, that rarest of gifts? How could I let my family down? My mother and her family were Eastern European refugees who came to this country with nothing. I had long carried the pressure and promise of their American dreams. But I no longer recognized myself. I was weak, lost, and scared.

Nine months after arriving in Oxford, I dropped out of graduate school and moved back in with my parents. Languishing in bed for hours at a time, I stared at dusty childhood trophies, paralyzed by depression and shame. The president of my college, when I called to explain, told me I had embarrassed our school. I had worked for her as a student assistant my entire senior year.

I found a therapist and began taking antidepressants. Before long, I came to understand two painful truths: First, I had become a Rhodes Scholar not because I wanted to study at Oxford but because I wanted to be a Rhodes Scholar. My decision was driven more by how the next life step looked to others than how it felt to me. I was doing what I thought I was supposed to, churning toward the next achievement. It never occurred to me to ask myself if I really wanted to do any of it. I had lost track of who I was and what I valued.

Second, my self-esteem had been built on winning awards. I had defined myself, and my self-worth, almost entirely by my success. When I suddenly encountered failure, I was shattered. I lacked the internal resources to cope with a setback. I had no idea how to fail.

After quitting the Rhodes, I hid this darker, more complicated item on my résumé for over a decade. I worried that if others knew I was a Rhodes Scholar dropout, my career would be discredited. I was convinced quitting defined my character, as if the years of hard work that came before it were suddenly voided.

I now know otherwise. Adolescence is a period marked by difficult transitions, and some of us make wrong turns. This chapter is about how the choice to change course, drop out, and, yes, quit can—with the right support and reflection—be the opposite of regrettable. It can be a spectacularly brave act of self-respect for your daughter. On the road to figuring out who she is, wrong turns are rarely dead ends. Whatever the reason—not the right school, not the right job, not the right time—a transition crisis can give your daughter the opportunity to reset, and figure out who and what she genuinely wants to become.

GRIT ISN'T ALWAYS GOOD

Americans have always prized persistence, and lately it has taken on a kind of worship. The character strength "grit," sticking with a long-term goal to its fulfillment, is all the rage. Extensive research by psychologist Angela Duckworth has shown that grit is a gateway to lifetime educational success.

But there are times when grit may be bad for you. In studies of youth, adults, and the elderly, Concordia University's Carsten Wrosch found that refusing to give up "unattainable goals" caused physical and emotional distress. A goal can slip out of reach when there is a mismatch between your skill set and objective, or if stress, whether age-related or from sudden life events, intervenes.

Wrosch found that adolescent girls who refused to change course showed elevated levels of the CRP protein, a marker of systemic inflammation linked to diabetes, heart disease, osteoporosis, and other medical conditions. These girls experienced more frustration, exhaustion, ambivalence, and depression.

By contrast, the girls who cut their losses had higher levels of well-being and lower secretions of cortisol, the "stress hormone." They were also more likely to reengage with new, more feasible goals, increasing their sense of purpose. "When people are faced with situations in which they cannot realize a key life goal," the researchers concluded, "the most adaptive response for mental and physical health may be to disengage from that goal."

Author and educator Alfie Kohn questions what is lost in our focus on grit. "What matters isn't just how long one persists, but why one does so," he wrote. "Do kids love what they're doing? Or are they driven by a desperate (and anxiety-provoking) need to prove their competence? As long as they're pushing themselves, we're encouraged to nod our approval." Doing what you've been told is the "path of least resistance," he argues. It takes courage to throw the brakes and go your own way.

Girls in particular learn early on to do what they are told. Tuning in to what others want earns them rewards from peers and adults, and punishment if they refuse to comply. Resisters are quickly labeled selfish or "conceited." This is why girls will give up their seat on the playground swings, let their friends pick the movie or mall this weekend, even look the other way when their feelings are hurt. They do it not only to keep the peace, be liked, or hold their place in the group. They also do it to survive. And it works.

When the payoff is that good, the habit seeps into other choices girls make: the classes they choose, majors they pick, schools they apply to, and jobs they take. If they do it enough times, and with enough rewards, they stop thinking about what they really want. The thread connecting them to their strongest desires wears down, thins out, then dissolves. Their choices are increasingly driven by forces outside of themselves. As the stakes get higher, so do the consequences if things don't work out: tuition and security deposits are lost, to say nothing of wellness and time.

Add to this the pressure to act like they have it all together, and the illusion that everyone else does. It leaves many girls suffering in silence, chained to decisions they've already come to regret, even while maintaining a saccharine front on social media.

The celebration of grit reflects a value judgment: deep focus on a task is preferable to trying new things, experimenting, and developing a breadth of knowledge. We've seen this most clearly in the "find-your-passion" obsession that dominates college admissions mania. Yet one of the most important developmental tasks of your daughter's adolescence is to form her identity, a journey that by its very exploratory nature is about pursuing goals that turn out to be unattainable. The College Application Industrial Complex may expect students to evolve without error but that doesn't mean life actually happens that way. Figuring out who she is will be more work in progress than nailed-on-the-first-try. These are moments when quitting may not only be wise but adaptive.

There is also the question of how ready she may be for big next steps like college, cross-country moves, and full-time employment. How she looks on paper may not match what's going on inside. Her GPA is far from a conclusive sign that she's ready to face down all that comes with a new opportunity.

When our kids are very young, we're encouraged to see development on a continuum. We are told that our kids will sit up, roll over, walk, and talk at different times. Somewhere along the way, we impose a rigid timeline on who we expect our kids to become and when. Wiggle room gives way to anxiety about keeping pace with others. By senior year of high school, it is a foregone conclusion that your middle-class child will matriculate at college the following September, then move along a uniform path to commencement, employment, and a new home. But kids are not all the same, and no amount of wishing, pressure, bribery, or therapy will bring them to a developmental line they are not ready to cross.

———

Emma had always been anxious: about standardized tests, the avalanche of work in her advanced placement classes, and the competitiveness of her soccer team. Most of all, she worried about college. Emma had scant success leaving home. There were few sleepovers, and no summer camp. "She's a homebody," her mother, Julie, told me.

But Emma managed a full course load, busy athletic schedule, and time with her boyfriend. When she applied and was accepted early to an elite college, she was stunned. She hadn't expected to get in. Emma dutifully blasted her news across social media; alone in her room, she beat back the fear that was beginning to take shape inside her. *Everyone goes to college and it's fine*, she thought. *I'll be a different person by the time I actually go.*

Willowy and poised, Emma now sat opposite me at a café, refusing an offer of coffee and remembering the fear that kept her in line throughout her senior year of high school. She recalled telling herself, *You never hear about people who don't go to college.* Not going was not an option.

As winter turned to spring, Emma allowed herself to be swept up in her peers' growing excitement about college. The admissions announcements of her friends and their families bordered on circus-like revelry. "There's this idea that when you go to college it's just immediate fun," Emma told me. "You're going to be a new person! With new friends! And have this amazing experience!" As her friends trumpeted their news, Emma tried to parrot it. "I was like, 'Everyone does this, I'm sure this is normal.'"

Julie saw through her daughter's front. She knew Emma had excelled until now precisely because she kept herself squarely in comfort zones. College would be a radical change. "Are you really ready?" Julie gently asked Emma. "Maybe you should take a gap year."

"No way," Emma said. "How embarrassing to stay home, when everyone else goes off to school. Who does that?" Julie backed down but worried quietly.

At the end of August, the family stuffed the car with everything of Emma's that it could hold. As Emma stepped gingerly into her dorm room, her roommate was mute and unwelcoming. Julie felt her stomach drop, but she knew the drill. A few hours later, she and her husband, Josh, walked down the stairs to let Emma start college on her own terms.

It was three days before Emma's denial shattered. She woke up one day, panic prickling through her, to understand this new life was now hers. "I felt so trapped," she remembered. The anxiety unfurled itself inside of her until it was all she could feel. "I would wake up in the morning and be like, 'Oh my God, I can't believe I'm here and not home,'" she told me.

Emma wept in her room as she pictured her family going about their days without her. She had panic attacks and called her parents five times a day, sobbing. "I can't stay here, I hate it so much, I hate the dorm, I hate the quad, I can't eat, I hate the food," she cried.

Freshman orientation was a disaster: mandatory friend-making events, hyperstructured days, "all the stuff she can't stand," Julie recalled. Emma used up most of her energy trying not to cry in public, clinging to the hope that the icebreakers would end and she could soon start her classes.

She was desperate to go home yet couldn't imagine actually doing it. "You never hear of anyone who does that," she told me. Her parents would lose God-knew-how-much money. And what would she do if she left? It was embarrassment and the judgment of others that scared her the most. "What would people think if I left?" she recalled thinking. "I just felt like such a freak."

Emma saw a therapist on campus. Over 150 miles away, her parents argued about what to do. Stick it out for a month, Josh said. Bring her home now, Julie countered. As Emma moved through her first day of classes, she felt like a ghost. The discipline and drive that had earned her a coveted place in college had disappeared, leaving a broken girl in its place.

It was a student resident adviser who sent Emma to see the freshman dean. The dean was no stranger to Emma's situation, and she explained the college's policy about withdrawing from school. "She acted like it wasn't weird at all," Emma recalled. "It was like, wait, this happens to people?"

Yes, it did, the dean told her, and there was a student she wanted Emma to meet. The young woman had also withdrawn in the first weeks of school and, after a productive year away, was now thriving on campus. "Hearing her story gave me hope that I could come back," Emma said. "She had been feeling all the same things as me."

The dean offered to call Julie and Josh and put Emma's meltdown into context. She assured them it was not exceptional, that their daughter could take time off and be welcomed back when she was ready. "That's what really changed it for them," Emma said. The financial loss would be nominal.

Three weeks after they first arrived on campus, Emma's family dismantled the dorm room they had assembled so carefully and packed up the car once more. Emma now knew two things: she wasn't alone, and she wasn't crazy. Freed of these burdens, she began to see the choice to withdraw in a new light, as perhaps the opposite of a cop-out. "I realized I wasn't running away, and that I was doing something for myself," she said. She began, for the first time, to feel hopeful.

On the one hand, Julie was proud of her daughter for rejecting the pressure to "do" college a certain way. On the other hand, was she doing the wrong thing by letting her come home? By now, news of Emma's aborted attempt at college had reached their close community of friends and family. The response was surprisingly muted. "You would not believe," Julie told me, "how many untraditional people, supposed progressives, are horrified at the idea of someone who goes to college and leaves."

No matter, she told herself. Focus on the real question: Would Emma ever be able to launch? Was she too messed up to leave the nest?

Then and there Julie became determined to redraw the boundaries in her relationship with her daughter. She would make Emma's withdrawal conditional on her confronting her anxiety and getting the help she needed to thrive away from home. It was a crucible moment for mother and daughter.

"She had to see a therapist, figure out her anxiety, and figure out what she wanted to do," Julie told me. She would make sure Emma did the work, and she knew it wouldn't be easy. "I had to step back," she recalled.

OWNING HER RECOVERY

One of the cruelest tricks of the adolescent brain is its ability to convince young adults that whatever moment they're in will define them forever. The past and future not only become irrelevant, but also seem to vanish completely from the mental dashboard. There is only now, now, now.

Back at home, Emma's resolve wavered. What kind of person had she been before this meltdown? It no longer seemed to matter that she had once worked hard to get into a good school, or that she was creative, smart, and social. All she felt now was the panic that she might always live, hamstrung, in purgatory between high school and college.

"I had been so in a bubble my whole life, of 'this is what you do next, you go from this school to this school.' I never had to make my own choices," she told me. "It was all easy, and now I had to ask, 'Well, what can I do to push myself?'"

Rites of passage like leaving home for college are vital anchors for teens. They establish routine during a period of stress and instability. When inner resources grow thin, social pressure nudges teens forward. But for those girls who finally must throw the brakes on that thing everyone else expects them to do, there is a second layer of pain to endure: self-doubt, isolation, and shame.

Shame is an extreme, toxic expression of remorse. It poses a double burden in the face of a setback: the experience becomes not just that I failed at a task, but that I have also failed myself. For Emma, the double burden was *I hate college, and I hate myself for hating college.* Thinking she was a bad person only sandbagged her ability to process the setback. It kept her tethered to a story that she was weak, pathetic, unworthy, and alone.

To recover, Emma had to confront two challenges: one, she had to learn to manage the anxiety that kept her from transitioning to college, and two, she had to revise the way she interpreted her experience. Emma had to stop judging herself for what was happening, and change the story she was telling herself about withdrawing. Even more than that, she had to consider the moment as a potential learning opportunity, not as a catastrophic end point. She had to own this process and take responsibility for her recovery. No one could do it for her.

Seeing the dean, then meeting the recovered student were two healthy first steps. Learning she wasn't "the only one," and that her problem wasn't exceptional, freed her from the weight of self-criticism. Beginning to forgive herself cleared the mental and emotional space she needed to begin moving forward again. It allowed her to drop the ruse of incessant high performance, and gave her permission to seek support.

The next step was to withdraw from college. To do this, Emma had to accept that she was not ready to be there. The goal had become unattainable for now, and the experience had pulled her too far away from who she knew herself to be. Finally, Emma had to believe there would be more beyond this excruciating moment.

As she sat in the unstructured quiet of her childhood home, two questions took shape inside her: *Can I acknowledge that I have things that I need to work on? How can I push myself to be in a better place than I was this year?* She felt something familiar begin to sprout: determination. Her old drive and discipline began to reassert themselves. She began weekly therapy appointments and continued her course of medication. Learning to live away from home would have to be gradual. Emma found a job in a nearby city and commuted by bus, often staying the night at the home of a family friend.

Months later, when Emma wanted to visit friends across the country, she felt terror at the idea of traveling so far on her own. But this time, Emma approached the challenge differently. Instead of pushing the feelings away, she paid close attention to mounting feelings of panic and dread. She focused on using the new tools she was learning in therapy to manage her feelings. "If this happens, I'll do that," she would tell herself. "If that happens, I'll do this." She would no longer chalk up her life's challenges to a generic diagnosis of "anxiety." Emma went to the source of the anxiety itself.

When Emma saw her friends at baggage claim, she was elated. It was a different kind of success than she had known before. It didn't rely on projecting an image of perfection but stayed closer to a more humble, authentic ground. It was a win she had worked carefully up to, instead of expecting herself to nail it effortlessly. Emma had revised her standards and taken the risk with a full embrace of her limits. It was her refusal to deny her weakness that gave her the courage to follow through.

Emma was discovering the courage that comes with vulnerability, and the success that comes with giving yourself permission to be ordinary. She adopted this stance again as she prepared to return to college. She softened her expectations: she would give it a semester, and if things didn't work out, she would transfer closer to home and forgive herself. She stayed in therapy, owning her fears and doing the hard work of managing her anxiety. "It was so different from the summer before when I'd been denying everything," she remembered. "I just had tool after tool of how I would make it work, and it felt really good."

Emma's new approach, along with the jarring events of that last year, also affected the way her parents watched from the sidelines. They, too, changed their expectations. They began operating from a different set of values, defining success and happiness for their daughter based on who she was, not on what they had been told she had to be. Now, they celebrated even the smallest victories. Did Emma have a good day? Was she passing her classes (note: not getting A's, just passing)? These became the new benchmarks of success.

Emma told me all this with a mix of embarrassment and pride. "It was kind of sad," she said sheepishly, "but it was also pretty great."

PARENTING THROUGH A TRANSITION CRISIS

For a moment, put yourself in your daughter's shoes: in the fall of her first year in college, around age seventeen or eighteen, she will sever her daily ties not only with her family of origin, but also with what one psychologist calls the "second family": the nurturing network of peers that she has built over a period of years, and which has provided a social safety net, activity partners, and academic support. Then she must relocate, sometimes to a new climate or time zone, and learn to adjust to a new schedule and a challenging workload. She must build a social network from scratch, all while trying to manage the challenge of separating from the old one.

For girls, this can be a particularly messy process. Consider the intimacy of girls with their closest high school friends. Their friendships are characterized by one-on-one connections and high levels of disclosure. They are more likely than boys to become upset when their friends have problems and to vicariously take on their distress. Finally, girls' self-esteem is vulnerable to the ups and downs of friendship.

Disentangling, separating, individuating—this isn't a smooth process for most girls, especially in the age of the smartphone. Social media now keeps girls preoccupied by their old networks as never before, at the very moment when they should be constructing new ones. For most girls leaving home, the break is hardly clean, and the emotional baggage of their transition may at times outmatch what fills their dorm rooms.

Girls who are the first in their families to attend college or who come from low-income backgrounds can be tight-lipped about their suffering while away from home. Unlike Emma, whose fear was self-oriented—she worried most about damage to her reputation and her own sense of self—these girls fear letting their families down.

"They definitely don't give themselves permission to struggle," says Marge Litchford, Smith's assistant dean of students, who oversees first-gen and first-year students. "They are the ones who got out, the ones who carry [the family's expectations] on their shoulders. They don't want to disappoint their mom." Changing course, to these students, is belittling the sacrifices that made their achievement possible. If they view themselves as their family's "way out" of poverty or the working class, and many surely are, acting on their suffering feels at best selfish, at worst putting their entire family at risk.

Their parents may be equally disinclined to speak up. These mothers and fathers worry about appearing too entitled to college administrators. They rarely resemble the privileged parents who are notoriously quick to pick up the phone on behalf of their daughters. They are far more inclined to defer to a school's authority than to question it. Ironically, parents of first-gen and low-income girls tend to be the least achievement-obsessed, Litchford said. "They want their daughters to be happy and do something they love," she told me.

Colleges want to hear from parents when their children are struggling. Without that partnership, girls may only come forward when they are too debilitated to continue. Older adolescents who receive "intense support" from their parents (emotional, financial, or practical assistance) at least once a week show higher reports of life satisfaction and better adjustment than adolescents who do not. We may be quick to condemn so-called helicopter parents, but it's important to understand that it's not parenting period that is a problem; it's a specific type of parenting. Helicopter parents do for kids what they can already do for themselves. When your daughter struggles in transition, a different kind of parenting is called for.

You will need to embrace the perspective that a setback isn't a detour from her path. It *is* her path. During this time, three points of intervention will help steady her and prepare her to move forward.

1. *Encourage her to forgive herself if self-criticism is immobilizing her.* Teach her the practice of self-compassion in chapter six. To be clear, you're not pretending this didn't happen. You are showing her that beating herself up is not productive, and that it will not motivate her to move forward and change her circumstance.

2. *Help her connect with her own values.* She will grow stronger when she is rooted in who she is, how she feels, and what she stands for, not who she is trying to be for anyone or anything else. Begin by asking her what she's proud of so far in the way she has handled this episode. What does that strength say about the kind of person she is? For me, as I left Oxford, I was proud of my commitment to going to therapy and reflecting on my choices. Celebrating her virtues will give your daughter a shot of motivation and hope.

    Ask her next about three values she wants to honor right now in her life. Friendship? Family? Honesty? Service? Talk together about ways she can align herself with what she cares about. This will increase her confidence and sense of self, both of which are likely running low. The goal of this work is not to get her to the next step. It is to stabilize her where she is, by anchoring her to her self.

3. *Enlist her in the response.* Ask her what she wants to do about the situation. Encourage her to brainstorm a few possibilities. Don't take "I don't know" for an answer. In this moment, good parenting feels like taking the steering wheel yourself. In fact, what she most needs is to reconnect with her own resourcefulness. She also needs to realize this moment won't last forever. If she's willing, map out some options. They don't have to be 100 percent doable or brilliant. They just have to be generated and owned by her.

This is not a call to overindulge her. You are still her parent. You retain the right to exercise your authority and narrate your values. As always, it will still fall to you to be the boundary drawer, "no" sayer, and deadline setter. You remain the container she pushes against as she wrestles with figuring out what is right and what is wrong. But she needs to stabilize first. Know that it may take some time to settle on the right mix of holding her and pushing her forward. If you can nurture and challenge your daughter in equal parts during this time, you will help her rebuild the confidence she needs to get back on her feet and start again.

WHAT SHE NEEDS YOU TO SAY

One summer during college, I took kayaking lessons on the Potomac River near my parents' home in Maryland. I loved the thrill of the rushing white water but had trouble staying upright. The secret, the instructor told me, was to lean into the waves.

"In?" I asked. "If I lean in, won't I capsize?"

"It feels like that," he said, "but you won't. Just try it."

I leaned a tiny bit and felt my body begin to fall toward the water. I yanked myself back. "Try again," the instructor said.

Eventually I felt what he was trying to teach me: it was only when I let my body do exactly what it wanted to resist that I would find the strongest position on the river.

The same is true in parenting a girl through a transition crisis. One of the best gifts you can give a girl—especially one who, day in and day out, navigates a world of overachievers—is permission to struggle. See her and love her as she is, not as you want her to be.

Giving in to her grief feels counterintuitive. Won't she just sink lower if you indulge her feelings? The answer is no. There is a difference between validating someone's pain and encouraging it. When you empathize with your daughter, you lay the groundwork that allows her to move through a challenge instead of beating herself up for it. You authorize and validate her experience. By reflecting back to her that she's not crazy, or alone, she's more likely to stay upright in the water.

But that is not what girls hear, see on their phones, or think. Most first-year college students are greeted with news of their peers' sparkling success: this class has so many valedictorians, and class presidents, elite athletes, acrobats, honor society members, and so on. At every stage, the expectation is that a young woman will be savvy enough to nail the right choice of college, pick the perfect major, land the most impressive job, score the best apartment in the hippest neighborhood, find the most awesome roommates, and love every minute of it (or at least says social media). There is no room for failure.

The most effective parents challenge this mythology and expose it for the fraud that it is. These are the parents who send their kids to college with the warning that it probably won't be the best four years of their lives. They say college is a place like any other, with its ups and downs and disappointments and moments of beauty. They tell their daughters to be patient as they build their new social life, and be prepared to go to bad parties, meet boring people, and be homesick as hell.

Everyone will be struggling, these parents say, so don't be fooled by the illusion that you're the only one who misses your old life or is having trouble adjusting to your new one. These parents give their girls permission to be torn, and torn up, about the next step. They confide their own stories of college and early real-world mishaps. They tell their girls there is nothing wrong with them for being unhappy, and that anything new that we do, especially a new learning experience, is supposed to be hard. That's part of what makes it a learning experience.

These parents disabuse their girls of the idea that success means never making a wrong turn. Finding out what you don't like or want to do is just as valuable as learning what you do. Bends in the road are part of the process; our inner compass grows more accurate once it knows where it doesn't want to go.

Getting somewhere on your own time doesn't mean you won't eventually get there. The analogy I use with my students is about speeding. Sure, I can do eighty on the highway to get where I'm going—but I risk getting a ticket or in an accident. If I drive the speed limit, I get there maybe ten or fifteen minutes later, but the loss of time is worth what I get back in safety, money, and sanity. The same is true of your journey through life. Is it worth risking your wellness to keep pace with someone else?

This is the moment when lowering the bar for your daughter, in your extraordinarily influential role as her parent, can go a long way. Give her credit for showing up, for making even small efforts when life feels hard. Focus on the little things she accomplished this day, or this week: Did she go to the gym? Hand in a paper on time? Do well on a quiz?

Likewise, work with her on setting reasonable (yes, small) goals. If she makes conversation with someone new on her hall, or goes to see a movie with a friend instead of curling up solo with Netflix, applaud. These are worthy steps that deserve recognition. Help her understand that she doesn't have to be freshman of the year in her first month at school. You may think she already knows it, but say it again—yes, even if she rolls her eyes. When you define success in these smaller ways, you give her both permission and a script to do the same.

THE DETOUR BECOMES THE PATH

For Emma, healing came through learning to manage anxiety. My challenge was different: I had to step off the achievement treadmill and find a way back to myself. My intrinsic motivation, that part of me that worked because I really wanted to, was nearly gone. I decided that if I was to change the situation, I had to figure out what truly mattered to me, and not because anyone wanted me to, or because it would win me awards. The answer came quickly. For years, I had been haunted by an incident in the third grade, when a girl named Abby made my best friends run away from me on the playground. Why did it bug me so much?

I started researching girls' aggression and found little written on the topic. I began interviewing women I knew about their memories of girl bullying. I was still sad, still confused about what to do next with my life, but I had constructed a set of learning goals inspired by the desire to master a skill, not win approval.

After those first months of brutal despair at home, I met an editor who was interested in my writing. Not long after that, I got a small advance from her publisher. I withdrew from the law school I had been slated to attend, and this time my parents were furious. My father shouted at me: "You're throwing away every opportunity you've been given."

I was shaken, but I kept walking. I suspected this book project would heal me and bring me back to myself. To earn extra money, I took short-term menial jobs. I moved to a mouse-infested apartment in Brooklyn and racked up credit card debt. But I knew what I felt most committed to in the world, and I was doing it. At the time, that was enough for me.

When I devoted myself to what I genuinely cared about, and when I let my heart guide me (as opposed to my need to accomplish), I found true success. Researchers studying motivation have confirmed this phenomenon: when you remove extrinsic rewards, you are forced to find out what drives you internally. When the University of Rochester professors Edward L. Deci and Richard M. Ryan decided to follow graduates two years after college, they found that students driven by a sense of purpose about their lives—a desire to "help others improve their lives, to learn and to grow"—were happier, more satisfied, and less anxious and depressed than they were in college. Students who pursued the extrinsic reward of money were more likely to be depressed, anxious, and demonstrate several other negative indicators of well-being. "It is those who are least motivated to pursue extrinsic rewards who eventually receive them," writes Daniel Pink, author of *Drive*.

It took me longer to realize that some success is not worth having, and that quitting is nothing to be ashamed of. According to Wrosch, knowing when to give up is an important form of self-regulation and best learned at this age, when the consequences of so-called goal disengagement tend to be less severe.

My misery was a critical signal that something in my life desperately needed to change. Today I am grateful for it. Girls have three choices when they hear that distress signal pulsing inside of them: Pretend it's not happening. See it as a sign that something is wrong with them. Or realize it means something is just plain . . . wrong.

If girls label distress as a sign there's something wrong with *them*, they miss the chance to attune to their own authentic needs and act with wisdom. They also revert to social comparison, obsessing over why others don't seem as unhappy or unlucky as they are. In these situations, parents must push their daughters to focus on their own lives and their own choices—and not worry about the other person down the hall or how happy everyone else seems. Everyone is different, and on her own track. Comparison is pointless and painful.

Instead, girls can choose to hear the signal inside them as a sign something is wrong, period. As parents, we must set the tone: when we help them bypass the shame and self-judgment, we bring them closer to a more clearheaded evaluation of their choices, and help them turn an existential crisis into an opportunity. We can start with language: instead of "dropping out" or "quitting," we can talk about "changing course" or simply "taking a break."

Taking time off from school can also help. According to the American Gap Association, high school burnout and a desire "to find out more about themselves" are two of the top reasons students take a break before starting college. Among the top three benefits of taking a gap year is developing "a better sense of who I am as a person and what is important to me."

It's also worth asking your daughter how she feels about the idea of college in the first place. The only people who tend to ask themselves if they truly want to go to college are the ones who have to fight the hardest to get there. But even if this next step is a given for your daughter, that doesn't mean she can't reflect on why she wants to go, and for what. The answer is not necessarily "so I can become an [x, y, or z career person]"—she doesn't need to know that yet— but rather an answer that suggests she sees genuine value for herself in the experience. If she can't answer these questions, pay attention and frame it as an opportunity to work with her on deeper reflection.

Some years ago I was speaking at a high school commencement in South Africa when I decided to share my Rhodes dropout story for the first time. (Yes, I was so afraid to share my story publicly that I had to do it in another hemisphere.) After I finished, there was a seemingly interminable pause. Then the students and their parents stood up and cheered.

That's the moment I decided I wanted to be a "work in progress" role model. Today I am determined to show my students and my daughter that the measure of a life is not a numerical score, nor how closely one can approximate a culturally imposed picture of success. Life is full of choices we make to keep moving forward, some foolish, some wise; it's what we make of where we find ourselves that matters so much more. And sometimes, giving up can set you free.

9

We Can't Give Our Children What We Don't Have

Parenting an adolescent can be painfully thankless work. A young adult's job is to reject your values, be frequently embarrassed by you, and be infuriatingly self-absorbed. When she was young, you were often an object of worship. Then the eye-rolling years hit, and you became a pain in the ass.

Young children provide reliable, instant feedback on your parenting. Tell them to do this and try that, and they often comply. Young adults, not so much. You will share rational, sane pieces of advice that come from your many years on this earth, only to have them accuse you of stupidity. You will question if, in fact, you are stupid, possibly until someone else reminds you that you are not.

"It's bad enough to be rebuffed by your daughter," writes psychologist Lisa Damour in *Untangled*, "it's worse that it happens right when you feel that she needs you the most." To parent a young adult is to make daily deposits of wisdom, modeling, discipline, and whatever else you can muster into your daughter, often for months, even years, without a dividend. She will never pat you on the back for telling her that she'll be happy anywhere she goes to college, or that the number of likes shouldn't define her worth. More likely, she'll tell you you're clueless or worse. Maybe you knew parenting wasn't a popularity contest; what no one told you is that you'd be sitting at the nerd table. The payoff almost always comes later, well into adulthood, when they remember things you have already forgotten, and thank you for something for which they once eviscerated you.

Adolescence thus requires a profound pivot in how you parent. First, you must come to terms with the fact that you can't control or fix your girl's challenges as you once did. Your daughter got hip to this a lot sooner than you did. For some time now, she has been less interested in your ability to fix her problem than whether you acknowledge how hard her problem is. Younger girls typically want your help, but older girls want your empathy. They want their feelings validated, and they want to be seen. They want you to say *how totally messed up this is.* They don't always want to be advised.

Adolescents also have, as girls like to say, "all of the feels." They have feelings to spare, feelings they could sell on eBay. Emotional intensity pours out of the adolescent brain unpredictably, and what adolescent girls want to do is expel those feelings onto you. "For many of the problems teenagers face," Damour has written, "dumping the feeling is a remedy unto itself." They empty themselves out, then move on, cleansed. We parents are less resilient. Our recovery time is much longer. We get the anguished phone call, hear the slammed door, and we are left with cartoon stars circling our heads, dazed at best, feeling like human punching bags at worst.

These changes demand redirecting your parenting energy away from the let-me-fix-it conversation and toward a more empathetic interaction, one that involves sitting with your daughter's pain and admitting that an immediate solution may not exist. It's a strategy simple in concept but harder in practice. We aren't wired as parents to sit on our hands while our children ache. We learn to parent by fixing and inevitably define our success by how well we have shaped our children's lives. It is no small task to tolerate their pain without trying to heal it.

The most effective work we can do to improve our parenting will always begin with ourselves. During this time, reflecting on your own habits and behavior—as both a role model and in your relationship with her—can be a useful redirection of your energy. However, if you are parenting a girl who navigates challenges unique to her identity, including discrimination, there are limits to what you can control. The responsibility for change may rest more with an institution than with your family. Your focus, as I explore later in this chapter, may look different.

Still, I am continually moved by Brené Brown's remark that "we can't give our children what we don't have." We can't teach girls what we ourselves don't know. If we want girls to understand life as textured and imperfect, we have to model acceptance and self-compassion. If we want our daughters to be willing and able to fail, we have to share our failures. So parents must learn to regulate their anxiety and calibrate their ambition thoughtfully, in concert with their daughters. Here are some important emotional support strategies you can offer your daughter as she navigates mid to late adolescence.

1. REMEMBER SHE'S STILL
WATCHING YOU

Recently my daughter's preschool teacher shared that in a moment of frustration, my daughter turned to a friend and warned imperiously, "If you continue using that tone, you're going to have to take a break." The teacher and I both laughed, and I blushed. We all have a story like that: a moment when our girls mimicked us hilariously, often embarrassingly.

As our girls age, we loosen the reins on what we say around them. We know "they've heard it before." Many of us stop thinking about that tendency to mimic. But we shouldn't. There is higher order mimicry still in play: the one where she watches how we respond to stress and take risks, how we speak to ourselves in the moments after a mistake, and how we talk about our appearance.

Do you remember when she was learning to walk? Those moments when she swayed like a drunken pirate, then tumbled hard to the floor? The first thing she did was look at you. In her gaze was a question: *How should I react to this? Is this bad?* If your face contorted in fear, if you gasped or covered your mouth, she had her cue. The wailing began. If you looked calm and comfortable, let her know she was okay, she was unperturbed.

Years later, we still cue our daughters by example in how to respond to stress. The tether between parents and girls remains strong, yes, even when they are teenagers. Especially when they are teenagers. When your daughter falls apart over a grade she wishes were higher, a college that didn't accept her, or a job she didn't get, she still wants to know, *How should I react to this? Is this bad?* The difference is that even as you tell her it's okay, she'll retort that it's not. Even as you tell her that you love her no matter what, she will snort and toss her hair like an angry mare. It is her job to do that as an adolescent. But she is still watching. She is still listening.

What are the traits or habits you want to model for her as she enters young adulthood? Think about the moments in your day when you can strategically show her a different way to navigate the world. If you hear yourself in the voices of the girls in this book, and many parents do, this process will ask you to do some work on yourself. One parent I worked with told me her default response to mistakes was to berate herself openly. She thought it was funny and self-deprecating, then realized she was modeling unhealthy self-criticism.

In our work together, she decided to rethink how she reacted when she made a mistake in front of her teenage daughter. "If I couldn't find my keys when we were leaving for school, I wouldn't say what an idiot I was out loud," she told me, even when she was secretly thinking it. "I would breathe, say that I was feeling anxious, but I wouldn't beat myself up."

When she noticed her daughter getting embroiled in college friend drama, Diane wondered if her daughter was too intolerant and quick to anger with her peers. When she spoke with her on the phone, Diane made it a point to share the ways she had accommodated a particularly difficult friend: how hard it was, and the value she gained in accepting someone as they were.

Another parent I worked with worried about her daughter's unwillingness to seek support when she struggled. This mother set a goal of asking for help in front of her daughter. "I'm asking your aunt to come and help me take care of your grandmother because it's too much to manage myself," she told her nineteen-year-old. She wanted her daughter to know she was strong and capable, but could also ask for what she needed.

Adolescents often talk about feeling a lack of control over their lives. As parents try to respond to the daily ups and downs of their daughters, they often feel the same way. Choosing one trait to model can anchor and focus you amid the chaos.

2. MODEL VULNERABILITY

At a West Coast school where I work every year, I noticed a father who showed up often to my workshops looking worried. He asked to speak. "I think my wife and I really screwed up," he began. They were both attorneys, both successful. One night, their high school daughter was inconsolable after bringing home a C on a science exam. He and his wife reassured her that it would be okay, that a bad grade didn't matter all that much in the scheme of things. That's when his daughter got angry.

"She said, 'You and Mom do everything right. You never make mistakes.'" He told the room, "I couldn't believe she thought that. That couldn't be further from the truth. We've screwed up a lot." He and his wife believed the best way to raise a competent daughter was to model excellence. They hadn't realized that by omitting their own setbacks, they had implied it wasn't okay for their daughter to have her own.

There's a famous quote I like from Marian Wright Edelman: "You can't be what you can't see." We use it to rally for minorities in leadership positions, so others can be inspired from afar, or mentored up close. But the quote applies equally to stories of our setbacks. If no one is out there saying they've screwed up, or taken a wrong turn, then how will girls know that it's actually okay to struggle? More important, how will they know *how* to move on, if they don't see anyone else around them doing it or talking about it?

When we work so hard to show girls role models for success, not to mention an artificially straight path to achieving it, we unwittingly fuel the silence and self-criticism that mark too many girls' lives. We deprive them of the chance to build the internal architecture they need to manage the demands the world is making of them, and which they inevitably make of themselves. For as long as she lives, she will still look at your face and ask the question, *Is this okay?* But as she gets older, you can answer that question with much more: with the robust, real story of your own life.

Boundaries are a must. The stories we tell shouldn't be so intense that our daughters feel compelled to parent *us*. Girls can be preternaturally good listeners, and even better at telling us it's okay to lean on them. The goal is to be vulnerable, not fragile, so she can bear witness to your realness without feeling uncomfortable or repulsed. In the security of that connection, knowing her parent is still her parent, your daughter will know she is not alone. It's one of the most important gifts you can give her in a dark moment.

3. REMEMBER THAT A TANTRUM IS A TANTRUM AT ANY AGE

When girls are upset, they genuinely appreciate when an adult asks this question: "Do you want my advice or do you want to vent?" Giving her the choice may feel mundane, but it can make a girl feel seen and understood. If you try this, though, you better be willing to listen. As one high school girl confided to me, "My mom *says* she's just going to listen, but after a while goes, 'Do you want my two cents?'" I have lots of sympathy for that mom, by the way, but if she keeps that up, her kid will stop taking her seriously.

When girls get agitated, conversations can cross a line to a place where dialogue is impossible. Many parents have told me their daughters are prone to stress-induced meltdowns about their workload, often late at night, often Sunday night, often as some assignment is coming due. The girls swing between rage, despair, and sorrow. They do not respond to reason or to gentleness. They insist you do not understand. They are inconsolable.

Like the tantrums of toddlerhood, you must not indulge it. When you attempt to negotiate with a girl in that state, you tacitly reward her behavior. You tell her it's acceptable to communicate like this when she is upset, and that she'll receive support from you no matter how she comports herself. You also send the message that she should indulge others behaving in this way. The reality is that she is most likely in a self-hating shame spiral, even if the way she shows it is by attacking you and everyone else (or, at the other extreme, withdrawing). Whatever the reason, she can't be productive or motivated in a state like this, and that's what she really needs to be.

A tantrum is a tantrum, no matter what the age. The best advice for dealing with it is to give a person her space until she is able to communicate with civility and self-control.

Your daughter needs to work through something painful mostly on her own, but with you close by to offer support as needed. If she can do that while she still lives with you, consider yourself lucky (though it won't always feel that way). In my work with college students, I see many young women facing struggle on their own for the first time many, many miles from home. Trust me when I say it's a lot harder for everyone that way.

No one likes watching their child suffer, and that's especially true when you've got an older, extremely articulate girl who is able, with heartrending clarity, to let you know precisely how much she hurts. As hard as this may be to face as parents, suffering is key to our children's learning, at any age. By adulthood we have learned that the price of some of our most important life lessons—the ones that make us wiser, tougher, and more capable—is pain, even heartbreak. It doesn't help that there are no moments in parenting when it's publicly acceptable to let your child suffer in the service of learning. The one exception is the controversial practice of sleep training, or letting your child "cry it out." According to its proponents, babies learn the "skill" of sleeping through the night when parents resist coming to their immediate aid every time they cry. Before they begin sleep training, parents are instructed to ensure their baby is well fed and dry, so they can be confident that hunger or a wet diaper isn't causing the crying. When the baby cries, the parents sit on their hands. Eventually, the baby gives up and goes back to sleep, and within a short time, begins sleeping through the night.

Now imagine the scenario with your young adult daughter in tantrum mode. She needs to learn a new skill that you can't teach her—in this case, the ability to calm herself under stress to a point where she can interact with you civilly. How can you ensure her basic needs are met while still letting her figure something out on her own? You might say something like this: *I am so sorry you are struggling. I really can see why you would feel this way, and I've been there myself [if that's true]. I know I can't understand exactly what you're going through, but I want you to know I love you and want to be here for you in any way I can. And [not "But"], it's really hard for me to be helpful when you're in this state. So I'm going to go to my room for a bit to take a break, and I'll be back to check on you soon.*

Then you leave. You really leave, you don't stand outside the door, and you wait ten minutes. You take some deep breaths, call a friend to talk you through it. You read a blog post and have a few sips of wine. You return, see how she's doing, reiterate your empathy, acknowledge her challenge. Bring her a snack.

4. REDIRECT CATASTROPHIZING

Once she's calm enough to talk, what often comes next is the catastrophizing: expecting the absolute worst thing that could happen next. *I'm going to fail the test. I'm going to get a B in this class and I won't get into X college. My life is over.* She'll do this for several reasons. First, it's the prevailing language of loss among her friends, how they process setbacks and bond over them. Second, when she exaggerates how awful something is, it becomes easier to distance herself from what's really happening. She can say "I'll never get into college" instead of "I am feeling disappointed, anxious, and scared, and I need to find a way to read twenty pages before class tomorrow." The first allows you to spin out and wonder about something too far away to do anything about. The second forces a concrete choice: What do I need to do right now?

Underlying the "my-life-is-over" dirge is also the belief that this shouldn't be happening to me—that I deserve and must be capable of more. Deep down, many high-achieving girls believe that if they only work hard enough, they should be able to get what they want. This is hardly surprising. Many have been told this repeatedly by their parents and teachers. While it's important to instill in girls a sense of their own potential, it can also distort their expectations of themselves, sending them off the deep end when they fall short of something they think they should ace.

In her wildly popular "Dear Sugar" advice column, author Cheryl Strayed chided a depressed writer in her twenties who was paralyzed by anxiety. *Why can't I write?* she asked Strayed. *And what if no one cares about what I write?* Instead of giving her a pep talk, Strayed called her out. "You loathe yourself, and yet you're consumed by the grandiose ideas you have about your own importance," she wrote to the woman. "You're up too high and down too low. Neither is the place where we get any work done. We get the work done on the ground level."

The same can be said for many a catastrophizing girl. They are down too low, imagining the worst possible outcome, and often up too high, expecting perfection from themselves. Your daughter needs your help to get to ground level. Try to respond to each statement with mindfulness: focus on her feelings and thoughts without judgment. You can engage her in two types of mindful conversations. The first focuses on the question: *What is happening right now?*

If she says, *My life is over*, focus on the emotions you observe: "I know you are so overwhelmed and anxious right now, and I'm sorry." You can *paraphrase* what you are hearing: "It sounds like you're really worried about getting into college." You can *empathize*: "I totally get why you would be upset about this." This dialogue should focus exclusively on trying to move her away from exaggeration without saying just that. Stay firmly in the present: don't forecast and look ahead by telling her everything will be okay, nor look back (*Yes, you probably should have studied harder*). Don't question her feelings (*Why are you so upset about this?*) or analyze (*You always get like this*). Don't invoke reason as a tool to talk her out of it (*Look at your GPA, of course you'll get into college!*). Don't deny how she's feeling, or minimize it. Just name the feelings and thoughts that are driving the hysteria. In this way, you're coaching her in how to stay with her authentic feelings and thoughts instead of exaggerating (or denying) them.

In the second mindful conversation, you can address a thornier question: *What does this situation mean?* This is where you help her interpret what has happened reasonably, and without drama. It might sound like this: *Yes, this exam grade may affect your final GPA and I get why you're worried about that. Yes, this may make it harder for you to get into that school. You will go to a good school no matter what. No, it may not be that school.* Under no circumstances should you indulge her catastrophizing by implying you agree with it. Help her face the reality instead of the distortion. Help her stay on the ground floor.

As always, don't expect a pat on the back. You may hear an exasperated "you just don't get it," and that's fine. You are trying to teach her something in this conversation: that stress is universal, and fairly constant, but it's what we do with it that matters. You are telling her that setbacks come with the territory of ambition and drive. It's the *meaning* we make of those setbacks that matters just as much. If she interprets failure in all-or-nothing ways, and decides that a bad grade means "my life is over," she short-circuits her ability to stay in the game by flooding herself with fear and shame. These conversations are a way for you to help her make meaning of the events of her life in healthy ways. Eventually, hopefully, someday she will mimic you, just like she did when she was a toddler.

5. REMIND HER IT'S NOT ALWAYS ABOUT HER

In a culture where racism, sexism, and homophobia continue to be rampant, it is vital for girls to know what is in their control and what isn't. This is a key component of resilience.

Parents here can take a page from the playbook of many of their African American peers. For generations, Black children have been brought up to have a critical race consciousness, a framework for dealing with prejudice and discrimination, which helps inoculate them against the spiritual toxins they will almost certainly encounter as they come of age in our society. "I would not have you descend into your own dream," Ta-Nehisi Coates writes to his son in his book *Between the World and Me*. "I would have you be a conscious citizen of this terrible and beautiful world."

Black parents prepare their children from a young age to train a critical eye on a racist and sexist culture, and equip their children to deal with cruel stereotypes and slights. They inculcate their children with the message that the disparate treatment they absorb isn't their fault and that they are not less-than. They are worthy but are growing up in a broken, unequal culture.

This parenting style is one of the reasons African American girls pose a stark contrast to their peers. In adolescence, when girls are known to lose self-esteem, Black daughters lose the least. Studies consistently show Black girls have higher self-esteem than white girls. They are among the most ambitious of any group of youth to lead, a trend that continues into adulthood.

Dr. Charlotte Jacobs has found in her research that Black parents protect their daughters not just by alerting them to racism, but also by reinforcing their self-esteem and confidence as Black girls. Renee, a twelfth grader at a predominantly white school, told Jacobs that her mother frequently told her to "Stand by what you think. Stay true to yourself." After telling Jacobs about the criticism she endured from some of her peers, Renee added, "I'm fine the way I am. I have supporters, and I know I have friends, and you know it's fine if I don't get everyone's approval, you know this is just—this is just me."

Teaching girls that not everything can be fixed, and that some systems may be beyond the reach of their ambition (right now), can be liberating. I was struck, after visiting a school in Ohio, when the assistant principal called me to share the students' biggest takeaway from my workshop. "You told them that all the toxic stress and craziness of trying to get into college wasn't their fault, and that they didn't need to fix themselves to deal with it," she said. "That meant so much to them. I could see how much lighter they felt afterward."

6. PRACTICE SELF-REGULATION

In his book *Age of Opportunity*, psychologist Laurence Steinberg argues that the central task of adolescence is to learn "self-regulation," or control over impulses, in order to achieve your goals. Dr. Marisa LaDuca Crandall, school psychologist, says parents of adolescents desperately need the same skill. Learning not to react openly to every challenge a daughter faces, she said, is "the hardest thing to do. As a parent, you have all your anxieties, you have all your psychological weight of what you did and what you didn't do, and what you want your child to do or not do, and the fears of what's going to happen if they do one thing wrong. There's all the catastrophizing that they're going to end up in a van by the river."

Anxiety can be contagious in families. Two researchers trained mothers not suffering from anxiety to act either calm or worried around their toddlers when a stranger appeared. After watching their mothers behave anxiously, the babies became fearful and avoidant with a stranger. Children and adults develop anxiety for all sorts of reasons—genetics, the temperament they were born with, or trauma—but it's also true that modeling matters.

The goal is not to erase worries, writes Lynn Lyons in her book *Anxious Kids, Anxious Parents*, but "to keep anxious fears from dominating our families." Lyons writes that anxiety is a response to the need for certainty and comfort. The problem, she writes, is that anxiety "wants these two outcomes immediately and continually," pushing us to do anything we can to stamp out what makes us feel out of control.

Parenting is nothing if not a long journey into constant, unpredictable change. By their very nature, children inspire uncertainty at every turn. Who will they become? Picture the child about to spill a glass of milk, or the homework left on the kitchen table. We see this, and we wonder: What does this mean for my child right now? It's often easy to soothe ourselves. We grab the milk, bring in the homework. The impulse is easy to indulge when they are young.

After the homework is left on the table a second time, then a third, and after the teacher has sent an e-mail, more dread-inducing questions make themselves known. Global questions emerge: What does this say about my child's character, potential, and future?

And the questions change as our girls get older. If she is a first-generation college student, an academic stumble may bring the question: *What if she can't make it in college?* You might then wonder: *What does this mean about her potential to succeed in life?* After a daughter moves to a new city and struggles to make friends, you might wonder: *What does this mean about her social skills?* Within moments, the what-if questions arrive. *What if other people don't like her?* Then the why-didn't-I's. *Why didn't I arrange more playdates? Should I have forced her to work at that summer camp?*

During a workshop on managing parental worry, I asked participants to share with me some of their global fears about their daughters. Their worries were profound and sad. Here's some of what they said in response to the prompt "What if my daughter . . . ?":

. . . Doesn't succeed in her passion?

. . . Lives her life with fear and insecurity and holds herself back?

. . . Is an academic underachiever?

. . . Isn't able to handle the stress of making decisions on her own?

. . . Is a quitter because she tends to get discouraged when faced with a difficult task?

. . . Is really annoying to other girls?

For many parents, these questions become a springboard for yet another leap, to a thought that is as anguished as it is self-critical: *What does this mean about me as her parent?* Here is what parents have shared with me. "What if I . . ."

. . . Am too impatient to help and overworried?

. . . Enable my child's dependency and don't allow her to fail?

. . . Can't make her feel better?

. . . Am too strict and mean, and am creating a submissive future woman?

. . . Feed into her negative behavior?

. . . Do not have the right answers?

. . . Have low self-esteem?

. . . Yell too much for her to listen?

It is no wonder parents struggle. Spiraling thoughts about the unknown feed a need for certainty that is so uncomfortable, and so strong, it must be fed.

How do parents quash the uncertainty? By solving the problem for their daughter: fix and remove the worry, and bring the homework to school. By losing their temper: release the anxiety as anger and shout at her. Or by withdrawing: recede into quiet denial or shame. We do this (and I have done all three) because we're at the end of our rope, because we want to protect our daughters or because we want to calm ourselves down.

In doing so we communicate a vote of no confidence to our girls. "It takes us away from what *is* to the what *if* or what *should* be," writes Dr. Shefali Tsabary in her book *The Awakened Family*. "We veer away from our children's natural way of being and impose our conditioning, beliefs, and fears on them instead." We send the message that we don't trust them to handle things on their own and that their fears about themselves are sound.

The next time fear like this grips you, ask yourself three questions:

1. How important is it for her to have this particular skill (or have it at a certain level) right now?

2. Will not having this skill right now affect her overall potential to develop and thrive?

3. Why is it so important for *me* that she has this skill, and at this level of proficiency?

In my own parenting, these questions ground me. They help me disentangle fear from fact, and myself from my daughter. They force me to stop and reflect about what kind of success I really want for her, what it means to "develop and thrive," and whether my daughter wants or needs something in the same way I do.

These questions sit me down, look me in the eye, and say, *Is this worth making both of you crazy for? Does this matter in the scheme of things?* The point isn't to step away or stop parenting. It's to step back and exercise caution, to check ourselves, remembering that our anxiety leaves a deep impression on even the most indifferent seeming teens. "Fear is the reason our parenting somehow manages to produce results that are the exact opposite of what we were aiming for," Tsabary writes. There have been countless times in your life as a parent that a blip or delay worked itself out on its own, or with a much lighter touch. Is this one of those moments?

7. TEACH COMFORT WITH UNCERTAINTY

Girls need their parents to model being able to sit with what you both don't have the answer to. They must learn to see that place of uncertainty less as something to escape from than as a normal, if uncomfortable, part of life.

One way to do this is to avoid making promises you can't keep. If you're not 100 percent sure a situation will go her way, don't guarantee that it will. Sure, it may calm her down in the short term, but it keeps her from practicing two vital life skills: recognizing that she is not in control of the way life turns out, and accepting that there are some answers she will not be able to know immediately. She needs to hear you say, "I don't know the answer," and watch you be peaceful in that unknown.

One of the hardest feelings to parent through is a girl's belief that life will *always* be this way. You can't be sure of what comes next, but you can tell her that things will change. Embracing uncertainty as her parent means holding, for both of you, the knowledge that this moment will pass. She will not always feel this way.

I coach parents to ask themselves a question when they are faced with a parenting challenge and feel anxiety begin to tighten its grip: *How would I parent if I were not afraid?* That is, if I knew that despite whatever was happening with my daughter, she would turn out just fine, what would I say and do differently in this moment?

The parents' strategy nearly always changes on the spot. The question lets parents pull back from historical worry and destructive future thinking, making room for openness and optimism. They can stay in the moment with their daughter instead of being hijacked by their own fear.

In moments of uncertainty, hold fast to the rituals that anchor you. Exert the control you do have. Prepare a meal she loves (and don't talk about anything stressful while you eat it). Do something fun together. If she needs it, give her a mental health day.

8. PARENT THE DAUGHTER YOU HAVE, NOT THE DAUGHTER YOU WISH YOU HAD

There are some parents whose ambition exceeds their children's. These are the parents who contest a school's decision not to accept a girl into an honors program, who insist that their girls are being treated unfairly. It does not make a girl feel respected or loved to have her parents proclaim that the world doesn't understand how fabulous she is. It makes her suspect that her parents don't think she is enough as she is, and that she must be more than she appears to be capable of at this moment in time. It becomes an indirect form of parental criticism: instead of criticizing the girl, they criticize everyone else around her.

The upshot, write Drs. Suniya Luthar and Barry Schwartz, is that teens believe parental pride is contingent on being a star. "Children come to feel that any failure to accomplish will seriously diminish the acceptance and esteem with which their parents regard them."

Knowing how and when to criticize a daughter is far from a science. It is also your right as a parent. That said, more than a decade of research on high-achieving youth has shown that kids who receive parental criticism for failures consistently show adjustment problems like depression, anxiety, substance abuse, and delinquency. Luthar has shown that when teens think their parents disproportionately value their successes over character traits like kindness and respect, their symptoms are more pronounced.

Emily's mother micromanaged her schooling. She regularly pried her daughter's book bag open to organize her loose papers. At the beginning of tenth grade, her mother designed a two-year plan with everything Emily needed to do to get into West Point, a school Emily had only mentioned a passing interest in. The two fought often about Emily's work ethic, and Emily struggled with depression in the bitter northeastern winter. She had a blocky foam chair that she cut with a pocketknife when she was angry.

When I asked Emily if fighting with her mom was getting to her, she said something telling. "I think I have to do [all this work] for my mom or for my school or whoever. But I've never been, like, I have to do this because I want to do this. I want to feel accomplishment from this thing. It's, I have to do this so my mom won't yell at me."

The constant bickering made Emily feel unseen for who she was. "She took me more seriously than I took myself," Emily told me. It felt, she said, "like I'm kind of a joke to myself. It kind of degrades me, making me feel as if I'm not serious enough and I won't understand what [life is like] in the real world. That I'm too childish."

Calibrating parental expectations is the work of attunement, or the way a parent carefully listens to and responds to the cues a child provides. Attunement lets a child know that you recognize and are responding to her unique needs. Healthy attachment establishes the foundation for trust, empathy, and understanding in relationships: the one you have with her, and the ones she will later have with others. When attunement is disrupted or unreliable, so is attachment. When attunement is conditional, anxiety increases. Children may change their behavior, but it is only to win back the connection.

Attunement is far from easy when you have a daughter in a high-achieving environment. A daughter comes home and says she just needs one more AP class or leadership role to round off her résumé. One more thing won't hurt, she might say. I can handle it. It's easy to give in, even when you think she needs more balance.

It's an ongoing dilemma: parents want their daughters to relax, but they also want them to keep pace with their peers. Others say their daughter's pressure is self-inflicted: "It's not me telling her to work this hard," they'll say. Yet many of these same parents, Renee Spencer and her colleagues found in a 2016 study, admit to pressuring themselves to provide the "very best" for their children so they can pursue success.

I spend a lot of time talking with parents in communities around the country about how to support their daughters through this maelstrom. One of the toughest questions for me to answer goes something like this: "I can't stand how much pressure she's under. I hate this. I don't know what to do. How can I help her thrive here?"

The question always makes me pause. I sense that the parent wants me to absolve her of responsibility for her daughter's challenges, to implicate the culture, the system, the school. I get it. Who wouldn't want their child to have the best opportunities in life, and why should anyone feel guilty as a parent for wanting that?

On the one hand, families make choices that reflect their priorities. Just as a couple's choice to settle down in a certain suburb or city often suggests professional ambition, the choice to enroll a daughter in an exclusive school may point to a family's desire to make their daughter competitive in particular ways.

But that's not the end of the story. In fact, there are ways to shield your child from the most toxic elements of a hyperachieving environment. Because parents often transmit their values indirectly, psychologists have begun to study the *perception* children have of their parents' values, regardless of what Mom and Dad say they are. For example, a parent may say kindness to others is paramount, but his actions focus attention on high achievement and status; this, researchers say, lets children know he values these traits more.

Last year, Lucia Ciciolla and colleagues published a study of how over five hundred predominantly white, upper-middle-class middle school students perceived their parents' values. They found that children were consistently healthier when they believed their parents showed "low emphasis" on achievement. Children's functioning declined when they thought their parents valued achievement over kindness to others; their adjustment problems ranged from acting out and learning problems to lower self-esteem, delinquency, aggression, and anxiety. The children who fared best? Those who perceived their parents as equally valuing kindness and achievement, or kindness above all.

It's important to note that emphasis on achievement is not the problem. It's when focus on success is paired with high levels of criticism, or when that focus trumps values of kindness and connection. Indeed, the study found that parents who emphasized achievement were also often critical of their children, sometimes harshly; this led to symptoms of anxiety and depression in girls.

Remarkably, the researchers found that children's academic performance did not suffer when parents were less focused on achievement. In fact, the opposite happened: their grades and teacher ratings bested the kids with even one parent who "disproportion-ately" valued achievement.

ENOUGH AS YOU ARE

The *New York Times* columnist Frank Bruni wrote a book about college acceptance mania called *Where You Go Is Not Who You'll Be*. To this I would add: where she goes, or doesn't, is not who you'll be as her parent. If you believe her success or failure is not a referen-dum on her worth or potential, you must embrace the same logic for yourself and your parenting.

At a parenting workshop on helping girls deal with college anxiety, I divided moms and dads into pairs, then asked them to do the "I love . . ." exercise I described in chapter one. For sixty seconds each, without interruption, each parent shared all the things they loved about their daughters. It sounded like this: "I love her sense of humor. I love the way she walks around the house singing to herself. I love how she is with her grandmother." I asked the parents how many of them named a quality that would get their kid into college. The answer was zero.

Your daughter has become who she is in large part because of the values you raised her with. Have faith in what you have given her. We compete and compare with other parents in part because we question or lose sight of what we stand for in our own families. When we disconnect from that compass, we lose our bearings and ballast. It is easy to lose sight of what matters when you're confronted with a daily onslaught of the latest GPA and test score. When you question if you are enough, it's a short walk to doing the same with your daughter. But she needs to hear from you that she is enough as she is, right now, aside from her achievements. There is no one with more access to her enoughness than you.

10

The Senior Year Slap in the Face: Life After College

If it's not about getting into another school or grades, how do I think about what makes me happy, where I want to grow, and who I want to be?

—FAITH, TWENTY-FIVE

On graduation day from college, a young woman faces a radical reversal of the rules of the College Application Industrial Complex. Up until that point, there was a well-defined path to follow if she wanted a successful life. If she took that class, did this community service project, wrote this kind of essay, or applied for that internship, her résumé would look good and her life would work out.

The Path was all-important. Who she was sometimes mattered less than what she was doing. The message she got, explicitly or implied, was that if she didn't do the right things, checking off certain boxes on her résumé, she'd lose at a game that everyone else had figured out how to win. The pursuit of the Path was exacerbated by professors, parents, and career development counselors who warned that veering off might result in an unfulfilled, unhappy life.

There was something soothing about this Path-centered way of living. Her goals were defined for her. She got to measure herself in a tangible way by watching her grades, internships, jobs, and activities pile up. Each time she did something right, she got insta-feedback.

But here's what the Path may not have given her: comfort with uncertainty. The ability to make a sound decision in the face of multiple compelling choices. Time logged in a world where skills like how to pay an electric bill are valued. Practice working without constant feedback about her performance. The humility to perform entry-level work such as answering phones and getting coffee. Acceptance of the tough reality that every step she takes won't be of value in and of itself—that sometimes she will have to make uncomfortable, seemingly thankless temporary moves, or find stepping-stones to the next, better place.

The alarm goes off senior year. Aaliyah, twenty-five, called it the "senior year slap in the face": that moment when you realize the Path as you've known it is ending. The questions race through girls' minds: *What if I can't get a job? What if the job I have doesn't lead to where I want to go? What if I hate grad school? What if I make the wrong choice? Why don't I know how to do this?* The questions arise not because there is no path, but because women expect there to be a *single* one. Uncertainty should invite curiosity and reflection, but instead it generates fear.

Anxiety skyrockets for these women, and who can blame them? Many have spent the last four years, and maybe their whole lives, in what students and grads call "a bubble." Sharon, twenty-seven, told me, "You're in this little bubble where you think the world is one way, and everything is right there and accessible, and everything is taken care of for you." Maybe you had a meal plan. Maybe you lived on campus. Maybe you never really made your own schedule.

Now, said twenty-two-year-old Morgan, "You have to
landlords and gas companies and employers and sudde
on your own."

For girls who have grown up with few resources, life
can be a radical change of fortune. Brianna paid her wa
public university, where she graduated with honors with
She served in student senate, worked in a private resear
as a tutor. Days after graduation, she was cleaning hotel i
houses, and taking care of her ninety-year-old grandmc
dementia. "You thought you were this great achiever who i
marks," she told me. "Then life spits you out and you're ba
and you can't walk down the hall and ask the career service
what you should do next. You're just kind of on your own
very stuck."

Remember Wile E. Coyote? When I hear young women c
their first years out of college, I picture him skidding off tl
hanging sheepishly in the air, suspended for that split second
plummeting to the ground.

"After you get a job, after you move out of your parents' l
then you just have to live this life that doesn't have any check i
or points or anything. It's just your life," Maddie, twenty-two,
me. "Now I have to decide when's the right time to move to a
job or reconsider what I'm doing." But figuring out your next n
is a tall order, isn't it, when you've been given a precise path to fol
and never really had to make your own way.

Whether mistakes will be made is not in question. What v
matter and make the difference is how you interpret them togeth
Too many women default to the I'm-not-enough response wh
things don't go as planned. They drown themselves in self-blam
"Everything that I thought was going to happen went wrong. Ev
erything," Jasmine, twenty-three, told me. "It was just unnerving
to know that I wasn't prepared. Like I did something wrong." They

interpret the inevitable, everyday ups and downs of life after college as personal failures.

Your number one job as a parent is to tell your daughter that uncertainty, bad choices, and wrong turns—all these will mark the next five to seven years of her life. The reality facing her is both terrifying and liberating. This isn't something she gets to control if she only works hard enough. It is her developmental task to survive the gray, undecided muck of her twenties. It's her job to not always know, and it's her job to be clumsy. It's your job to stick with her, not let her shame herself, and keep reminding her how hard it is to go from a life where everything was planned and structured (college) to one that isn't.

You must promise her that she will figure it out slowly and get there eventually, and that one day she'll look back and realize that every step was getting her closer to where she needed to be.

Why didn't anyone warn me? she will ask. The truth is that no one really can. Like becoming a parent, plunging into the Real World isn't something you can do much to prepare for. She has to do it, just like you did when you became her parent, with all the mistake making, self-doubt, and unexpected moments of joy and triumph that being a parent entails. This journey is more uncertain than it's ever been for young adults, who until a few decades ago knew exactly what life held in store for most of them in their twenties: marriage, children, and steady, long-term jobs. "Adolescence is longer today than it has ever been in human history," writes Laurence Steinberg. Untethered to spouses and children, as they once were a generation ago, twentysomethings are today called "emerging adults" by psychologists, who have created a new developmental stage to describe this unique period.

And like parenthood, the Real World may enjoy a mythical status that, in practice, turns out to be untrue. Some girls enter college expecting the "best four years of their lives," only to realize that

college is far from that. Others dream that life after college will be filled with liberty and exploration, only to be disappointed. They discover that, despite upholding their part of the contract, working their tails off and getting good grades, they are bitterly betrayed by postgrad jobs that don't work out as planned, or at all.

This is a bittersweet moment for you and your daughter. Independence comes with fear and freedom, for both of you. Jasmine described the dilemma elegantly: "I feel empowered in the fact that I'm an adult who's in charge of her own life. At the same time it's really scary because it means I'm responsible for my whole life."

The metrics of success change, for nearly everything. "If it's not about getting into another school or grades," Faith, twenty-five, said, "how do I think about what makes me happy, where I want to grow, and who I want to be?" You need to be aware of the dramatic changes your daughter is confronting so you can help her transition out of college and embrace the challenges of the so-called Real World.

THE POSTCOLLEGE LIFE NEVER UNFOLDS ALONG A LINEAR PATH

Throughout this book, girls describe a split-screen mentality about their work: they focus on whatever they are doing in the moment, while keeping in mind whatever they have to do next. This is a multitasking maneuver, yes, but it also develops a habit of needing to know the next step at all times. It equates knowing what's next with control and effectiveness.

The idea that you should always have your next step in mind implies that you think each step leads seamlessly to the next, and that you should *know* exactly what those steps must be. This kind of reasoning no longer works after graduation. If knowing what's next becomes all-important for your daughter, she may force decisions that don't reflect what she really wants or is ready for. In the short term, that can feel like a comfort. In the long term, it can become a costly mess.

Implicit in the assumption that "I should know what's next" is the belief that girls should spring forth from college fully formed like Athena from the head of Zeus, armored up and ready for battle. "I thought college was supposedly the time when you developed your identity and then you could enter the real world," Faith told me. By this reasoning, it's a girl's fault if she doesn't have her life figured out by senior year. This can leave women feeling self-critical at best, and unwilling to seek support at worst.

Isabel was embarrassed by the need to network with alumnae from her alma mater. "I thought I would apply and get hired right away," she told me. "I have the mindset. I have been trained, I'm prepared, I should be able to do this myself."

All this can scare women away from taking steps that aren't a sure thing. "I've seen a diminished willingness to start life with all kinds of unknowns," said Stacie Hagenbaugh, director of Smith's Lazarus Center for Career Development. "This is a generation that thinks, 'Unless I have that job, unless it's a known jump, I'm not going to take that leap.'" For example, new graduates will not move to a city and *then* find a job, even though living locally increases their chances of getting hired.

Some are so paralyzed they won't even walk into the career services office. "They get to the edge of a cliff and they get stuck," Hagenbaugh said. "Many of them shut down. They're overwhelmed by the unknown, the fear, the not having the answer for what's next." Compassion is key here. "They've been so overprogrammed," Hagenbaugh added, echoing the comments of many higher education professionals I interviewed. "Everything's been decided for them. They've always known what's next."

Your daughter will need to hear from you about times in your life when you moved forward into a gray space without knowing the outcome.

Let her know that fear is not a reason to ride the bench and that you will have her back emotionally if things go sideways. If that involves moving back home for a time, it should happen for the right reasons: she needs time to think, save some money, recover from burnout. But home shouldn't be a proxy for confronting uncertainty. It shouldn't be a way to circumvent flexing the muscle of not knowing.

EVERY STEP WILL BE GOOD IN SOME WAYS, BUT ALMOST NEVER IN ALL WAYS

High-achieving girls fantasize about their first jobs in ways that closely resemble romantic myths. In the world of Disney and rom-coms, true love happens at first sight and lasts forever. So it should be, some girls reason, with that first job.

Cue the needle scratching on a record, because this will almost never be how her first job will play out. Just like she'll have to kiss a lot of frogs before she finds her prince or princess, she'll land in jobs that are unfulfilling, overwhelming, boring as hell, beyond wrong for her, and everything in between. This isn't her fault. It is a reality of adulthood. Life throws us unexpected curveballs. Sometimes there is little more to say.

The reason why this is so hard for your daughter is that in college, every step seemed to have a clear value in and of itself. When I talk with young women suffering at work, many ask the wrong questions. They want to know, *Why isn't this job giving me what I need? Where did I go wrong?* What she needs to ask instead is, *How can this job get me where I want to go next? What is this job teaching me about what I want and don't want?*

To continue the romance analogy, heartbreak teaches us what we truly want and need. The same is true of crap jobs. And just as it's not fair to expect your partner to be perfect, no job will meet every one of our needs. To give up an opportunity because it doesn't seem "just right" may mean giving up a lot of opportunities and missing out on one that could have been pretty good. "Pretty good," in your early twenties, is pretty damn great.

That's not to say your daughter should stay in a job where she's miserable. But it may mean temping to make money in a new city while she applies for a job, or taking a position that only gives her some but not all of what she wants. It can mean embracing a world-view that doesn't constantly put outcomes and destinations at the top of every list. It understands her path in terms of a journey. It is a road that winds, and it is a road that can totally bite. But it is a road that she must trust is taking her where she needs to go.

Morgan passed up an AmeriCorps job for a nanny position she quickly regretted taking. At first she beat herself up for making the wrong decision. Over time, she realized the misstep taught her lessons she didn't know she had to learn: how to make decisions based more on logic than on emotion. The need to be fiercely honest with herself about her choices. Learning to ask for help with challenging cover letters. And embracing the reality that "sometimes you have to make sacrifices to get where you want to go. It means sometimes you won't get exactly where you want. You're going to do things that aren't the most appealing work, but they'll prepare you for what you want to be doing."

In the world of home buying, real estate experts advise you to come up with the three must-haves you want in a new home—the stuff you can't (or don't want to) live without. It's a useful question here, too: What are the three most important things you want from a job?

I asked this question of Abby, a twenty-two-year-old senior

economics major and cross-country runner, who is also one of my babysitters. We were on a run together through icy New England woods with my dog. She panted for a while, then said: "I want to be near my friends, either from high school or college. I want to do something related to the environment. And I want to do something that directly affects people's lives, like finding someone housing." Her criteria were fair: not so specific that only a few jobs would work, and not so wide-ranging that no job could ever satisfy her. The question asks you to zero in on what matters to you most, but it makes clear that no one job, just like no one house, will ever offer anyone everything.

FROM SEXISM TO RACISM AND BEYOND, THE WORKPLACE IS FULL OF VARIABLES IMPOSSIBLE TO CONTROL

In high school and college, hard-driving young women exercise vigorous control over their lives. They decide how hard they work or study, and most function in a (presumably) meritocratic system where effort and intelligence are rewarded in reasonably predictable ways.

In the Real World, how smart you are and how hard you work won't protect even the highest achieving woman from things beyond her control. Jasmine, twenty-three, was recruited by a college trustee to work in public relations in Washington. The interview process was full of red flags, but Jasmine persisted. Within three months she was being bullied by her boss, who said things like, "I know you think you're better than everyone because of your education, but you're not."

Jasmine is African American and believed her boss's treatment had racist undertones. She was scared to say anything. Eventually she found the courage to leave with her parents' blessing, with loans coming due and no savings. She began taking classes to gain student status, and got an internship that eventually became a job in the White House.

Had Jasmine not believed she could control these variables, she might never have left the job. "I would never be here [at the White House] if I had stayed, or listened to my boss tell me that I wasn't good enough."

THE DAYS OF HAND-HOLDING ARE OVER

In college, your daughter would offer up her best self in her work, by taking an exam or writing a paper, and there was swift feedback from professors. At school, Morgan told me, if she applied to something but didn't get it, professors "would at least reach out and say, 'Hey, you didn't get in, sorry.'"

Out in the job market, positive affirmation is gone. So is the hand-holding. Alyssa graduated magna cum laude with a degree in American studies from a New England college. She spoke at her commencement and sang the national anthem. "It was the highest of the high coming out [of college]," she told me over coffee. "I was convinced there was no way an employer would see my résumé and turn me down. I truly thought I could do anything."

She sent out résumé after résumé. Crickets. As the months wore on, her hope deflated with her ego. "It feels like, does what I do have any value or worth in this world?" she said.

In the Real World, résumés and calls may be met with the crushing sound of silence. You offer up yourself, and "you don't even hear from people," said Isabel. *They don't respond.*

Isabel would obsessively refresh her e-mail after submitting her résumé. She fought hard against the growing dread that this was her fault and that she was a failure. A constant stream of rejection or silence makes it hard to keep up the incessant self-promotion required to thrive as an applicant. "It's really hard after accruing all this great stuff [in college] to then confidently talk about it, especially if it's not amounting to anything," Faith said. I can't count the number of young women who have described this kind of rejection to me as "crushing."

Rejection in the job market forces a reckoning with the ways young women have assigned value to themselves. For years, grades and scores were tangible measures of worth, not unlike the way "likes" became concrete measures of popularity on social media. When the numbers evaporate, so does the avenue to a sense of satisfaction and self-worth. "We get caught up in achieving to succeed, but then when the achievements go away we don't have that thing inside of ourselves to hold us up," Faith said.

Morgan and Isabel have both worked on reminding themselves of their own value irrespective of someone's response to their applications. Isabel tries saying the words out loud: "This is not my fault." She reaches out to her family for support when she finds herself hungry for affirmation. Morgan works on internal affirmations that connect her to why she is enough as she is. "You have to keep your own sense of, 'I'm still a great person and have lots of value,'" she told me, "in a way you don't have to in school because you're always having your hand held."

In *Playing Big*, Tara Mohr tells women to accept the feedback of others as information about the people giving the feedback, not as a definitive statement about your work, or you. The same can be said of the "feedback" from a job inquiry. When you don't get a response, Isabel told me, "It's good to think about the needs of that particular hiring person, and not necessarily what you're bringing, because otherwise you'll feel that you're not good for anything that's out there."

AMAZING STILL HAS TO GET COFFEE
AND ANSWER PHONES

Older adults talk a lot of trash about the work ethic of young adults, who are regularly labeled entitled, unwilling to pay their dues, and arrogant. They balk at entry-level positions. They project a sense that "I've worked really hard, I've done all these things, I shouldn't have to answer phones. I shouldn't have to consider an administrative assistant job," a director of a college career services center told me. I admit I have seen this myself. When I was hiring for a position at the nonprofit I cofounded, I was astonished by the high-minded tone of the cover letters I received. Twenty-two-year-olds with the ink drying on their degrees identified themselves as "sociologists." I would finish reading cover letters describing the candidates' vast experience and expertise, and assume they were written by applicants twenty years out of college.

This actually shouldn't surprise anyone. This generation of young adults has been pressured to brand themselves into ever more perfect packaging, to embellish their résumés so that they appear as fabulous and exceptional and as admissions-worthy as possible. They are pushed to do this by well-meaning parents, college counselors, and career services centers. Is it no wonder, then, that they expect to do and be more when they graduate? If you have been told to represent yourself as the most extraordinary person around, why take a job where you do little more than file, answer phones, and take notes at meetings?

Humility may be in short supply when a young woman takes her first job. This deserves compassion, not scorn, and patience as she learns to make the transition to reality. Help her understand that acting as if she's beyond her job can repel colleagues who might promote her. It can also diminish the workplace relationships that make tough first jobs manageable and even fun.

SOCIAL MEDIA IS CURATED. EVERYONE STRUGGLES IN THEIR OWN WAY AND AT DIFFERENT TIMES.

If social media is important in college, it becomes even more critical afterward. As friends go their separate ways, they rely more and more on their phones and laptops to connect. Job applications are submitted electronically, and interviews take place on video chat. During times of transition and social rupture, feedback online can compensate for a profound relational loss. "I don't have that constant feedback from thirty professors and twenty friends," Tala, twenty-three, explained. "I turn to social media really because I don't have all those people. I don't just count the likes. I look at who's liking."

But social media, with its feeds teeming with announcements of new jobs, new apartments, moves to new cities, and grad school admissions, can be downright brutal in the first years after college. "So happy to announce that I already have a job after graduation," goes a typical post. "So excited to see what this opportunity holds and so grateful for all the guidance and advice I have received along the way." Social media cruelly reproduces the messages of the College Application Industrial Complex: its carefully curated posts represent life as a seamless transition from college with the perfect job, or city, or school, or roommate, or apartment—and then marriage, babies, and degrees for everyone, seemingly, but you.

If your daughter is struggling, social media will dig the knife in even deeper. "You see the rose-colored, glossed-over version [of life] on Facebook that makes it look like they're partying it up in the city they're living in, living in luxury, having the greatest life ever, and it makes you think, 'What am I doing wrong?'" Morgan told me. You compare yourself to others and wonder how you measure up. "You question, 'Am I doing the age-appropriate thing right now?'" Jasmine said. "'Am I on the right track?'" What most women don't realize is that you can make any decision look confident and "right," just like you can make your arms look thinner if you stand at the right angle. It's all about how you portray it, and social media offers a million ways to pretend.

The community social media offers is largely plastic. It produces precisely the opposite of what women need after college: authentic connections with people whose lives and feelings resemble their own. As picture after picture, and post after post portray unblemished lives, women sink lower into isolation. "You think everyone else has got it together so you don't want to be the one to say that you don't," Sharon said.

Social media is "me, me, me." What young women need during this time is a "me, too." Face-to-face connecting with others opens up real conversations. Morgan discovered that being vulnerable with friends yielded a very different story than the one she saw online. "They're miserable," she said of her friends. "They have long hours, they have pretty bad relationships with their bosses in terms of being expected to do everything, and often they're not happy." Real conversations about what's actually happening diminish shame and the impulse to retreat into not-enough. This is especially true for nonwhite, low-income, queer, and first-generation women.

THE UPSIDE OF POSTCOLLEGE LIFE

The College Application Industrial Complex too often creates an environment where young adults disengage from what they actually want to do and learn and be. This happens just at the moment when they should be becoming directors of their own lives, not performers. Advised to focus on external expectations, many disconnect from the internal compass that tells them things like: *I lose track of time when I do this activity. I don't want to work in this lab all night.*

I could read books like this all day. Some trade gut feelings for what they are told will make them successful. Others choose safer paths instead of rockier, more exciting roads. Some lose touch with themselves and what they stand for.

After college, some will repress their ignorance of themselves and blindly take the next step. The wiser, luckier ones will suffer through the vertigo of realizing they have no clue. If they give themselves a chance to ask hard questions of themselves, they will get to a next step they feel genuinely good about.

Like many of her peers, Isabel had focused most of her attention outward: she monitored her friends' achievements online and worried about pleasing her family. Now, when she applies for a new opportunity, Isabel sits down and thinks about how she feels about it. "Am I feeling this way because this is what I really want?" she asks herself. "Or because my parents would be happy, or because my friends would brag about me, or because I'm going to get calls from my college to be interviewed [for the alumnae magazine]?"

Isabel tries to understand if her motivation is external or internal: Is she doing it for herself or for someone else? The key is taking her own voice seriously: believing that what she wants matters as much as any other competing interest. For girls, this is a paramount concern, especially for the women who grapple with the desire to please their parents. Faith had worked at a foundation for three years. She wanted badly to please her mother, a first-generation American from Korea, but she balked at her mother's traditional view of success. "How do I explain to my mom that growth isn't necessarily accumulating graduate degrees or being senior management?" she asked me. "I'm searching for what fulfills me." Daughters of immigrants who enjoy more opportunity than any generation before them told me they were haunted by the pressure to do right by their elders.

As hard as life can be after college, it also comes with perks. There is more free time. If your daughter is not in school, she can leave her work at the office. Morgan, who initially took the wrong job, reclaimed her autonomy in her free time. She began drawing again and taking regular walks. A graduate of my Leadership for Rebels course, she practiced a nightly check-in with herself. "I make a conscious effort to see if I like what I'm doing regularly during my evenings and weekends. If I don't, I change it," she told me. Facing rejection as she applies for jobs is painful, but it has also made her a lot tougher. "Now, when I don't get something I want, I'm able to realize that I have worth without that one acceptance. I try and remind myself that applying taught me something about myself and that I will have wins and losses. The more I do it," she said happily, "the easier it becomes."

CONCLUSION
"DEAREST DAUGHTER: LEAN INSIDE"

I was sitting with students on a midterm study break, listening to them talk about all-nighters and exam overload, when a question popped into my mind.

"What do you guys see as a happy life?" I asked. There was uncharacteristic silence in their dorm living room.

"I just want to be outside," one finally said.

"I want to have good relationships. Friends and family and community."

"I want to stay in touch with my family wherever I go."

"I want to have time to explore the place I'm in. I want to sit down and read all kinds of books. I want to immerse myself wherever I am."

"I really want a cat."

"I want to feel like I'm doing something good for the world, whatever size that world is. Good for other people, or the environment, but I want a positive impact."

Watching them draped across couches, slippered feet dangling off their chairs, I felt something shift in the room. It was clear few of them had reflected on this question. As they spoke, their voices grew stronger and more animated. Their hope and inspiration were palpable.

The driven, hardworking girls I met while writing this book rarely spoke about their futures in terms of what made them happy. Instead, they constantly battled messages exhorting them to be *more*. The *more* they felt compelled to become lay somewhere off in the future: more miles on the treadmill tomorrow, more hours in the library next semester, more social media–worthy posts on Saturday night. *More* was the future they were told to aspire to. It was not a *more* they had created, nor was it one they authentically desired.

Our girls will begin to feel that they are enough as they are when we help them replace the culture's toxic voice of *more* with their own vision of a fulfilled life—one that doesn't choose external rewards over purpose and connection to others. For if we have long known that good girls are taught to repress their feelings in order to be liked, what I learned in writing this book is that they must also defer to someone else's definition of success. It is a Faustian bargain. As Anna Quindlen has written, "If your success is not on your own terms, if it looks good to the world but does not feel good in your heart, it is not success at all."

One of the most popular classes taught at Harvard was about something many of its hard-driving students lived without: happiness. A leader in the field of positive psychology, Professor Tal Ben-Shahar told his rapt students that happiness was the ultimate currency in life—more than wealth, achievements, or material possessions—and that they should live their lives in a way that maximized it.

Happiness, Ben-Shahar argued, is a two-part equation, achieved when we find the right balance of meaning and pleasure, and when we are engaged in an activity that has both present and future benefit. These are pursuits that both absorb us and require us to contribute to the world beyond ourselves (Stanford's William Damon called this *purpose*).

As I interviewed girls living in the College Application Industrial Complex, and the undergraduates who had just left it, I was struck by how the very terms of their lives ran opposite to everything we know about happiness. Developing a sense of meaning is replaced by the relentless pursuit of outside rewards. Students are pushed to disregard the journey of learning in order to fixate on the end result. To avoid failure, they steer clear of the challenges that can lead to the peak learning experience of "flow." They experience a sense of being loved not for their intrinsic selves but for their accomplishments. If they possess unusual interests that don't meet the Complex's criteria for success and college admission, these interests are ignored and frequently atrophy.

I often ask my students to plug their daily activities into this happiness "equation." Ben-Shahar offers as concrete a recipe as we may ever find for feeling good in your life. How much of what they do each day combines genuine pleasure and meaning? What proportion of a given week is what they want to do versus have to do? Their schedules are dominated by "have-tos."

My five-year-old daughter loves puzzles. She spends hours on the living room floor forming scenes of princesses, unicorns, and jungle animals. Sometimes I sit with her and watch her turn a single piece this way and that, working to find the fit. She is preternaturally patient and focused. When she finally figures it out, she lets out an ebullient, gusty "YESSSSS!"

There is no better sound than that *yes.* It is the yes of a challenge she had the authority to choose, a risk faced and squarely taken. It is a reward earned through persistence and commitment. It is her yes, and it is for her and no one else.

I want all girls to have access to their own yes. I don't want my daughter to lose hers. It's our job as parents to clear the space for them to find it. We are girls' best hope in the face of the most toxic messages they hear. We must stand up for them, either at the dinner table when they express outrage or when we implore them not to give up on a treasured "want-to" in their lives.

This is not a call for you to sabotage her ability to excel. To the contrary: I tell all my students to continue to compete and shine. But no girl should have to sacrifice her self-worth, wellness, or curiosity in exchange for distinction. I hope this book will help you keep her from making that terrible trade.

No matter how much things change for girls, the bedrock of raising them well remains as vital as ever. First, your willingness to listen to and empathize with your daughter will matter more than anything you *do* to fix a problem on her behalf. What every girl wants from adults is validation for her challenge without judgment, empathy for her feelings, and fellowship in her struggle. This is what she will remember, even when you can do little to change the obligations the outside world enforces.

Second, no matter how damaging this culture, or how loud its voice of *more* rings in her ears, she is still listening to you. She still cares about what you think, even if every gesture and sigh and eye roll suggest otherwise. And what she needs to know, more than anything else, is that who she is right now is enough for you. I have come to see that the most meaningful, if not revolutionary, success we can nourish in our girls is helping them see that they are enough, exactly as they are—that at the end of the day, wherever they've landed, they are enough because they are good friends or sisters, because they made eye contact with someone who sits alone at lunch, because they feed the dog when everyone else forgets to, because they don't give up when they fall down.

What if our girls could accept and honor exactly who they are today? What if they could remember that they still matter, no matter what? To me, that's the beginning of true success.

ACKNOWLEDGMENTS

To the inimitable Gails: Winston, you are a dream. I feel lucky every day to be guided by you. Ross, thanks for sticking with me through every hill and valley, for being a peerless thought partner, for your sparkling integrity, and for loving me and my kid.

To the friends and colleagues who read drafts and offered critical feedback along the way, thank you for making this book so much better: Emily Bazelon, Dr. Marisa LaDuca Crandall, Blaine Edens, Lilly Jay, Armistead Lemon, Dr. Donna Lisker, Marge Litchford, Dr. Suniya Luthar, Julie Mencher, Peggy Orenstein, Maya Bernstein Schalet, Dr. Julia Taylor, and Jessica Weiner.

I am grateful to the Wurtele Center for Work & Life at Smith College for giving me the time and space to ask new questions, take risks, and listen to young women's voices. I also thank Hannah Durrant, Stacie Hagenbaugh, and Julianne Ohotnicky for their patience, teaching, and good humor; and Ellen Carter and the Stoneleigh-Burnham School for their ongoing partnership.

Dr. Tara Christie Kinsey and the Hewitt School have gifted me with a community in which I can learn, be challenged, and teach. I am proud to be a Hewitt girl. Simone Marean and Girls Leadership have been steadfast thought partners, and I am grateful to get to work with them on behalf of girls every day.

Thank you to my hardworking research assistants: Lindsey Chou, Shanila Sattar, and Leanne Arsenault, who helped guide this book to completion.

To my kickass, loving village, the people who love me no matter what and slay me six ways to Sunday: Julie Barer, Gwen Bass, Maggie Bittel and Barry, Henry and Owen Daggett, Nicole Bourdon and Josh Levy, Judith Holiber and Kim, Jake and Rachel Warsaw, Cathie Levine and Josh, Benji and Ruby Isay, Jane Isay, Julie Koster, Becky Shaw, Pamela Shifman and Lee Schere, Sam and Colleen Taylor, Daniella Topol and Joe Slott.

Elita Baker and Alex Viera, thank you for loving and teaching our girl, and taking such good care of us both while I worked on this book.

To my family: Josh and Tony, Dad, Lia, Jaynie and Scott, and Ziggy. Finally, to my mother, Claire, whose fierce care of me and my daughter created a space in which this book could come to life.

I couldn't have done this without you.

APPENDIX

Age and Disclosed Racial Identity of Interview Subjects

Name	Age	Race/Ethnicity
Rebecca	16	White
Lily	16	White
Tala	23	Lebanese American
Emily	16	White
Hannah	19	White
Casey	20	White
Jennie	20	White
Jessica	16	White
Isabel	27	Cuban Immigrant
Maya	18	White
Kayla	19	White
Natalia	18	White
Alexis	20	White
Vivian	20	South Asian American
Grace	17	White
Haley	26	White
Anna	19	Biracial (Chinese and White)
Bianca	17	Hispanic
Kaitlyn	24	White
Amira	17	Indian American
Iyana	17	Black
Kavya	16	South Asian American

Lauren	16	White
Amy	16	Korean American
Katie	19	White
Jessie	19	White
Morgan	22	White
Lee	19	African American
Hadia	19	Arab American
Anu	27	Sri Lankan Immigrant
Silvia	19	Mexican American
Jordan	22	White
Jasmine	23	African American
Avesha	16	Sri Lankan American
Allison	17	White
Harper	16	White
Joanna	17	White
Claire	22	White
Phoebe	21	Chinese American
Julia	21	Hispanic
Kelsey	21	White
Nora	19	White
Zoe	16	White
Maggie	22	White
Jahleese	21	Biracial (African American and Puerto Rican)
Sadia	19	Bangladeshi American
Aaliyah	25	African American
Sharon	27	White
Maddie	22	White
Faith	25	Korean American
Alyssa	23	White

Abby	22	White
Nicole	21	Hispanic
Emma	18	White
Brianna	22	White

SELECTED BIBLIOGRAPHY

Afifi, Tamara, Walid Afifi, Anne F. Merrill, Amanda Denes, and Sharde Davis. "'You Need to Stop Talking About This!': Verbal Rumination and the Costs of Social Support." *Human Communication Research* 39, no. 4 (2013): 395-421.

Archard, Nicole. "Adolescent Girls and Leadership: The Impact of Confidence, Competition and Failure." *International Journal of Adolescents and Youth* 17, no. 4 (2012): 189-203.

Armstrong, Elizabeth A., and Laura T. Hamilton. *Paying for the Party: How College Maintains Inequality.* Cambridge, MA: Harvard University Press, 2013.

Aronson, Joshua, Carrie B. Fried, and Catherine Good. "Reducing the Effects of Stereotype Threat on African American College Students by Shaping Theories of Intelligence." *Journal of Experimental Social Psychology* 38, no. 2 (2002): 113-125.

Asser, Eliot S. "Social Class and Help-Seeking Behavior." *American Journal of Community Psychology* 6, no. 5 (1978): 465-475.

Atlantis, Evan, and Kylie Ball. "Association Between Weight Perception and Psychological Distress." *International Journal of Obesity* 32, no. 4 (2008): 715-721.

Bagrowicz, Rinako, Chiho Watanabe, and Masahiro Umezaki. "Is Obesity Contagious by Way of Body Image? A Study of Japanese Female Students in the United States." *Journal of Community Health: The Publication for Health Promotion and Disease Prevention* 38, no. 5 (2013): 834-837.

Baker, Buffy, Katy Bowers, Jess Hill, Jenny Jervis, Armistead Lemon, Maddie Waud, and Adam Wilsman. "How an Online Gradebook May Impact Student Learning, Development and Mental Health at Harper Hill." Harpeth Hall School. Unpublished manuscript, last modified 2016.

Barstead, Matthew G., Laura C. Bouchard, and Josephine H. Shih. "Understanding Gender Differences in Co-Rumination and Confidant Choice in Young Adults." *Journal of Social and Clinical Psychology* 32, no. 7 (2013): 791-808.

Ben-Shahar, Tal. *Happier: Learn the Secrets to Daily Joy and Lasting Fulfillment*. New York: McGraw-Hill, 2007.

Bettina, Spencer, Caitilin Barrett, Gina Storti, and Mara Cole. "'Only Girls Who Want Fat Legs Take the Elevator': Body Image in Single-Sex and Mixed-Sex Colleges." *Sex Roles* 69, no. 7-8 (2013): 469-479.

Blattner, Meghan C. C., Belle Lang, Terese Lund, and Renee Spencer. "Searching for a Sense of Purpose: The Role of Parents and Effects on Self-Esteem Among Female Adolescents." *Journal of Adolescence* 36, no. 5 (2013): 839-848.

Bluth, Karen, Rebecca A. Campo, William S. Futch, and Susan A. Gaylord. "Age and Gender Differences in the Associations of Self-Compassion and Emotional Well-Being in a Large Adolescent Sample." *Journal of Youth and Adolescence* 46, no. 4 (2017): 840-853.

Boepple, L., and J. K. Thompson. "A Content Analytic Comparison Of Fitspiration And Thinspiration Websites." *International Journal of Eating Disorders* 49, no. 1 (January 2016): 98-101.

Booth, Alison L., and Patrick Nolen. "Gender Differences in Risk Behaviour: Does Nurture Matter?" *Economic Journal* 122, no. 558 (2012): F56-F78.

Boyd, Danah Michele. "Taken out of Context: American Teen Sociality in Networked Publics." *Dissertation Abstracts International Section A: Humanities and Social Sciences* 70, no. 4-A (2009): 1073.

Brougham, Ruby R., Christy M. Zail, Celeste M. Mendoza, and Janine R. Miller. "Stress, Sex Differences, and Coping Strategies Among College Students." *Current Psychology* 28, no. 2 (2009): 85-97.

Brown, Brené. *Daring Greatly: How the Courage to Be Vulnerable Transforms the Way We Live, Love, Parent, and Lead.* London: Penguin, 2013.

———. *The Gifts of Imperfect Parenting: Raising Children with Courage, Compassion and Connection.* Louisville, CO: Sounds True, 2013. Audiobook, 2 compact discs; 2 hrs., 6 mins.

Brown, Z., and M. Tiggemann. "Attractive Celebrity and Peer Images on Instagram: Effect on Women's Mood and Body Image." *Body Image* 19 (2016): 37-43.

Byrnes, James P., David C. Miller, and William D. Schafer. "Gender Differences in Risk Taking: A Meta-Analysis." *Psychological Bulletin* 125, no. 3 (1995): 367-383.

Calmes, Christine A., and John E. Roberts. "Rumination in Interpersonal Relationships: Does Co-Rumination Explain Gender Differences in Emotional Distress and Relationship Satisfaction Among College Students?" *Cognitive Therapy and Research* 32, no. 4 (2008): 577-590.

Calogero, Rachel M., Sylvia Herbozo, and Kevin J. Thompson. "Complimentary Weightism: The Potential Costs of Appearance-Related Commentary of Women's Self-Objectification." *Psychology of Women Quarterly* 33, no. 1 (2009): 120-132.

Carlson, Cassandra L. "Seeking Self-Sufficiency: Why Emerging Adult College Students Receive and Implement Parental Advice." *Emerging Adulthood* 2, no. 4 (2014): 257-269.

Chang, Janet. "The Interplay Between Collectivism and Social Support Processes Among Asian and Latino American College Students." *Asian American Journal of Psychology* 6, no. 1 (2015): 4-14.

Chou, Hui-Tzu Grace, and Nicholas Edge. "'They Are Happier and Having Better Lives Than I Am': The Impact of Using Facebook on Perceptions of Others' Lives." *Cyberpsychology, Behavior, and Social Networking* 15, no. 2 (February 2012): 117-120.

Ciciolla, Lucia, Alexandria S. Curlee, Jason Karageorge, and Suniya S. Luthar. "When Mothers and Fathers Are Seen as Disproportionately Valuing Achievements." *Journal of Youth and Adolescents* 46, no. 5 (2017): 1057-1075.

Ciesla, Jeffrey A., Kelsey S. Dickson, Nicholas L. Anderson, and Dan J. Neal. "Negative Repetitive Thought and College Drinking: Angry Rumination, Depressive Rumination, Co-Rumination, and Worry." *Cognitive Therapy and Research* 35, no. 2 (2011): 142-150.

Clance, Pauline R., and Suzanne Imes. "The Imposter Phenomenon in High-Achieving Women: Dynamics and Therapeutic Intervention." *Psychotherapy Research and Practice* 15, no. 3 (1978).

Clonan-Roy, Katie, Charlotte E. Jacobs, and Michael J. Nakkula. "Toward a Model of Positive Youth Development Specific to Girls of Color." *Gender Issues* 33, no. 2 (2016): 96-121.

Coffman, Katherine Baldiga. "Evidence on Self-Stereotyping and the Contribution of Ideas." *Quarterly Journal of Economics* 129, no. 4 (2014): 1625-1660.

Cokley, Kevin, Germine Awad, Leann Smith, Stacey Jackson, Olufunke Awosogba, Ashley Hurst, Steven Stone, Lauren Blondeau, and David Roberts. "The Roles of Gender Stigma Consciousness, Imposter Phenomenon and Academic Self-Concept in the Academic Outcomes of Women and Men Coping with Achievement Related Failure." *Sex Roles* 73, no. 9–10 (2015): 414-426.

Damon, William. *The Path: How Young People Find Their Calling in Life*. New York: Free Press, 2009.

Damour, Lisa. *Untangled: Guiding Teenage Girls Through the 7 Transitions to Adulthood*. New York: Penguin Random House, 2016.

Dariotis, Jacinda K., and Matthew W. Johnson. "Sexual Discounting Among High-Risk Youth Ages 18-24: Implications for Sexual and Substance Use Risk Behaviors." *Experimental and Clinical Pharmacology* 23, no. 1 (2015): 49-58.

Davila, Joanne, Rachel Hershenberg, Brian A. Feinstein, Kaitlyn Gorman, Vickie Bhatia, and Lisa R. Starr. "Frequency and Quality of Social Networking Among Young Adults: Associations with Depressive Symptoms Rumination and Corumination." *Psychology of Popular Media Culture* 1, no. 2 (2012): 72-86.

Deci and Ryan cited in Henderlong, Jennifer, and Mark R. Lepper. "The Effects of Praise on Children's Intrinsic Motivation: A Review and Synthesis." *Psychological Bulletin* 128, no. 5 (September 2002): 774-795.

De Vries, Dian A., and Jochen Peter. "Women on Display: The Effect of Portraying the Self Online on Women's Self-Objectification." *Computers in Human Behavior* 29, no. 4 (2013): 1483-1489.

Dixon, Wayne A., Kimberly G. Rumford, Paul P. Heppner, and Barbara J. Lips. "Use of Different Sources of Stress to Predict Hopelessness and Suicide Ideation in a College Population." *Journal of Counseling Psychology* 39, no. 3 (1992): 342-349.

Dunkley, David M., Kirk R. Blankstein, Jennifer Halsall, Meredith Williams, and Gary Winkworth. "The Relation Between Perfectionism and Distress: Hassles, Coping, and Perceived Social Support as Mediators and Moderators." *Journal of Counseling Psychology* 47, no. 4 (2000): 437-453.

Dweck, Carol S. "Is Math a Gift? Beliefs That Put Females at Risk." In *Why Aren't More Women in Science?: Top Researchers Debate the Evidence*, edited by Stephan J. Ceci and Wendy M. Williams. Washington, DC: American Psychological Association, 2007.

———. *Mindset: The New Psychology of Success*. New York: Random House, 2006.

Eagon, Kevin, Ellen Bara Stolzenberg, Joseph J. Ramirez, Melissa C. Aragon, Maria Ramirez Suchard, and Cecilia Rios-Aguilar. *The American Freshman: Fifty-Year Trends, 1966–2015*. Los Angeles: Higher Education Research Institute, UCLA, 2016.

Economos, Christina D., Lise M. Hildebrandt, and Raymond R. Hyatt. "College Freshman Stress and Weight Change: Differences by Gender." *American Journal of Health Behavior* 23, no. 1 (2008): 16-25.

Elliot, Andrew J., and Marcy A. Church. "A Motivational Analysis of Defensive Pessimism and Self-Handicapping." *Journal of Personality* 71, no. 3 (2003): 369-396.

Engeln-Maddox, Renee, and Rachel H. Salk. "The Demographics of Fat Talk in Adult Women: Age, Body Size, and Ethnicity." *Journal of Health Psychology* 21, no. 8 (August 2016): 1655-1664.

Flanagan, Caitlin. "How Helicopter Parenting Can Cause Binge Drinking." *The Atlantic*, September 2016.

Florin, Todd A., Justine Shultz, and Nicolas Stettler. "Perception of Overweight Is Associated with Poor Academic Performance in US Adolescents." *Journal of School Health* 81, no. 11 (2011): 663-670.

Frazier, Patricia A., and Laura J. Schauben. "Stressful Life Events and Psychological Adjustment Among Female College Students." *Measurement and Evaluation in Counseling and Development* 27, no. 1 (1994): 280-292.

Fredrickson, Barbara L., Tomi-Ann Roberts, Stephanie M. Noll, Diane M. Quinn, and Jean M. Twenge. "That Swimsuit Becomes You: Sex Differences in Self-Objectification, Restrained Eating, and Math Performance." *Journal of Personality and Social Psychology* 75, no. 1 (1998): 269-284.

Gay, Robin K., and Emanuele Castano. "My Body on My Mind: The Impact of State and Trait Objectification on Women's Cognitive Resources." *European Journal of Social Psychology* 40, no. 5 (2010): 695-703.

Gentile, Brittany, Shelly Grabe, Brenda Dolan-Pascoe, Jean M. Twenge, Brooke E. Wells, and Alissa Maitino. "Gender Difference in Domain Specific Self-Esteem: A Meta-Analysis." *Review of General Psychology* 13, no. 1 (2009): 34-45.

"Girls' Attitudes Survey," Girlguides UK: London, 2014.

Gnaulati, Enrico. "Why Girls Tend to Get Better Grades Than Boys Do." *The Atlantic*, September 18, 2014.

Goswani, Sweta, Sandeep Sachdeva, and Ruchi Sachdeva. "Body Image and Satisfaction Among Female College Students." *Industrial Psychiatry Journal* 21, no. 2 (2012): 168-172.

Grabe, Shelly, and Janet Shibley Hyde. "Body Objectification, MTV, and Psychological Outcomes Among Female Adolescents." *Journal of Applied Social Psychology* 39, no. 12 (2009): 2840-2858.

———. "Ethnicity and Body Dissatisfaction Among Women in the United States: A Meta-Analysis." *Psychological Bulletin* 132, no. 4 (2006): 622-640.

Grabe, Shelly, Janet Shibley Hyde, and Sara M. Lindberg. "Body Objectification and Depression in Adolescents: The Role of Gender, Shame, and Rumination." *Psychology of Women Quarterly* 31, no. 2 (2007): 164-175.

Hankin, Benjamin L., Lindsey Stone, and Patricia Ann Wright. "Co-Rumination, Interpersonal Stress Generation, and Internalizing Symptoms: Accumulating Effects and Transactional Influences in a Multiwave Study of Adolescents." *Development and Psychopathology* 22, no. 1 (2010): 217-235.

Harackiewicz, Judith M., and Andrew J. Elliot. "Achievement Goals and Intrinsic Motivation." *Journal of Personality and Social Psychology* 65, no. 5 (November 1993): 904-915.

Haydon, Katherine C. "Relational Contexts of Women's Stress and Competence During the Transition to Adulthood." *Journal of Adult Development* 22, no. 2 (2015): 112-123.

Hesse-Biber, Sharlene, Patricia Leavy, Courtney E. Quinn, and Julia Zoino. "The Mass Marketing of Disordered Eating and Eating Disorders: The Social Psychology of Women, Thinness and Culture." *Women's Studies International Forum* 29, no. 2 (2006): 208-224.

Hicks, Terrence, and Samuel Heastie. "High School to College Transition: A Profile of Stressors, Physical and Psychological Health Issues That Affect the First-Year On-Campus College Student." *Journal of Cultural Diversity* 15, no. 3 (2008): 143-147.

Hicks, Terrence, and Eboni Miller. "College Life Style, Life Stressors and Health Status: Differences Along Gender Lines." *Journal of College Admission* 192 (2006): 22-29.

Hinkelman, L. "The Girls' Index: New Insights Into The Complex World Of Today's Girls." Ruling Our eXperiences, Inc. Columbus, OH: 2017.

Holland, Grace, and Marika Tiggemann. "A Systematic Review of the Impact of the Use of Social Networking Sites on Body Image and Disordered Eating Outcomes." *Body Image* 17 (2016): 100-110.

Holt, Laura J. "Attitudes About Help-Seeking Mediate the Relation Between Parent Attachment and Academic Adjustment in First-Year College Students." *Journal of College Student Development* 55, no. 4 (2017): 418-423.

Homan, Kristen, Daniel Wells, Corrinne Watson, and Carolyn King. "The Effect of Viewing Ultra-Fit Images on College Women's Body Dissatisfaction." *Body Image* 9, no. 1 (2012): 50-56.

Homayoun, Ana. *Social Media Wellness: Helping Tweens and Teens Thrive in an Unbalanced Digital World.* Newbury Park, CA: Corwin Press, 2017.

Hudd, Susan S., Jennifer Dumalao, Diane Erdmann-Sager, Daniel Murray, Emily Phan, and Nicholas Soukas. "Stress at College: Effects on Health Habits, Health Status and Self-Esteem." *College Student Journal* 34, no. 2 (2000): 217-227.

Kalpidou, Maria, Dan Costin, and Jessica Morris. "The Relationship Between Facebook and the Well-Being of Undergraduate College Students." *CyberPsychology Behavior and Social Networking* 16, no. 7 (2011): 183-189.

Kay, Katty, and Claire Shipman. *The Confidence Code: The Science and Art of Self-Assurance—What Women Should Know*. New York: HarperCollins, 2014.

Klein, C. K., S. Sherman, L. Galinsky, R. Kaufman, and B. Bravo. *Work on Purpose Curriculum*. New York: Echoing Green, 2013.

Krueger, Katie S., Meghana Rao, Jeanna Salzer, and Jennifer C. Saucerman. "College-Age Women and Relational-Aggression: Prevalence and Impact." In *Wisconsin Women's Studies Consortium Women and Gender Studies Conference*, Madison, WI: 2011.

Lahey, Jessica. *The Gift of Failure: How the Best Parents Learn to Let Go So Their Children Can Succeed*. New York: HarperCollins, 2015.

Lam, Desmond, and Bernadete Ozorio. "The Effect of Prior Outcomes on Gender Risk-Taking Differences." *Journal of Risk Research* 16, no. 7 (2013): 791-802.

Laudricella, A. R., D. P. Cingel, L. Beaudoin-Ryan, M. B. Robb, M. Saphir, and E. A. Wartella. "The Common Sense Census: Plugged-In Parents of Tweens and Teens." San Francisco: Common Sense Media, 2016.

Leadbeater, Bonnie J., Sidney T. Blatt, and Donald M. Quinlan. "Gender-Linked Vulnerabilities to Depressive Symptoms, Stress and Problem Behaviors in Adolescents." *Journal of Research on Adolescents* 5, no. 1 (1995): 1-29.

Leary, Mark R., et al. "Self-Compassion and Reactions to Unpleasant Self-Relevant Events: The Implications of Treating Oneself Kindly." *Journal of Personality and Social Psychology* 92, no. 5 (May 2007): 887-904.

Liang, Belle, Terese J. Lund, Angela M. Desilva Mousseau, and Renee Spencer. "The Mediating Role of Engagement in Mentoring Relationships and Self-Esteem Among Affluent Adolescent Girls." *Psychology in the School* 53, no. 8 (2016): 848-860.

Liang Belle, Terese Lund, Angela Mousseau, Allison E. White, Renee Spencer, and Jill Walsh. "Adolescent Girls Finding Purpose: The Role of Parents and Prosociality." *Youth & Society* (2017).

Lim, Lina. "A Two-Factor Model of Defensive Pessimism and Its Relations with Achievement Motives." *Journal of Psychology* 143, no. 3 (2009): 318-336.

Lisker, Donna. "Effortless Perfection." Unpublished manuscript, last modified March 2017. Microsoft Word file.

Luthar, Suniya S., Samuel H. Bankin, and Elizabeth J. Crossman. "I Can, Therefore I Must: Fragility in the Upper-Middle Class." *Development and Psychopathology: A Vision Realized* 25, no. 4 (2013): 1529-1549.

Luthar, Suniya S., and Lucia Ciciolla. "What It Feels Like to Be a Mother: Variations by Children's Developmental Stages." *Developmental Psychology* 52, no. 1 (2016): 143-154.

Luthar, Suniya S., and Adam S. Goldstein. "Substance Use and Related Behaviors Among Urban Late Adolescents." *Development and Psychopathy* 20, no. 2 (2008): 591-614.

Luthar, Suniya S., Phillip J. Small, and Lucia Ciciolla. "Adolescents from Upper Middle Class Communities: Substance Misuse and Addiction Across Early Adulthood." *Development and Psychopathy* (2017): 1-21

Lyman, Emily L., and Suniya S. Luthar. "Further Evidence on the 'Costs of Privilege': Perfectionism in High-Achieving Youth at Socioeconomic Extremes." *Psychology in the Schools* 51, no. 9 (2014): 913-930.

Lythcott-Haims, Julie. *How to Raise an Adult: Break Free of the Over-Parenting Trap and Prepare Your Kid for Success.* New York: Henry Holt and Company, 2015.

Maatta, Sami, Jari-Erik Nurmi, and Hakan Stattin. "Achievement Orientations, School Adjustment and Well-Being: A Longitudinal Study." *Journal of Research on Adolescents* 17, no. 4 (2007): 789-812.

Mahalik, James R., Rebekah Levine Coley, Caitlin McPherran Lombardi, Alicia Doyle Lynch, Anna J. Markowitz, and Sara R. Jaffee. "Changes in Health Risk Behavior for Males and Females from Early Adolescence Through Early Adulthood." *Health Psychology* 32, no. 6 (2013): 685-694.

Marsh, Imogen, Stella W. Y. Chan, and Angus MacBeth. "Self-Compassion and Psychological Distress in Adolescents: A Meta-Analysis." Unpublished manuscript, last modified July 13, 2017. Microsoft Word file.

Martin, Andrew J., Herbert W. Marsh, Alan Williamson, and Raymond L. Debus. "Self-Handicapping, Defensive Pessimism, and Goal Orientation: A Qualitative Study of University Students." *Journal of Educational Psychology* 95, no. 3 (2003): 617-628.

Martin, Courtney E. *Perfect Girls, Starving Daughters: The Frightening New Normalcy of Hating Your Body.* New York: Free Press, 2007.

Meier, Evelyn, and James Gray. "Facebook Photo Activity Associated with Body Image Disturbance in Adolescent Girls." *CyberPsychology Behavior and Social Networking* 17, no. 4 (2014): 199-206.

Mensinger, Janell Lynn, Deanne Zotter Bonifazi, and Judith La Rosa. "Perceived Gender Role Prescriptions in Schools, the Superwoman Ideal, and Disordered Eating Among Adolescent Girls." *Sex Roles* 57, no. 7-8 (2007): 557-568.

Merianos, Ashley L., Keith A. King, and Rebecca A. Vidourek. "Body Image Satisfaction and Involvement in Risky Sexual Behaviors Among University Students." *Sexuality and Culture* 17, no. 4 (2013): 617-630.

Mohr, Tara. *Playing Big: Find Your Voice, Your Mission, Your Message.* London: Penguin Publishing Group, 2015.

Neff, Kristin. *Self-Compassion: The Proven Power of Being Kind to Yourself.* New York: HarperCollins, 2011.

Niederle, Muriel, and Lise Vestserlund. "Gender and Competition." *Annual Review of Economics* 3 (2011): 601-630.

Niemiec, Christopher P., Richard M. Ryan, and Edward L. Deci. "The Path Taken: Consequences of Attaining Intrinsic and Extrinsic Aspirations in Post-College Life." *Journal of Research in Personality* 73.3 (2009): 291–306. PMC. Web. 30 Oct. 2017.

Nolen-Hoeksema, Susan. *Women Who Think Too Much.* New York: Henry Holt and Company, 2004.

Orenstein, Peggy. *Girls & Sex: Navigating the Complicated New Landscape.* New York: HarperCollins, 2016.

Peralta, Robert L. "Alcohol Use and Fear of Weight Gain in College: Reconciling Two Social Norms." *Gender Issues* 20, no. 4 (2006): 23-42.

Pink, Daniel H. *Drive: The Surprising Truth About What Motivates Us.* London: Penguin, 2011.

Pittman, Laura D., and Adeya Richmond. "University Belonging, Friendship Quality, and Psychological Adjustment During the Transition to College." *Journal of Experimental Education* 76, no. 4 (2008): 343-361.

Pomerantz, Shauna, and Rebecca Raby. *Smart Girls: Success, School, and the Myth of Postfeminism.* Oakland, CA: University of California Press, 2017.

Poon, Wing-Tong, and Sing Lau. "Coping with Failure: Relationship with Self-Concept Discrepancy and Attributional Style." *Journal of Social Psychology* 135, no. 5 (1999): 639-653.

Recalde, Camila Tili. "Keep It Casual: A Sexual Ethics for College Campus Hookup Culture." Senior honors thesis, Wesleyan University, 2016.

Rose, Amanda J. "Co-Rumination in the Friendships of Girls and Boys." *Child Development* 73, no. 6 (2002): 1830-1843.

Rose, Amanda J., Rebecca A. Schwartz-Mette, Gary C. Glick, Rhiannon L. Smith, and Aaron M. Luebbe. "An Observational Study of Co-Rumination in Adolescent Friendships." *Developmental Psychology* 50, no. 9 (2014): 2199-2209.

Rutledge, Christina M., Katherine L. Gillmor, and Meghan M. Gillen. "Does This Profile Picture Make Me Look Fat? Facebook and Body Image in College Students." *Psychology of Popular Media Culture* 2, no. 4 (2014): 251-259.

Salk, Rachel H., and Renee Engeln-Maddox. "'If You're Fat, Then I'm Humongous!': Frequency, Content, and Impact of Fat Talk Among College Women." *Psychology of Women Quarterly* 35, no. 1 (2011): 18-28.

Sax, Linda. *The Gender Gap in College: Maximizing the Development Potential of Women and Men*. San Francisco: John Wiley & Sons, 2008.

————. "Her College Experience Is Not His." *Chronicle of Higher Education* 55, no. 5 (2008): A32.

Sheu, Hung Bin, and William E. Sedlacek. "An Exploratory Study of Help-Seeking Attitudes and Coping Strategies Among College Students by Race and Gender." *Measurement and Evaluation in Counseling and Development* 37, no. 3 (2004): 130-143.

Skelton, Christine. "Gender and Achievement: Are Girls the Success Stories of Restructured Education Systems?" *Educational Review* 62, no. 2 (2010): 131-142.

Slater, Amy, and Marika Tiggemann. "A Test of Objectification Theory in Adolescent Girls." *Sex Roles* 46, no. 9-10 (2002): 343-349.

Smith, Rhiannon L., and Amanda J. Rose. "The 'Cost of Caring' in Youths' Friendships: Considering Associations Among Social Perspective Taking, Co-Rumination, and Empathetic Distress." *Developmental Psychology* 47, no. 6 (2011): 1792-1803.

Spencer, Renee, Jim Walsh, Belle Liang, Angela M. Desilvia Mousseau, and Terese J. Lund. "Having It All? A Qualitative Examination of Affluent Adolescent Girls' Perceptions of Stress and Their Quests for Success." *Journal of Adolescent Research* (2016).

Steiner-Adair, Catherine. "The Body Politic: Normal Female Adolescent Development and the Development of Eating Disorders."

Journal of The American Academy of Psychoanalysis 14, no. 1 (1986): 95-114.

Stress in America™: Are Teens Adopting Adults' Stress Habits? 2014, American Psychological Association.

Taylor, Julia V. *The Body Image Workbook for Teens: Activities to Help Girls Develop a Healthy Body Image in an Image-Obsessed World.* Oakland, CA: New Harbinger Press, 2014.

Taylor, Kate. "Sex on Campus: She Can Play That Game." *New York Times,* July 12, 2013.

Thompson, Sharon H., and Eric Lougheed. "Frazzled by Facebook? An Exploratory Study of Gender Differences in Social Network Communication Among Undergraduate Men and Women." *College Student Journal* 46, no. 1 (2012): 88-98.

Tompkins, Tonya L., Ashlee R. Hockett, Nadia Abraibesh, and Jody L. Witt. "A Closer Look at Co-Rumination: Gender, Coping, Peer Functioning and Internalizing/Externalizing Problems." *Journal of Adolescence* 34, no. 5 (2011): 801-811.

Tsabary, Shefali. *The Awakened Family: How to Raise Empowered, Resilient, and Conscious Children.* New York: Penguin, 2016.

Twenge, Jean M. *iGen: Why Today's Super-Connected Kids Are Growing Up Less Rebellious, More Tolerant, And Less Happy—And Completely Unprepared for Adulthood.* New York: Atria, 2017.

Van Zalk, Maarten, Herman Walter, Margrett Kerr, Susan J. T. Branje, Haka Stattin, and Wim H. J. Meeus. "Peer Contagion and Adolescent Depression: the Role of Failure Anticipation." *Journal of Clinical Child and Adolescent Psychology* 39, no. 6 (2010): 837-848.

Weiner, Jessica. *Life Doesn't Begin 5 Pounds from Now.* New York: Simon Spotlight Entertainment, 2006.

White, Erica Stovall, and Danielle M. Boyd. "Where and When I Enter: A Study of the Experiences of African-American Girls in All-Girls' Independent Schools." Laurel Center for Research on Girls, 2015.

Wilson, Reid, and Lynn Lyons. *Anxious Kids, Anxious Parents: 7 Ways to Stop the Worry Cycle and Raise Courageous and Independent Children*. Deerfield Beach, FL: Health Communications Inc., 2013.

Yamawaki, Niwako, Brian Tschanz, and David Feick. "Defensive Pessimism, Self-Esteem Instability, and Goal Striving." *Cognition and Emotion* 18, no. 2 (2004): 233-249.

Yarnell, Lisa M., Rose E. Stafford, Kristin D. Neff, Erin D. Reilly, Marissa C. Knox, and Michael Mullarkey. "Meta-Analysis of Gender Differences in Self-Compassion." *Self and Identity* 14, no. 5 (2015): 499-520.

Zhang, Kaili Chen. "What I Look Like: College Women, Body Image, and Spirituality." *Journal of Religion and Health* 52, no. 4 (2013): 1240-1252.

INDEX

ABOUT THE AUTHOR

RACHEL SIMMONS is the author of the *New York Times* bestsellers *Odd Girl Out: The Hidden Culture of Aggression in Girls* and *The Curse of the Good Girl: Raising Authentic Girls with Courage and Confidence.* Cofounder of Girls Leadership, a national nonprofit, she is a leadership development specialist at Smith College and is the Girls Research Scholar in Residence at The Hewitt School in New York. She lives in western Massachusetts with her daughter.